Nonprofit Governance

The Why, What, and How of Nonprofit Boardship

John Tropman
University of Michigan

Thomas J. Harvey
University of Notre Dame

Co-published by Corby Books
Notre Dame, Indiana

University of Scranton Press
Scranton, Pennsylvania

Nonprofit Governance

Copyright © 2009 by John Tropman and
Thomas J. Harvey

10 9 8 7 6 5 4

Manufactured in the United States of America

Co-published by Corby Books
A Division of Corby Publishing
P.O. Box 93
Notre Dame, Indiana 46556
and
University of Scranton Press
Smurfit Hall 103
Scranton, Pennsylvania 18510

Library of Congress Cataloging-in-Publication Data

Tropman, John E.
  Nonprofit governance : the why, what, and how of nonprofit
  boardship / John Tropman, Thomas J. Harvey.
      p. cm.
  Includes bibliographical references.
  ISBN 978-1-58966-199-8 (pbk.)
  1. Nonprofit organizations–Management. 2. Boards of directors.
  3. Corporate governance. I. Harvey, Thomas J. II. Title.
  HD62.6.T75 2009
  658.4'22–dc22
                                        2009010025

Nonprofit Governance

Table of Contents

Foreword

The nonprofit sector in the United States of America boldly reflects one of the centerpiece values of the American Revolution, namely, the value of free association. The Founders of the Republic had an inherent distrust of intrusive government. Indeed, the Boston Tea Party marked an immediate and direct response to the government extreme of taxation without representation. The longer term response was the importance placed on voluntary association as a societal value for problem solving and for enhancing the quality of life at every level of community from neighborhood to nation. Voluntary association is the overarching point of organizational identity for all nonprofits, regardless of their widely disparate missions in the fields of health, education, social welfare, human rights, philanthropy or the arts. In the United States, we value individuals working together in organized ways to serve the common good. We even use tax policy to encourage and incentivize the development of such collaborative associations.

The scale of this reality is measurable. The nonprofit sector in the United States involves 1.7 million organizations that are designated by the Internal Revenue Service as nonprofits with operational, annual budgets over $1.5 trillion. This altruistic sector employs 10% of the nation's workforce and recruits an equal number of volunteers in their board governance, in their programs, and in their gathering of financial resources.

Perhaps the most unique feature of the nonprofit sector that distinguishes it dramatically from the for-profit or governmental sectors is exactly the responsibility of placing the governance of every nonprofit organization in the hands of community volunteers, volunteers who by definition, do not receive any financial compensation. This reality gives the nonprofit sector its historic value in being rooted in the vision of the founding architects of the United States of America.

In spite of, and in contrast to, this extraordinary celebration of the human community coming together to serve the greater good, voluntary governance has an abundance of problems that are beginning to

Foreword

draw the attention of scholars, such as Lester M. Salamon, the author of *The State of Nonprofit America*, of leading sector organizations such as the Independent Sector, which recently released a list of 33 best practices, many of which address remedial ways to avoid dealing with board inefficiencies, and, lastly, of the managers of too many typical nonprofit organizations. Just over a year ago, the Mendoza College of Business sponsored a seminar for recently appointed CEOs of nonprofit organizations. On the final day there was a session on Board Development. The majority of those in attendance expressed high levels of frustration at the functioning of their boards. So much so that the faculty professor teaching the session quipped, "As I listen to you, I am feeling less like a business school professor and more like Dr. Phil!" His comment provoked a moment of laughter, but, more importantly, it provoked in many of us, who can improve the situation, a renewed commitment to bring the reality and functioning of nonprofit boards to attain the quality performance levels that the value of voluntary association in American Society deserves.

In this spirit, I welcome this newly published book, *Nonprofit Governance*, designed to offer an array of creative tools for nonprofit boards to improve their performance. The book's authors are John Tropman, Ph.D., a tenured professor at the University of Michigan's highly reputed Graduate School of Social Work and an Adjunct at Michigan's Ross Business School, and Thomas J. Harvey, MSW, President Emeritus of Catholic Charities USA and currently the Director of the Master of Nonprofit Administration Program at one of the nation's top business schools, the University of Notre Dame's Mendoza College of Business. These men have drawn on eight decades of experience in leading, educating, governing, and advising some of the best known nonprofit organizations in the country.

Other such authors, such as John Carver, speak to the philosophical underpinnings of the nonprofit governance. Harvey and Tropman address the nitty-gritty of how to maximize the effectiveness of board functioning by using the best insights of group theory, organizational behavioral research, and good old-fashioned common sense.

Foreword

As the Dean of a business school that places great value on results, I will predict that, if the leaders of today's nonprofit organizations use this book, the results will not only be measured in improved efficiencies, but also in the quality of life in the communities where these organizations serve the common good.

Carolyn Y. Woo
Dean
Mendoza College of Business
University of Notre Dame

Preface

John Tropman and Tom Harvey have written an authoritative and complete reference for the directors of nonprofit boards. If I had this book 30 years ago, before founding the first of several businesses and nonprofits, the world would be a better place, with less frustration and waste. I only realized the value of a board a few years after the start of my first business when my first real board provided feedback for a strategic plan. They ripped it to shreds. And it came out better because of that criticism. After reflecting on their feedback, I realized how much I had paid over the years for my business education of trial and error. From then on, I always had boards comprised of the best people I could find and I listened to them.

When I was 40, I took a sabbatical from business and went back to the University of Michigan, receiving a dual Ph.D. in Organizational Psychology and Social Work. It was there I met John Tropman. When I finished, I felt it was time that I give back, and I started working with nonprofits, first as an advisor and finally starting and running a number of "successful" non-profits over the next several years. I always had a board of directors; I used them for advice, community contacts, fundraising, and developing partnerships and collaborations.. I believed that I was fairly proficient, until I read the pre-release version of this book.

Then I read it again. I seldom read books twice (sometimes not even once!), but this book is so very helpful on so many levels. I gained a much deeper understanding the second time through. I excerpted parts of the book and worked with the Earth Force CEO to think through our coming restructuring. This book then became our reference as we sat back and reflected on our board structure. Vigorous, diverse directors are a vital *sine qua non* for vigorous high performing nonprofits.

I realized how recruiting directors to act in areas beyond their wallets and address books would pay high dividends to the nonprofits with which I was, and am, associated. At first, Earth Force staff resisted what appeared to be the board involvement in the operations of the organization. As we read more closely, we realized the role of oversight from talented, involved people who represent varied perspectives did not have to be oppositional or result in micro-management. The nature of the oversight depends on the relationship the CEO establishes with her/his board; in our case that role was welcomed by the CEO. This oversight also brings dividends if your board is diverse enough, as suggested, to include people from the population you serve as well as business people, professionals, and philanthropists. Your board can offer unique perspectives from the population you serve, from the community, and from various professionals' advice.

Another section, we found very useful, was how to run a meeting. I was familiar with John's earlier book on meetings, but merging meeting management with the various roles on the board provided an opportunity to excerpt sections for the board manual, which included a written model for the board members to follow in their specific roles.

Earth Force had a rather complex board structure, with a national board of directors and local advisory boards. Using ideas from this book, we were able to create a new national structure, including standing committee designation for the local advisory boards with specific delegated responsibilities from the national board of directors. The local committees, will become our outer circle—what in the book is called the leadership circle—a great source of new directors. The result: the same board members are more involved, generous and dedicated to the success of our local sites.

We continue using this book with our current board, creating a truly great partnership with some very talented people. Though we are at the beginning of this restructuring, early returns suggest that this deeper involvement is resulting in a board that is more generous, and helpful; there seems to be a mutually beneficial partnership developing as opposed to the board being one more job for our very busy CEO.

Harry A. Ford, Ph.D.
Earth Force, Inc.

Acknowledgments

We want to thank our wives, Penny and Karen, for their contributions, support, and forbearance. In each case, they have served on boards and contributed their experience and perceptions of needed information, problems, and issues.

We want to thank our students at the Universities of Michigan and Notre Dame who looked at and responded to portions of this volume. Lloyd Hitoshi Mayer and Tom Croxton did outstanding jobs with the legal issues chapters.

We want to thank the many nonprofit executives and nonprofit directors who contributed their insights to the board process. Special thanks goes to Dan Magnuson, CEO of the Counseling Center of Milwaukee, for his thoughtful contributions to the ideas and dimensions of boardship.

Elmer J. Tropman,
In Memoriam

1975

Elmer J. Tropman, John's father and coauthor of the first edition, died at the end of February 1993, during the middle of this project. He was a coauthor of the first edition of this book. Elmer received his master's in sociology and certificate in social work from the University of Buffalo, Buffalo, New York. He served as CEO of the Council of Social Agencies of Buffalo and Erie Counties, New York, and CEO of the Health and Welfare Planning Association of Pittsburgh and Allegheny County. Upon retirement, he developed and directed the Forbes Fund of the Pittsburgh Foundation. His working life emphasized, encouraged, and enhanced human services management.

There was, however, an initial draft, and his corrections, emendations, and suggestions inform every page. He was a United Way CEO for many years and, following that, embarked on a second career as a foundation CEO. He thus had long board experience; indeed, the impetus for a "board book" was originally his. A whole career of "boardship" is represented here—from the CEO's perspective as well as that of the director-director. During his final illness, he expressed sadness that he could not see the project to completion. I know he was joyful that the first edition came to fruition, and is even more joyful that the project

Elmer J. Tropman...In Memoriam

continues to move forward so that people can use it to help in achieving better boards and a more enhanced realization of civic purpose. Tom Harvey offered a personal recollection to the readers of this book.

Nonprofit Boards: What to Do and How to Do It reflects John Tropman's life commitment as an educator at one of the nation's finest universities. The book also reflects his lifetime opportunity to be a student of his father, who was a master at promoting civic engagement and community problem solving. For many years, Elmer J. Tropman was the CEO of the Health and Welfare Planning Association of Pittsburgh and Allegheny County in southwestern Pennsylvania. As a resident of that area, I frequently had the privilege of being involved in community projects undertaken through the leadership of Elmer Tropman. Admirers of Mr. Tropman's abilities coined the term, the "Tropman touch." It designated not only efficiency in the inefficient and sticky work of community problem solving and of community development, but also the knack for getting the right people to the table...and with staying power.

This book will permit another generation of nonprofit board directors to enjoy the social well-being that comes from the Tropman touch!

1992

A Note on Terminology

In this book we use the standard terminology for the organizations in the "third sector" or the "interdependent sector." Commonly, most citizens and scholars call organizations that are not corporations or sole proprietorships, or governmental agencies, "nonprofits." However, from our perspective there are several problems with this language. For one thing, "nonprofit" is a tax status in which the government allows exemption from taxes (a "tax expenditure or a number representing what the entity would have paid in taxes if it paid taxes") in return for the contribution of a social benefit of some kind. Therefore, we prefer the phrase "social enterprise organizations" or "social benefit organizations," but that phrase might engender some confusion so we are sticking to the more common usage.

A second problem comes with the phrase "nonprofit." Social enterprise organizations should make "profit"—we prefer the term "surplus" so that they can innovate and improve their product lines. And many do have surpluses of various kinds, from cash in the bank to large multibillion dollar endowments. It is our position that social benefit organizations should seek surplus in operating revenue so they have income to invest in the organization. This is a good thing.

Part I: Context

Society and Community

American society has been, historically and characteristically, and is contemporraneously, oriented toward the individual and his or her needs and achievements. Groups also have been a part of the American tradition. (De Tocqueville mentioned the American penchant for "associations" was already well established in 1825). This penchant has expanded into a sector of global uniqueness – the American nonprofit or voluntary sector.

In 2006, according to the Independent Sector (Independent Sector.org), America had 1.9 million nonprofit organizations with budgets of more than $5,000. They fall into eight major groups:

Arts, Culture, and Humanities –
   museums, symphonies, community theaters, etc.
Education and Research –
   private colleges and universities, noncommercial research institutions, etc.
Environmental and Animals –
   zoos, wildlife organizations, environmental groups, etc.

Health Services
>   hospitals, public clinics, etc.

Human Services
>   housing and shelter programs, youth programs, social
>   agencies, etc.

International and Foreign Affairs
>   overseas relief, etc.

Public and Societal Benefit
>   private and community foundations, civil rights organiza-
>   tions, civic, social and fraternal organizations

Religion
>   houses of worship and auxiliary services

Financially the nonprofit sector plays a huge role in the American (and world) economy. In 2004, it employed 9.4 million persons; when we add volunteers, the number increases to 14.1 million. In financial terms, the total expenses for 2004 were $1 trillion. Of that, about $260 billion was of charitable giving (2005 figures.).

However, in spite of our historical affinity for them, groups in their various forms (teams, collectivities, communities, committees, and, of course, boards) and contemporary size and importance have occupied a subdominant position in the American psyche. We prefer the "mountain man" mythology to that of the "wagon train" (Tropman, 1998). It is perhaps for this reason that we tend to ignore the needs that collectivities have, and the skills that are needed by participants to optimize collective performance. Nowhere is this more striking than in the contemporary diminishment of the ideas of "meetings" and "committees." The _New Yorker_ has dozens of cartoons about committees, and meetings all referring to their lack of utility, their time consuming/time wasting nature, and their general problem as a social form through which accomplishment is created. "I did not get any work done today" a common phrase runs, "I spent it all in meetings."

Yet groups have more strength different from, and greater than, individuals. For one thing, they correct errors by providing a plurality of perspectives. Brainstorming can get many good ideas on the table for discussion. Second, they provide social support. People need to have social support and validation for the ideas and concepts they express. Ideas are not usually presented fully formed but rather are elaborately constructed, bit by bit, by others, like a snowball rolling downhill, gaining in size as it goes. The conceptual snowball picks up an idea here and there as it rolls along, resulting in a well-rounded concept. Then, too, groups foster competition for respect, which provides a stimulus for greater effort (Tropman, Johnson, & Tropman, 1992).

But each of these strengths requires management. Having a multitude of perspectives is not useful if people do not begin with correct information. Social support and concern for cohesion can lead to groupthink and pressures to conform (Janis, 1972; 1983), and competition can result in destructive self-dealing effects where the interests of the board as a whole become subordinate to individual ego needs. In short, groups can perform in a superior fashion to individuals, if they are properly managed.

In spite of their potential problems, groups today are vital to the successful functioning of the contemporary nation-state and modern organizations. American society has particular needs and problems in this area, because of our tendency to regard the individual as most central.

When one thinks of "groups," many different kinds come to mind, including teams, communities, committees, and, of course, boards of directors. Boards of directors are an important group in our society. They make decisions about a range of matters appropriate to their organization. However, in recent years, both corporate and nonprofit boards have been shown to be deeply flawed in many dimensions (Tropman, 2004). "Governance," as the currently popular word has it, was only randomly existent in many boards. Cozy interlocking directorates brought to mind the concepts of "The Power Elite" developed by the sociologist C. Wright Mills in the 1950s (Mills, 1952). Self-serving, self-dealing relationships on corporate boards between "inside directors" (company management) and "outside directors" (supposedly independent, respected, and knowledgeable citizens) seemed common. Spectacular company collapse, driven apparently by overreaching management and flaccid and/or complicit directors, has become a staple of the media. Exxon, Qualcom, Health South, and Adelphia, among others, have become common names to those interested in ethical governance (Tropman, Schaefer, Zhu, 2006). So problematic and excessive were the company transgressions that Congress passed the Sarbanes Oxley Act requiring publicly traded companies to adhere to certain procedures designed to ensure more robust attentiveness to ethical practices. Many states are passing legislation carrying over the requirements of Sarbanes Oxley to nonprofit application, even though the fit is not perfect. (Take a look at the chapter on legal issues in the appendix. For more information on nonprofit implications, check the material on boardsource.org.)

Nonprofit organizations have not been exempt from problematic practices. The United Way of America found serious problems among it successes, and its CEO resigned and was imprisoned in the 1990s. The details of these difficulties were detailed in John Glasser's book, *The United Way Scandal* (Glasser, 1992). Problems occurred at other United Ways (Ann Arbor and Lansing, MI, Catholic Charities (San Francisco), Capuchin Food Kitchens (Detroit) to name a few (Tropman and Schaefer, 2004). The fact that there were virtually no ethical standards for board governance per se has contributed to these problematic behaviors. (The Independent Sector developed a task force which has developed a proposed list of 30 ethical principals for boards. [Independent Sector.org] These are listed in the Appendix as well.)

With all this activity, boards are trying to take more of a leadership role, asserting themselves, and seeking active ways to make the responsibility real to themselves and to their publics. But large questions remain: "What are boards supposed to do?" Nonprofit boards are especially needful of direction and assistance here because they most often can least afford professional help.

Chapter 1

The Contemporary
Nonprofit Board

You have heard it said. You have probably even experienced it. When many people look at the same thing, they do not all see the same thing.

Reasons for this phenomenon have been offered for centuries. A favorite explanation for why we perceive things so differently dates to Thomas Aquinas, the 13th-century saint and sage. He is remembered as a theologian, philosopher, metaphysician, and physicist in an age when disciplines were not yet sharply delineated. More importantly, he was one of those gifted people who could reduce profound and complex ideas to simple levels for comprehension.

In terms of differing perceptions of the same reality, Aquinas noted that something is received according to the disposition of the receiver or, in Latin, id quod recipitur, secundum modum recipientis recipitur. To make his point, Aquinas filled a glass with water and observed that water takes the shape of the glass. He then applied this simple principle to human communication. Obviously, personal experiences shape our "glasses" and will play a big role in what we see or hear and how we perceive it.

Psychology assumes that individuals perceive things differently. The Rorschach test helps us assess how widely perceptions vary. Inkblots with the same shapes, but with no special meanings, are placed before different people. The people are asked to interpret what they see in the inkblots. Different people see very different things!

As common as this phenomenon is, truth be told, many things that look alike or sound alike are actually very different. It is not always a matter of perception. Nowhere is this more evident than in the world of nonprofit organizations.

The nonprofit sector is not a monolithic reality. The term nonprofit describes a range of organizations differing in size, scale, and scope—from the largest and most powerful universities and foundations to the smallest and least-funded neighborhood organizations. They also vary widely in mission. Some enhance the lives of communities through the arts and humanities; others focus on problem solving through health, education, or welfare programs; still others promote civic engagement. Regardless of their differences in purpose or policy, they all have, or are expected to have, a board of directors.

All boards share common responsibilities. We identified seven. Legal compliance, of course, goes without saying. We have two appendices devoted to that topic. The remaining six are as follows:

- Ensuring trusteeship of public purpose;
- Establishing vision, mission, and goals;
- Making and overseeing policy;
- Selecting and evaluating the CEO;
- Assuring the organization's financial wellness; and
- Introducing strategic planning, change, and entrepreneurship.

A more extensive and ambitious list was developed by BoardSource (formerly the National Center for Nonprofit Boards) in a 2005 monograph, entitled *The Source: Twelve Principles of Governance that Power Exceptional Boards,* (http://www.boardsource.org/

files/thesource.pdf). BoardSource lists the constructive partnership of the board and the chief executive as the number one principle for success in nonprofit governance and management. (The others are as follows: 2] mission driven, 3] strategic thinking, 4] culture of inquiry, 5] independent mindedness,6] ethos of transparency, 7] compliance with integrity, 8] sustaining resources, 9] results oriented, 10] intentional board practices, 11] continuous learning, 12] revitalization.) We discuss the connection between our list and theirs in the introduction to Part 3.

BoardSource serves the nonprofit sector by providing resources for effective nonprofit boards. Thus, it should not be taken lightly that its fundamental principle unequivocally sees the effectiveness of the board and chief executive as interdependent.

The role of the executive is also seen as crucial by John and Miriam Carver (whom we discussed earlier). Their work preceded the BoardSource effort and may well have influenced the BoardSource document. The Carvers are two of the most well-known theoreticians on nonprofit board governance. They see the delegation of its authority into one executive (by whatever title) as the board's ultimate and, in a sense, only decision. The Carvers stress the board's personal charge of accountability for the organization's success to one Chief Executive Officer, who, in effect, becomes the board's one employee. Because of the widespread use of Carver's Policy Governance Model in nonprofit organizations, an appendix will offer a consideration of its basic framework.

Beyond these general commonalities, however, boards are not the same. They differ in composition, size, and the quality of their functioning. For good or evil, depending on the situation, a nonprofit board may not be what it seems.

A prevailing difficulty facing many nonprofit organizations, and the nonprofit sector itself, lies in the ambiguity of their expected roles in the United States today. Our society traditionally has had three distinct sectors, each with a special purpose. Their boundaries are shifting, and ambiguity is the result. Much of the nonprofit sector's ambiguity comes from changes in the other two major sectors in this society, namely the public sector (the government) and the for-profit sector. With shifts in public policy priorities, and with a growth of for-profits in activities historically identified with nonprofits, nonprofit boards must not only be competent in the programs of their organizations, but in translating the value of these programs to the public. *Nonprofit Governance* is not a blueprint for dealing with such challenges. Nonetheless, the book focuses on strengthening the people involved on nonprofit boards to function in the best possible way to deliver their programs and to overcome the challenges that come from a litigious and changing environment.

To give weight to this priority—namely, strengthening the people involved on nonprofit boards—this practical book will repeat, over and over again in different contexts, that the power of the board to act and lead is not found in individuals nor in individual responsibility, but in the social interaction of the group. Thus if directors search for theories that can assure the best organizational behaviors and successful outcomes, they would be well served in reviewing the basic dynamics of group process.

Throughout this text, there runs an underlying assumption that the most successful boards function well as a "group." Group theorists hold that any group must deal effectively with two challenging problems if it is to function well. They are the problem of authority and the problem of intimacy. Let us look at each of them.

The authority problem has little to do with hierarchical authority. Rather group theory uses "authority" as a designation of rights or powers by the members of the group to each other. Perhaps an example will best make the point.

In a residential youth-serving organization, the teenagers will live in clusters of perhaps 10 or 12. When these clusters or "groups" are first formed, there are frequent outbreaks of tension and even of violence. If good group process happens, such tension will begin to diminish as the authority problem is dealt with. Gradually the group will decide who can change the TV channel; who is the best athlete, the brightest student, the one who decides the dress code, or picks the snack menu, etc. When the cluster obviously has assigned these various acceptable roles for each member of the group, then it has dealt with the authority problem.

The intimacy problem does not refer to romantic intimacy. It merely tests whether members of a group accept and like each other enough to work together after the authority problem has been resolved.

The example from the child welfare living situation may seem a stretch in comparison to the "group" that makes up a nonprofit board, but it is not. Informal roles are assigned to board members. When this is done well and with maximum buy-in, the board moves quickly to having the needed intimacy to work well together.

In light of the importance of boards dealing effectively with the problems of authority and intimacy, we should consider proven methods of helping the group's process. One of the most common techniques involves having an annual or biannual board retreat that is mandatory for all directors.

A board retreat differs radically from a normal business meeting. By design, a board meeting should only take one or two hours. A board retreat often covers a day or two.

The purpose of a board meeting is to make policy decisions based on researched facts in an efficient manner. In contrast, a retreat is less about efficiency and decisions and is more about awareness—awareness of the organization's mission and identity and awareness of each other's commitment to that mission. While the business meeting seeks to answer fact questions like how many dollars are available to deliver what services to whom at what locations? A retreat asks the more open-ended questions like who are we? What is our purpose? How do we attain the purpose?

Such questions take time and demand trust. As the board deals with them, it usually also deals with and resolves the authority and intimacy problems of the group. One of the most obvious outcomes of a well-orchestrated retreat will usually be seen in the better functioning of business meetings. As the directors accept each other's roles and like to work together, they tend to cooperate better in handling the group's business.

In light of these insights from group theory, one may ask how often the problem of authority must again be addressed. And the answer is, every time the board adds a new director. Thus boards would be well served if they hold their annual or biannual retreat shortly after new directors are appointed so that they will be part of the group experience. It may be equally important for a board not to replace a director who may die or resign. It is better to function well with one fewer board member than to reopen and renegotiate the authority problem. If it is not possible to defer the selection of one or more new board members, then a very careful orientation process should be designed to integrate the new members not just into the board's business, but into its group process.

In writing this volume, the authors have drawn on their many years of experience in practice and in the classroom to craft a readable, usable text to strengthen the contributions of board members. Taken seriously and used well, the valuable tool can make quality performance the norm for board functioning. Though educational in purpose, this book is written in a conversational style that reflects the authors' awareness of practice as well as principle.

The environment for nonprofit organizations has changed in many ways. For example, a few generations ago, lawsuits against nonprofits were rare. Not so today. In the past, the Congress of the United States gave little attention to the organizational and functional accountability of nonprofit organizations, other than through Internal Revenue regulations. Now a senate committee has given sufficient scrutiny to the issues that the Independent Sector, an advocacy network for nonprofits, felt the need to publish 31 principles for effective nonprofit governance. These are listed with commentary as an appendix of this book.

Another appendix, written by law professor, Lloyd Mayer, addresses the whole range of legal issues with which a nonprofit board should be familiar, or at least, should insist that its legal counsel is. Nonprofit boards must be more sophisticated in dealing with organizational challenges. In doing so, they need competence.

In the legal arena, boards may need to conform very carefully to specific regulations. The Mayer and Independent Sector appendices will be invaluable to such compliance. However, in many areas of board activity, boards will have options. Throughout its many chapters, *Nonprofit Governance* tries to suggest tips that will lead to best practices. In fact, the tips come from proven best practices in the field today.

Chapter 2

Theory and Principles of Nonprofit Governance

Introduction

From colonial times forward, American society has been comprised of private organizations, governments, and non-governmental organizations (NGOs) which began as associations, and have now emerged as the "nonprofit sector." The balance between what government does, what the private sector does, and what nonprofits do is shifting constantly. The recent movement toward "privatization" has been based on the idea that the private sector and the nonprofit sector can perform tasks better than government. For the nonprofit sector, it is important to consider the ways in which it is governed, the ways in which that governance should be guided and the aims for which it should strive, and the importance of that function beyond the organization itself.

Boards of directors are much more complex, intricate, and involved than people usually understand. Through the board, the pluralism of American values is (hopefully, but too often infrequently) expressed and democratic involvement in decisions affecting individual lives is orchestrated. These democratic imperatives interact and

13

intertwine with the regular board chores of making policy decisions for the nonprofit /human service organization.

Becoming a director is a challenge and a responsibility. So much depends on the board, it seems. Whether we are talking about a profit-making organization or one that is nonprofit, the role of the director seems of increasing importance, yet steeped in ambiguity.

Despite these important large-scale social functions, as well as the crucial day-to-day decisional functions, board directorship is treated casually, even shabbily. Nearly everyone involved with nonprofit organizations conspires in this casualness and shabbiness—directors who accept board positions without proper scrutiny and review; those of us who extend invitations for seats on boards in a thoughtless, offhand manner; CEOs who place education and training for their boards at the bottom of their lists of priorities; and society itself, which tends to undervalue group activities. Nonprofit organizations, whether they be philanthropic or human service, must receive effective leadership, stewardship, and trusteeship from their boards of directors if they are to survive.

Few areas of the modern organization have been as ignored as the board of directors in terms of research, training, or operating guidelines, though more materials are becoming available every day. Those who seek to learn more in this area to hone and improve it are to be commended. It is not a job full of praise and thanks. Rather, one is likely to be greeted with indifference, uncertainty, and lack of concern.

In this chapter we look at the issues of governance from a theoretical perspective, and suggest some principles (as opposed to practices, which come later) that boards should seek to follow.

The Political Theory of Governance

Philosophically, nonprofit nongovernmental organizations have a value history that is as old as the history of the United States itself. Settlers fled from Europe to get away from governmental oppression. Once here, they "fled" further west to seek opportunity. The nature of the American Revolution revealed a deep seated suspicion of government. Thus early on there was a high priority given to the right of association. John Adams, the nation's second president, gave such value to the right to association that he insisted on its inclusion into the Massachusetts's Constitution. Here it is:

"The body politics is formed by a voluntary association of individuals: it is a social compact, by which the whole people covenants with each citizen, and each citizen with the whole people, that all shall be governed by certain laws for the common good."
John Adams, President, 1797-1801, Preamble, Constitution of the Commonwealth of Massachusetts.

That great analysis of America, Alexis De Tocqueville's *Democracy in America*, made a similar observation in 1835.

"Americans of all ages, all stations in life, and all types of dispositions are forever forming associations. There are not only commercial associations and industrial associations in which all take part, but others of a thousand different types—religious, moral, serious, futile, very general and very limited, immensely large and very minute. Americans combine to give fetes, found seminaries, build churches, distribute books, and send missionaries to the antipodes. Hospitals, prisons, and schools take shape in that way. Finally, they want to proclaim a truth or propagate some feeling by encouragement of a great example, they form an association. In every case, at the head of any new undertaking, where in France you find a government or in England some territorial magnate, in the United States you are sure to find an association." Alexis de Tocqueville, *Democracy in America*, ed. J.P. Maier, trans. George Lawrence (Garden City, NY: Anchor Books, 1969), 513-17.

Beyond the issue of citizen rights and cultural dispositions, "association" is about the philosophy of organizing society so that individuals can work together to meet their needs and those of their communities. In other words, the nation encourages its people to create mediating structures between the power of government and the needs of the people. The sociologist William Kornhauser talks about these "secondary associations" as an essential buffer between the vital ties of primary associations (family) and the tertiary connections of citizens to "mass society"(Kornhauser, 1959). Associations, then, occupy an historically important place in American society.

From a theoretical perspective, associations are a part of American political governance, a key way that citizens carry out functions that government is not currently carrying out, or could not carry out. Other societies which do not have a "third sector" often find themselves facing one or both of two problems. One problem is that the actions/nonactions become more fateful and highly charged—too much rides on what government does, or does not, do. As people are members of many groups, partisanship tends to dissipate.

The second problem is the "mass society" problem. The lack of mediating structure (Kornhauser's secondary associations) creates a lack of filtering from the top down and the bottom up, a situation which can lead to overly powerful governmental bodies and a mindless citizenry.

Nonprofit governance, then, plays an important part in this political drama. It is a far bigger role than most directors imagine. While "associations" have their "work" (to be discussed in a moment), they have a higher political purpose as well. Boards of directors, then, are heir to the long American tradition of Association, and need to act in ways that honor and respect that tradition.

Relevant Work—The Focus of Governance

One large set of such associations engages collectivities of citizens to solve problems, to enhance the quality of life through health, education, and welfare programs, and to entertain through museums, theatres, and symphonies and even, to protest public polices! It has often been called the Voluntary Sector, or, more recently, the third sector, or the nonprofit sector. Voluntary is not used in the sense of doing an altruistic activity for no salary, although historically this situation might have been more true than today. Rather it is used to signify the empowerment that comes from organized voluntary association to serve the common good[1]. And it is at the level of nonprofit boards that we find such voluntary association. Individuals unite in voluntary association to accomplish some mission to the benefit of society. Many associations—membership organizations are one example—are formed for the membership. Nonprofit organizations are formed to produce a social benefit, not personal gain. No doubt individual directors secure pleasure from their contribution to board work, and also from the appreciation they receive from that work. However, directors are really "trustees" of community capital, entrusted into their care for the accomplishment of a social benefit. It is not their organization, nor their money. It is not "about them." Rather, it is about the work. "The Work" is the bundle of products and services offered by the organization. Governance needs to ask questions such as the following:

- "Is the 'work' working?"
- "How could we do this work better?"
- "Is there other work that we should also be doing, or that is more important than the work we are now doing?"
- "Are we collaborating and sharing with others who are doing similar or complementary work?"
- "What part of the work we are now doing should we stop doing?"
- "Are the specific users of our work, as well as the larger community, benefiting from our work?"

Asking questions such as these will help the organization achieve a high ROSI – Return On Social Investment.

Exceptional Work – The Goal of Governance

The goals of governance should be higher than being ethical, evidence based, nimble, and relevant. Organizations should strive always to be exceptional. To aim to exceptionality, there needs to be

---

[1] In the contemporary nonprofit sector, serving on a board (directorship) is one of the important elements of uncompensated activity. The other large segment is the simple donation of time to the nonprofit organization's task needs.

a measure or standard against which directors can look. To us, the very best list is the one provided by Peter Vaill, in his thought-provoking article, "The Purposing of High Performing Systems" (Vaill, 1982). We have adapted Vaill's list slightly, and added two variables. The governing directors of voluntary organizations should drive the organization to meet at least two of the following standards:

1) BENCHMARK—They are performing excellently against known external standards.
2) POTENTIAL—They are performing excellently against what is assumed to be their potential level of performance.
3) IMPROVEMENT—They are performing excellently against where they were at some previous point in time.
4) PEER JUDGMENT—They have been judged by informed observers to be doing substantially better qualitatively than other comparable systems.
5) EFFICIENCY—They are doing what they do with significantly less resources (sic) than it is assumed they needed to do what they do.
6) EXEMPLARS—They are perceived as exemplars of the way they do whatever they do and thus become a source of inspiration to others.
7) HIGH CULTURE—They are perceived to fulfill at a high level the ideals for the culture within which they exist.
8) THE ONLY ONES—They are the only organizations that have been able to do what they do at all, even though it might not seem that what they do is a difficult or mysterious thing.

To these of Peter Vaill, we would add the following:

9) LEADERSHIP POSITIONING—Their processes and procedures (compensation, human resources, technology, training, among other important processes) are ahead of the curve, not behind the curve.
10) NON-EXPLOITATIVE—They accomplish these tasks without exploiting workers or the environment.

Nonprofit boards have a huge assignment. They are responsible individually for their organizations, and for guiding those organizations toward doing their work, rather than deviating from their mission, and doing that work in an exceptional way. In accomplishing these tasks, they become part of the American political system itself, something that has always been true but, in our view, has been poorly understood in recent times.

With this background, it is now possible to proceed to look at the sector itself, and the organizations within it. From there, we can consider better practices, and ways to use those practices to achieve exceptionality.

Part II: Closer Context

The Organization of "Nonprofits" and "For-Profits"

This second part of the discussion of context moves from the society and community level to the organizational level. Here, we look at the differences between for-profit and nonprofit organizations. We also examine some systemic problems in nonprofit/nonprofit board performance which se the stage for the competencies coming up in the next section.

Chapter 3

Nonprofit and For-Profit Organizations: Differences and Similarities

Introduction

For many years, the "common sense" of the American organizational world was that a sharp distinction existed between the for-profits and not-for-profits. The for-profit was interested in bottom-line calculations, and the not-for-profits were oriented to "providing service." At the CEO level, the senior manager was called a CEO or president in the for-profit, and the CEO at the not-for-profit. At the board level, board participants were "directors" in the for-profit firm, and board members for the social nonprofit/human service organization.

There has been something of an evolution in the actual name of the "head" of the nonprofit organization. In the early part of the 20th century "Secretary" or "General Secretary" was the common designation. This title evolved into "CEO" in the middle to later part of that century. Then, within the past 30 years or so, the name has changed again to "CPO" ("Chief Professional Officer" and then again to CEO "Chief Executive Officer" and also "President." Frequently the "head" is CEO and President, something that is a bit of overkill in our view, but becoming common. One force driving this change was to achieve titular parity with corporate counterparts. Confusion comes in two ways here, however. One is that the term President was reserved for the Chairperson of the board (aka CVO, or Chief Volunteer Officer). Now we must take care to be sure which "President" we are talking about in a nonprofit. Second, as the names have changed, there have been subtle (and not so subtle) changes in expectations of the role of the CEO/President. The older, "Secretary" designation referred to a position that was clearly subordinate to the board. The "CEO" moniker implies a person who is "co responsible" with the board, and, in some instances, is actually a voting member of the board.

This Chapter looks at the differences between the not-for-profit and for-profit agencies, and especially, their boards.

Nonprofit boards have a unique place in the structure and functioning of American society. Millions (1.9 million in 2006, actually) of voluntary organizations exist—from churches to schools and universities, from foundations to small storefront operations (independendentsector.org). In many ways, they are quite similar to for-profit organizations, but they have many differences as well. We consider here some of these similarities and differences, as well as the main responsibilities of nonprofit boards.

Key Similarities

For the most part, nonprofit and for-profit organizations are the same, as organizations. Each has goals, and each seeks to maximize these goals. The fact that the goals may be different is less significant than commonly supposed. If there is no income, there is no organization. If there are no products, there is no income, whether you are a restaurant or a foster care organization.

Both organizational types need to "run" their organization—introducing new products, pruning old ones, and improving those they are keeping. They face a series of common problems, from managing change, to seeking to influence their relevant environments, to developing an organizational structure that is sufficiently firm to be recognizable and sufficiently nimble to respond to environmental upheavals. Each needs to perform "environmental scans" to apprise themselves of relevant environmental elements. Each needs strategic direction, capable CEO leadership, and robust governance. Each needs to hire and fire staff.

Key Differences

There are some vital differences, however. While these are not the only ones, they are the ones that we see as most significant, because, singly and severally, they tend to heavily impact the culture of the organization and give a distinctive sense.

Legal Status

Nonprofit organizations have a different legal status. They are exempt from taxes, in exchange for which they serve, as organizations, a civic rather than a personal purpose. How they define this civic purpose is an important question, as is how they know whether they achieve this goal. But the situation is not completely either-or. Nonprofit organizations are entitled—and indeed expected—to look after their own survival. And, although for-profit organizations serve primarily personal purposes, they also have civic duties to consider, especially when one of their products has a flaw, is tampered with, or experiences similar difficulties.

Customer Duality

A second difference involves customer duality—users/payer unity or difference. In for-profits, the user—the customer—is most often the payer. Nonprofits usually have two "customers"—users (clients, consumers, customers) and payers (governments, donors, and users as well). This complicates the nonprofit's job because the nonprofit/human service organization often has to harmonize conflicting customer preferences around the same product. There are other implications to this difference. Over time, the "golden rule" tends to obtain: she who has the gold, rules. This gradual identification means that agencies gravitate toward funder preferences rather than that of clients, unless significant refocusing is done. In addition, at least for those clients who are not paying themselves for their services, it is difficult for the user to demand better quality of a free good. Absence of user demands simply exacerbates the focus on funder preferences.

Stakeholders Rather than Stockholders

A third difference lies in the larger accountability structure. When we broaden the issue of "accountability," beyond payers and users, we come to the difference between stakeholders and stockholders. Public for-profit organizations have owners—stockholders—who invest in the organization to make gains for themselves. Stockholders are a vital group of stakeholders. Stakeholders is the community that has an interest in the organization—these include employees, customers, suppliers, cities, and states that get the organization's tax dollars, locales where the organization has facilities, among others. Whereas nonprofit organizations must keep civic purpose in mind, the for-profit must keep personal purpose in mind and interpret its needs to itself and to the public.

Nonprofit organizations have stakeholders but not stockholders. In the for-profit case, stockholders (or owners if the organization is privately held) are a dominant force. In the nonprofit case, stockholders are absent, but stakeholders are vital. The problem here is that it is much more difficult to crystallize the ambiguous and often conflicting preferences of the stakeholder community.

Volunteer Workforce

A fourth difference is that the nonprofit uses volunteers as part of its delivery structure, while for-profits do not. These organizational features mean that nonprofits have to manage two workforce systems—a paid and an unpaid group. These volunteers are at both the level of service (doing the actual work of the nonprofit/human service organization, such as providing transportation, cooking, cleaning, keeping records, etc.) and at the director level.

Affectively Charged Culture

Fifth, nonprofit organizations tend to have a culture that is more affectively charged than for-profits do. On the employee side, people who work for nonprofits tend to see their work as a "calling" in addition to a job or career. They seek to "make a difference" and want that kind of psychic income (meaning, affirmation, sense of purpose and importance) as well as cash income. They are frequently motivated to work for social justice, to "repair the world," to right wrongs they see in the communities and societies in which they live, and even in a global context.

Of course, employees in both for-profits and not-for-profits seek meaning in and through work. However the importance of socially contributory meaning in the nonprofit workforce seems to be significantly greater.

Volunteers have a similar sense of calling and wish to make a difference to the employees. They chip in significantly. In 2006, the value of volunteer time as calculated by The Independent Sector was around 250 billion dollars.

This workforce's emphasis on social significance and helping complicate the management tasks for nonprofit CEOs and managers because staff and volunteers care deeply about their tasks. However, caring deeply does not clarify *what* it is that needs to be done; *how* it should be done; or *decide* when one is doing enough. It also opens the door for exploitation on the compensation side of nonprofit employees, on the grounds that "you do not come into nonprofit employment to get rich."

On the organization side, nonprofit agencies tend to be "mission driven." Such motivation can, of course, be a good thing, unless it creates a subculture (which it can do) in which sensible management practices are ignored.

The Higher Standard

Sixth, for better or worse, is expectations. Nonprofits are often held to higher standards of behavior. This expectation extends beyond organizational purpose itself to include staff and the place of work. Office quarters cannot be plush, CEO and other compensation is lower, and perks are fewer than is sometimes true in the for-profit sector.

Wicked Problems

Seventh, an argument could be made that the work of the nonprofit/human service organization and board is truly harder than that of the for-profit firm, or at least provides truly unique challenges. Why should this statement be true? Rittle and Weber (1973), in looking at public managers, make the point that public managers deal with what they call "wicked problems" and we think this analysis applies to nonprofits as well. In wicked problems, the subject matter at hand is beset with a number of particular difficulties that make it extraordinarily difficult work.

- There is no definitive formulation of a wicked problem
- Wicked problems have no stopping rule
- Solutions to wicked problems are not true or false, but good or bad
- There is no immediate and no ultimate test of a solution to a wicked problem
- Every solution to a wicked problem is a "one-shot operation"
- Every wicked problem can be considered a symptom of another problem
- Wicked problems have an innumerable (rather than an exhaustible describable) set of potential solutions; there is not a well-described set of permissible operations that may be incorporated into the plan
- The existence of a discrepancy representing a wicked problem can be explained in numerous ways. The choice of explanation determines the nature of the problem's resolution

The result of the fact that human problems tend to be wicked ones is a problem-set of exquisite difficulty from the governance perspective.

Unique Board Structure and Composition

Finally, eighth, there are differences at the board level[2]. Corporations tend to call their board persons "directors" while nonprofits tend to call their board participants "members." Corporate directors are typically compensated, while nonprofit directors are typically not. Corporate boards have inside directors while nonprofit boards have all outside directors. An "inside" director is an officer of the company, such as the CEO, CFO, etc. In nonprofit boards, the CEO and other nonprofit/human service organization officers may sit on the board, but are most typically *ex officio*, rather than voting members. Typically all directors (inside and outside) vote on corporate boards, while in nonprofit boards only the outside directors vote. It is our view that employees of the nonprofit/human service organization who sit with the board should NOT vote, a view we extend to corporations as well. And the legal obligations of profit and nonprofit directors may be construed differently. Certainly, in both cases, following the law is such a basic injunction that one thinks it hardly needs mentioning. If the law is not crystal clear, however, differences of approach develop. For this reason, many nonprofit organizations take out liability insurance so that their directors' own personal resources will not be exposed as a result of their actions as directors[3].

Conclusion

There are, therefore, similarities and differences. We need to think about them with care, because several issues come to mind.

Even though differences exist, they are not differences that make a difference. Within the human condition, for example, some differences make a difference (skin color, for example) and others seem not to (eye color, for example).

Secondly, the within group differences might be as great as the between group ones. Profits and nonprofits have a significant

---

[2] We mentioned the diffeences in nomenclature for the organizational "head" above.
[3] The appendix details some of the considerations that nonprofit directors may want to take into account.

variation in scope and scale. Nonprofits range from huge ones (like Bill Gates Trust—39 Billion in 2006; and the Bill and Melinda Gates Foundation—29 Billion in 2006; the University of Michigan with a budget of 4+billion in 2006, to small store front operations that have tiny budgets and sometimes no paid staff. For-profits have similar ranges of scope and scale.

The industry focus may also matter. Within the nonprofit sector, there are great differences in focus, from churches, health and hospital organizations, museums, art and cultural organizations, environmental groups, to human service organizations.

Then too, in almost each of these areas, one can find nonprofits and for- profits doing similar work. Some child care organizations are for-profit; some are not. Some counseling agencies are for-profit, some are not. Some nursing homes are for-profit; some are not. Some hospitals are for-profit; some are not.

At the director level, both not-for-profit and for-profit boards have to oversee the organization, and seek to make decisions that allow it to operate at maximum effectiveness (doing the right things) and efficiency (doing things right). CEOs in each organization have to manage and lead their organizations with the same goals of effectiveness and efficiency.

We mention these similarities and differences because, although this book is aimed at the nonprofit director, almost everything in it applies to the for-profit director as well. Today, to paraphrase Gilbert and Sullivan[4], "the director's lot is not a happy one," and all directors are seeking direction and assistance. Indeed, the landscape of both for-profit and nonprofit directorship has changed substantially in recent years. For one thing, there have been the high profile scandals in each sector that have shaken the foundations of probity and rectitude that were thought to have characterized directors on both sides of the fence. Legislative attention has brought many ethical lapses to the public's attention as well as internet blogs that detail corporate and nonprofit abuses.

---

[4] The Pirates of Penzance, Act II.

Chapter 4

Governance-Related Problems in Contemporary Nonprofit Human Service Organizations

Introduction

As we undertook updating the research on which this volume is based, we came across one universally agreed upon point: Boards of directors are deeply flawed. They seriously underperform and malperform virtually everywhere. While there were many prescriptions for improvement, no one really thought they were doing well. We ourselves interviewed many directors and CEOs which provided anecdotal confirmation of this trend in the literature.

Board Ineptitude

Let's start where the buck stops. Nonprofit boards are in need of much—really huge—improvement. While for-profit boards have much to answer for, and have been poor performers in many cases, nonprofit boards are, amazingly, worse. They are worse because, in effect, they have no oversight. They are, in effect, like public servants. Insulated as both groups are from the "political" process, they are insulated, as well, from accountability and responsibility. No one "fires" a nonprofit director (board member). Many times we have worked with boards which are out of legal compliance, having members sitting for two or three terms past their allowed timeframe (usually a maximum of two terms, or six years) because no one has the courage to tell them to move on. To this abuse we can add scores of others. For example, board members often have no idea what they are to do individually and collectively. Their processes and meetings become a venue for expressing and implementing private agendas. They are typically "run" by the most socially "powerful" person on the board. Status and deference operating as they typically do, other members defer to the socially prominent. Even the best ones fail in many areas and the worst ones are abysmal. They create, as W. Edwards Deming said, "incalculable loss." Among their most egregious failures is setting the direction for the organization and reviewing the CEO. As important, the boards do not care about management in the largest, most positive sense, providing vision and strategic guidance for the nonprofit/human service organization and the CEO[5]. This charge may be a bit unfair—board members do not come to their positions as callous individuals. But, in the absence of personal competence (competence = knowledge + skill) or board/guidance they resort to their default position, pushing their own agenda. A related problem is that there is no set of standards, and we are talking about lots of people here. If each of the 1.9 million nonprofits mentioned in the Preface had 10 board members, 19 million Americans would be serving as nonprofit directors, about the population of Australia. And 10 would be a conservative estimate. Fifteen is a more common average, meaning that about 28.5 million would be in the director group! (Of course, many have fewer than 10). Twenty-eight million plus folk with big responsibilities and no practical or ethical guidance is a scary thought—especially when they manage a trillion dollars. It is actually amazing they have done as well as they have. This situation is beginning to change,

---

[5] We use nonprofit/human service organizations as a capturing phrase because in a sense, all nonprofits are human services organizations—but the HSOs that we want to highlight are those that deal with the press of daily human problems.

however. In the US, The National Center for Nonprofit Boards is making important strides in training, and The Independent Sector is developing a list of ethical guidelines (see Appendix 2). But it still takes more training and testing to get a life-saving decal from the Red Cross than it does to become a nonprofit director. We have a long way to go.

The Organizational Legacy of Board Ineptitude

The inept, unguided, untrained, and particularistic nature of nonprofit governance—to which we have taken a "ho-hum" attitude in the past has had some serious consequences for the sector as a whole. The problematic items below are, of course, not characteristic of every nonprofit, but in our experience are broadly representative of the problems and issues besetting the sector, hampering its efficiency and effectiveness, driving its costs up and its successes down, and making it like a constant struggle. The sampling of problems we are mentioning here are largely deficiencies—in CEO education and preparation, human resources and technology gaps, lack of customer input, poor evaluatio—ones which the boards should have addressed. None are recent, and each and all are lamented in conversations with directors and CEOs around the country. However, the accepted view seems to be similar to that about the weather—it is what it is and nothing can be done. The whole issue has the feel of a self-fulfilling prophecy, where we create the very thing we fear by the attitudes we have about it and the actions we (do not) take as a result.

The CEO/CEO/CPO and the Top Team Are Often Untrained or Maltrained

Nonprofit/human service organization CEOs lack managerial training to help them in their tasks. For one thing, there is little administrative training either in the degree program (MSW curricula), as they are on the way to a CEO position (management certificate and post-grad programs) or when they are a CEO (continuing education programs). There is a bit of a vicious circle here. It is not available because "we cannot afford it." We cannot afford it because the boards do not believe it counts, even though some of the board members have themselves, through their commercial organizations, enjoyed such training. Because the boards do not think it counts, the CEOs do not either. Because the CEOs do not, they do not press their boards; you can see where this goes ... nowhere. Hence, CEOs are, by and large, untrained in management and leadership competencies.

If this situation sounds bad, it is. Unfortunately, it is, actually, worse. They are maltrained. In the absence of training, CEOs use the skills at the last position as appropriate for the new one. Let me explain. Organizations exist in three broad skill bands—the technical band, the managerial band, and the institutional band. This means that there are two kinds of managers in social work agencies—the top team and the top person. What happens frequently is that an excellent technical person—a worker say, but it could be a teacher, an engineer, a whatever—is, because of that excellence, promoted into the managerial ranks. This promotion is based upon the assumption, held by the promoters and the promotees, that the new job is an **extension of**, rather than **different from**, the old job.

As many organizational observers have pointed out, there are qualitative shifts as one crosses levels, which require qualitatively different skill sets. In fact, being good at your old job may, in effect, disqualify you for your new job. Why is that? The answer is that whatever we are good at becomes our "default" style. Under stress, which the move to a new job certainly is, we are more likely to resort to that default style, other things being equal. That means that the therapist, upon becoming director, "defaults" to therapeutic-style skills and styles as a **manager**. This is something all of us have seen as social workers. We may even have done it. Indeed, so common is this phenomenon that an early diagnostic version of it emerged as "The Peter Principle." This "principle," developed by Lawrence J. Peter, sought to explain why so many managers were incompetent (Peter, 1970, 1972; Kane, 1970). He observed that organizations structured incompetence by promoting employees until they reached their level of incompetence. There they would remain.

Use of the default style is encouraged by more than just stress, though. Here is where training comes in, or more accurately, does not come in.

And here again there is progress. "Nonprofit Management" is a growth area in American Higher Education. Centers around the US (Indiana University, Case Western Reserve University, and others) are under vigorous development. And there is a National Network of Social Work Managers that has a list of competencies and provides certification. But the need is great.

The CEO/CEO/CPO and the Top Team Are Cast Adrift

Because of the board problems and the training problems just mentioned, the CEO/CEO/CPO and the top team are in many ways left to "twist slowly in the wind." This point connects, of course, to the board, which is supposed to provide policy direction, on the one hand, and CEO appraisal, on the other, and which rarely does either. CEOs are surrounded by high and often unexpressed expectations. Praise is meager; criticism voluminous. Here again, progress is on the horizon. For example, The Amherst Wilder Foundation in Minneapolis is taking a leadership role in making it easy to use materials available to CEOs and their staffs in a variety of key areas. (Their training and publishing arm has spun off into the Fieldstone Alliance).

Continuing Education Programs for the Nonprofit CEO Are Few

Given the large number of nonprofit human service organizations, one would expect a flourishing "industry" of post-degree training and education programs. If the front-end training is thin, perhaps, once on the job, managers and CEOs could build skills with a seminar here, a workshop there, over the course of their careers. Sadly, this is not the case. The "big" systems—the United Way of

America, the Girl Scouts, the Child Welfare League of America, and so on—have CEO training programs for "their" CEOs. These are, of course, to be encouraged and expanded. But outside of this effort, social work managers and CEOs find it difficult to find programs, and to pay for them when they do find them. This kind of situation is another way in which managers are left adrift. The Alliance for Children and Families has developed a very successful program—The CEO Leadership Institute—which runs yearly at The University of Michigan and provides CEO training and education to more than two dozen CEOs annually.

The Executive and Managerial Mindset Is Underrepresented in the Nonprofit Culture

Nonprofit work seems to be focused on helping people and communities with problems or reshaping social policy. Somehow "managing" or "governing" does not seem like a meaningful task— mission, not management, is the call. The idea seems to be that, because our hearts are pure and our intentions good, "management" is somehow not needed. Somehow, many nonprofit participants—paid and volunteer—apparently feel that good intentions are enough. They forget, of course, that the road to hell is paved with good intentions.

And this lack of attention to management issues has very negative consequences for the nonprofit participant. That "participant"— clients, customers, consumers, employees—on the ground experiences and feels the effects of bad management. Hundreds of participants with whom we have talked complain that their's is badly run and/or badly governed ... and then they go on to give chilling example after chilling example. Yet the "felt problems" of bad management have not translated into support for good management.

The Human Resources Function Is Underdeveloped

Not only is the management function underrated, the worker function is underrated. Oddly, for organizations addressing issues of social betterment, the typical nonprofit has underdeveloped human resources function aimed at helping their own workers. Perhaps the volunteer tradition that began our field and that continues to this day may have something to do with the under appreciation of the employee herself or himself.

Fiscal Knowledge Is Limited

Such limited training as CEOs and future CEOs do receive for CEO and managerial roles is very shy on financial management skills, including accounting. Many nonprofit CEOs say that finding a good CFO is one of their hardest tasks.

Technological Development Is Lagging

What is true for financial management is also true for technology. Nonprofits are 20th century at best. Computer-based applications, email and web-based activities are a long way from standard at most social agencies. Equipment is often second- or third-generation, technology knowledge limited, and technology based activities the subject of a series of running jokes about "the computer this" and "the computer that."

The Voice of the Customer Is Largely Silent

For some reason social work has never embraced the program and services assessment mindset either. (Could it be because our clients were poor and it did not matter)? CEOs all too often became apologists for lackluster nonprofit/human service organization performance rather than leaders down the road of better quality.

Evaluation Is Heavily Process-Based Rather than Results-Based, Focusing on Outputs Rather than Outcomes

Connected with the issue of "customer" evaluation is the issue of the results of human intervention. Are we, at the end of the day, adding value, helping people, making a difference? Famous wit Dorothy Parker's comment applies here as well. When told that the American president Calvin Coolidge had died, she is supposed to have asked, "How can they tell?" This question applies to nonprofit human service organizations specifically. "Are you helping?" "And how can you tell?" Doing good is not enough. One needs to do it right, and do it well! Such evaluations procedures as are largely in place tend to be of a process nature—we "saw" so many clients, we have so many children in our center, etc. But does anyone get better? On THAT question we often have little to share. Not all process measures are problematic—hot meals served, women given shelter, etc., are some examples of acceptable evaluations. But overall, evaluation needs to be drastically improved. Outcomes need to be the focus—are we actually achieving results? Activity measurement—outputs—is important but not the same as outcomes.

Conclusion

This book is about boards and their responsibilities. The point of including some detail here about the organizational issues facing nonprofits is that poor, inept, do-what-you-feel-like, well-intentioned governance has really bad consequences, bad for the mission, bad for the clients and users, bad for the employees, and for the community and society. Improving governance can have a magnitude of positive effects that make the board better, and the nonprofit/human service organization as well.

Part III: What to Do

Competencies: The Basic Responsibilities of Boards

Overview

We define competencies as the combination of knowledge plus skill. We think of boards as falling into four categories –

- those with the knowledge of what to do and the skill to put that knowledge into practice;
- those with knowledge of what to do but have a lack of skills to apply that knowledge usefully and create accomplishments;
- those with skills but limited knowledge of what they are supposed to do;
- those with neither the knowledge nor the skill to work efficiently or effectively.

The first group we calmly call the *articulated board*; it oversees and guides organizational accomplishment. The second group we call the *"fire, ready, aim" board.* They know what they want to do, they have mission clarity and a strong sense of their responsibilities, but lack the skills to work efficiently. The third group we call the SALY board – Same As Last Year. They continue to do what they know how to do, regardless of its appropriateness. Robert K. Merton called this situation "means ritualism"(Merton 1958). The last group we call the *"good intensions" board.* They have good intensions, but no clear idea of what to do or how to do it.

We see two kinds of important knowledge. One is mission definition, crispness, and clarity. Keeping the mission in front of each director, the board itself, and the organization is an important task of the board. Failure to do so leads to mission creep, a widening gap between what the organization wants to do and thinks it is doing and what the organization is actually doing. One might also call these "organizational ends."

Nonprofit organizations can pick their own mission, or ultimate goals. Regardless of what mission they select, there are certain instrumental goals that each board needs to address. For the first edition we interviewed directors and chairs who had reputations as outstanding directors to develop perspectives on the subject, synthesizing their views and using them in conjunction with the writings of others. For this edition, we followed the same procedure, with newer literature and more conversation. We found the original areas largely valid, but made one addition—assure financial wellness and integrity—and combined two previously separate ones—strategic planning and entrepreneurship.

The result is a series of six key areas of board-governance responsibility.

The six responsibilities detailed here allow boards to exceed their basic legal requirements and achieve substantive success.

One might ask how these six relate to the 12 principles that BoardSource identified as characteristics of "exceptional" boards. Their approach identifies 12 areas of work, as follows our six, to be discussed in detail and in subsequent chapters. There is a good match between the 12 and the six.

BoardSource	Tropman/Harvey
Constructive Partnership	Civic Purpose
Mission Driven	
Strategic Thinking	Vision/Mission/Goals
Culture of Inquiry	
Independent Mindedness	Make/Oversee Policy
Ethos of Transparency	
Compliance With Integrity	Hire/Evaluate CEO
Sustaining Resources	
Results Oriented	Assure Financial Wellness
Intentional Board Practices	
Continuous Learning	Strategic Planning/Change
Revitalization	
	Legal

BoardSource goes a step further. Within each dimension they use an equation: Responsible Boards X Source of Power = Exceptional Boards.

There are behaviors under responsible boards matched with a leveraging process which results in exceptional board performance. Here is one example, their first, from Constructive Partnership:

Responsible Boards	X Source Power =	Exceptional Boards
Articulate a Clear Statement Of mission	Use Mission and Values in Decision Making	Sharply Address Community Needs

We have huge respect for BoardSource, but have three concerns as well. First, their system is detailed and complicated, though still very good. Second, our sense is that most boards are aspirationally responsible but actually problematic. Hence, our first major national goal should be to get the majority of boards into the responsible area. But there is no problem in setting goals for us all. Thirdly, BoardSource does not address in this document the "how to do it" element. We feel this is an omission, and can leave readers feeling a bit "lost." That said, it is excellent work and a touchstone volume.

41

Let us turn now to a more detailed discussion of our "significant six."

Basic Responsibilities

First, of course, boards must meet legal requirements and conditions. Mayer and Croxton discuss these in the appendix. These requirements, however, are the absolute minimum that a board seeks to achieve. Beyond legal obligations, six responsibilities are basic and crucial:

1. Embody and enact trusteeship of civic purpose
2. Articulate vision, mission, and goals
3. Making and overseeing policy
4. Select and evaluate the CEO
5. Assure financial wellness and integrity
6. Introduce strategic planning, change, and entrepreneurship

To carry out these responsibilities, the board needs some tools. One set of techniques involves the structure and culture of the board. The other set involves the board meeting itself.

What to Do

Too often, those of us who wind up on boards don't know what to do. People we have interviewed about governance complain that their boards—including themselves and their fellow directors—are ignorant about their responsibilities. Based on these discussions, and the writings of others, we have identified the key responsibilities of boards.

Embody and Enact Trusteeship of Civic Purpose

The board of directors, particularly the voluntary board, represents the embodiment of a larger civic purpose and is the vehicle through which civic impulses for the betterment of the community are expressed. These are flowery phrases, surely, but they do represent something of the importance of the overall mission and role of the directors and the organization. It is because of civic purpose— as opposed to the personal—that society, through government, grants tax exemption to nonprofit entities. Part of the trusteeship role is legal integrity and compliance. As collective entities, boards have legal responsibilities under state statutes. Individual directors are responsible—ethically and sometimes legally—for the conduct of the corporation as well. The appendix addresses legal obligations in detail.

Articulating Vision, Mission, and Goals. Boards and directors have the responsibility of developing and affirming the longer term purpose of the nonprofit/human service organization (its particular civic purpose or function) and shorter term missions and goals. Vision, and the shaping of organizational purpose to that vision, is a crucial board activity, one more frequently lost than not. The responsibility of the board is to articulate the organization's vision, translate that vision into a mission, and fashion goals from that mission that embody the vision and make it real. The board is also responsible for changing the vision when the time is appropriate.

Make and Oversee Policy. Policy is the vehicle through which vision and mission are effectuated. Policy is written, approved by the board, provides a basis for action, and is current. The board of directors makes overall policy for the organization. It is important that the board remain on the policy level. The problem of what is a policy decision and what is an administrative decision occurs frequently, and Chapter 8, on policymaking, provides useful concepts to keep policy and administration in their corners.

While not micromanaging administration, the board, usually through its committee structure, must oversee the implementation of policy to some degree. Contemporary boards often fail in both the policymaking and oversight aspects of their responsibilities. They avoid decisions, making them too late or not at all. Often, they do not ask enough questions of the CEO, and they sometimes fail to check the implementation of policies they have made.

Select and Evaluate the CEO. One of the most important responsibilities that boards have is to select the CEO of the organization and to evaluate that person on a regular basis. Too often, the first of these tasks is done poorly and the second is not done at all. Poor selection results from the fact that most boards don't select CEOs regularly or frequently. Hence, whatever accumulated wisdom exists about the selection process tends to be lost in the interim. The search process overall, the legal requirements that may surround it, the useful practices to follow—all are forgotten.

As we said, boards often fail to evaluate the CEO. Once they hire the CEO, not much more is heard from the board until, perhaps, the CEO is fired. Signals sometimes come in the form of lower or higher salary increments but cannot substitute for a sit-down, talk-through of the past year's accomplishments and problems. And the lack of evaluation experience is an additional sign of the lack of experience that boards display in the hiring process.

Entrepreneurship and Innovation. Nonprofit/human service organization vitality is not manufactured by doing the same thing again and again. Rather, agencies need innovation and periodically may need to be reinvented (Naisbitt & Aburdene, 1985). Directors are responsible for changing the organization to keep it current. That is major change. But the board also needs to champion minor change—the kind of day-to-day improvements that everyone talks about, but few do much about. Transforming the system and tweaking the system—both are necessary.

Assure Financial Wellness and Integrity. Assuring and ensuring the financial well being of the organization is an important part of the governance responsibility. For one thing, as we noted in the discussion of civic purpose, nonprofits are the beneficiaries of tax expenditures on the part of the citizens. Nonprofits need to be sure that their value proposition exceeds their subsidy. Secondly, nonprofits are the custodians of gift dollars and gift time. These need to be well used.

Third, for many nonprofits, their clientele is vulnerable and not able to advocate as well for themselves. Special care need be taken that financial problems do not interfere with the stream of service.

Fiscal Health has two major parts. One is attending to the income, the other attending to the expenditures. In the first case, the board may engage in development, personal gifts, etc. What matters is not the mode—different boards take different paths—but the fact that there is regular attendance to this issue. (And this does NOT mean approving monthly budget statements.) Expenditures of course are the other side of the coin, and care must be taken to make sure they are appropriate. That is especially the case in mission driven organizations, where some of the businesses a nonprofit/human service organization might run are subsidy businesses.

Then there is the audit function. Outside firms are used to assess the fiscal integrity of the nonprofit/human service organization and to apply standard tests to the its fiscal performance. The board needs to have an executive session at least once each year with those auditors.

Finally, the directors individually need to improve their own knowledge and comfort with fiscal matters. This improvement can be part of the training in a board development program, discussed in Chapter 12.

Strategic Planning, Change, and Entrepreneurship. Boards have a fundamental responsibility for positioning the nonprofit/human service organization for the future as well as the present, for tomorrow as well as today. They chart the course of their organizations. Such a process involves strategic planning. Every couple of years, the board should reassess the organization's strategic goals, adding goals if needed and removing outdated goals as appropriate. Strategic planning involves change in the organization's mission. As important, however, strategic change also requires changes to an organization's structure. The structure of the nonprofit/human service organization needs to be aligned with its mission and product lines. As Henry Mintzberg, the famous organizational analyst, would put it, "Fit is it." This nostrum means that the role of the board may change as the strategic goals change. As part of the strategic planning process, the board also needs to encourage development and innovation within the nonprofit/human service organization. Such responsible risk taking requires budgetary support, another piece of the organization's fiscal health.

Exercise 1: Grade Your Board

Consider the responsibilities of boards and the skills for better boardship. Rate your board on each (A = Excellent, B = Good, C = Average, D = Poor, F = Failure). If you are not sure, put DK ("don't know").

Basic Responsibility	Grade
Meets legal requirements	_____

Regular Responsibilities	
Is a trustee of civic purpose	_____
Articulates mission, vision, and goals	_____
Makes and oversees policy decisions	_____
Selects and evaluates the CEO	_____
Assures fiscal health	_____
Introduces strategic planning, change, and entrepreneurship.	_____

If your board rates less than A in any category, what do you think the problem(s) is (are)? How could these problems be solved or managed?

Chapter 5

Embody and Enact
Trusteeship of Civic Purpose

Introduction

The first main area of board responsibility is the role of trustee-ship (Greenleaf, 1973). Trusteeship extends beyond the minimum legal requirements for avoiding lawsuits. The trustee holds corporate charter for the benefit of the community (as tax exemption makes nonprofit organizations "instruments" of government, as discussed in Chapter 2). This idea is implied in the term civic group. Trusteeship speaks to the larger issues of responsibilities and obligations and the various constituencies that must be considered.

Social Responsibilities

Although the realm of an organization's social responsibilities is, as yet, unclear and subject to much discussion and concern, the question is nonetheless pertinent whether one is talking about seat belts, toxic waste, or responsibilities to staff for adequate salaries. The nonprofit and charitable board has an impressive burden of social responsibility because of its "public" (or semipublic) role through its tax exemption. Expectations thus vary.

The issue becomes even more complex because the people and causes for which the nonprofit works almost always involve the less powerful, the disadvantaged, or the vulnerable. For example, in a board designed to promote youth services, should youth be on the board? If they cannot legally serve on the board, is an ex officio role or a youth advisory committee structure appropriate? If the organization serves a cultural group, should members of that group be on the board, be the whole board? The problems are difficult. Charitable organizations or nonprofit public benefit corporations that receive charitable contributions are responsible to donors as well as to receivers and to the community. And those responsibilities are enmeshed in organizations' larger responsibilities to society.

The concept of trusteeship means that society has delegated to a particular board the accomplishment of a civic purpose. The board must think through the way in which it conducts its business and organizes itself so it may carry out this civic purpose. Boards can take several approaches to accomplishing this. One is through the very composition of the board itself.

Trusteeship through Board Composition

Boards are created to direct organizations in carrying out their "public benefit" responsibilities. Board directorship is often approached as a way to bring resources to this commitment. There are many approaches to creating a board. People with personal wealth who can personally contribute to an organization constitute a "money board," a prime financial resource to the nonprofit/human service organization.

Sometimes, organizations recruit people with prestige rather than, or in addition to, personal wealth to add luster, acceptance, and "class" to the board and, hence, to the nonprofit/human service organization purpose as a whole. The "prestige board" helps legitimize the organization. Organizations sometimes seek people with knowledge and experience in a particular field. The "professional board" seeks expertise.

48

In some cases, those most affected by the actions of the organization in question become drivers; hence, the "stake-holder board" or "client board." So, one question about board composition is whether one has the people one needs. And how does one know who is needed, anyway?

Some organizations try to sidestep this issue by putting everyone but Mr. Kitchen Sink on the board. This practice leads to "show boards" or "trophy boards" of 50, 60, 70, or more directors. This feeble attempt to solve the problem of directorship through quantification almost always, and sooner rather than later, leaves the board directorship bored! And the bigger the board, the more likely the organization is run by a small elite—sometimes an executive committee, sometimes "managing committees." One organization was ultimately run by a "noncommittee" of the most "important" people in town. Good boards seem to have 12-18 directors for both representation and decision-making purposes.

To accomplish trusteeship, the board itself must become the instrument of trusteeship. One way to approach trusteeship, then, is to have a board of appropriate directorship and size.

Trusteeship Through Community Representation

But everyone cannot be on the board, especially if the size is modest. How, then, can one create involvement on the one hand while maintaining suitable size?

As an alternative to "board stuffing," we recommend establishing a visiting committee, leadership circle, or advisory board—a larger group of people who join a circle around the board. No fee is necessary to join, just a declaration of interest. The circle can provide a broad base for testing trusteeship ideas and is the source of new directors. (See the section on recruitment later in this chapter.)

The Leadership Circle usually convenes annually. Appointing committees from the circle can augment the strength of the board. When directors leave the board, they can join the visiting committee as emeritus directors, giving them special honor without the board losing their expertise. New directors of the leadership circle can work to become future directors. Membership in the leadership circle is distinct from being an actual director. There must be a clear distinction between a leadership circle—which broadly represents the community and has input to the board of directors— and the board itself. This is one reason why we usually refer to the board as directors, not members—to verbally reinforce the role that they have in law and in fact. Those in the leadership circle, and in other "advisory" groups that the organization may set up from time to time, can have "members."

Thus, boards achieve a balanced composition that is representative of the whole community through a two-tier structure rather than seeking to accomplish all purposes through a single-tier structure.

This two-tier structure would look something like Figure 1.

Figure 1
The Leadership Circle

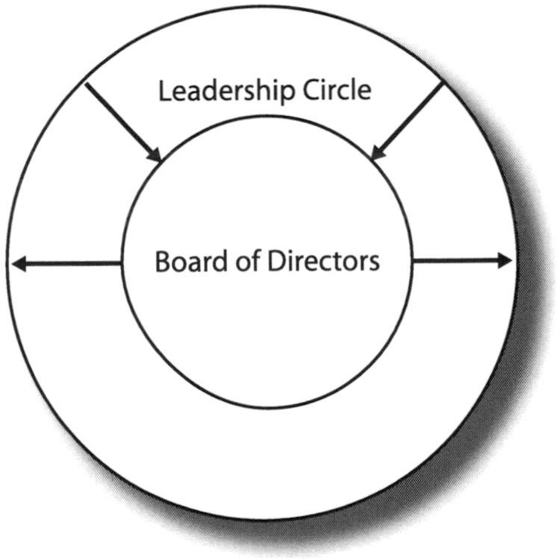

Trusteeship through Membership Organizations

Some nonprofits use a membership model. Typically one becomes a "member" of the organization (a person can become a member or an organization can become one). There are often member services and "the membership" frequently approves new directors at an annual meeting.

Trusteeship through Advisory Commissions and Hearings

If the board requires input from a particular segment of the community, but that segment is not represented on the board (for example, the African American, Asian American, Latino, or elderly communities), the board can establish a special advisory committee. Developed on an as-needed basis, such ad hoc arrangements can advise the board and undertake missions at the board's request. When issues of great public interest arise, the board can hold or organize public hearings, forums, or special sessions to obtain appropriate input. It is important to remember that advisory groups and public sessions are advisory to programs, not to governance itself.

Trusteeship through Quality Participation

Boards cannot accomplish their responsibility for trusteeship with lackluster directors participating haphazardly. The criteria for board directorship should be interest, competence, and a willingness to participate. Then, of course, the question of knowledge arises. Do prospective directors know what to do? Can they do it? Will they do it? Hopefully, the answer is yes. If so, board decisions are more likely to be of high quality.

Trusteeship through Quality Decisions

One way to assess successful trusteeship is by asking if the board is making policy decisions of high quality. Although assessing the quality of a decision is difficult, doing so is important. A board is a decision-making body. Its first goal is to make decisions. Boards often do not meet this standard, or they do not meet it in a timely or honest fashion. The board that delays making decisions or that rubber-stamps CEO proposals is not meeting this qualification. Even more, the board should aim for high-quality decisions. High-quality decisions expand and enhance the board's ability to carry out the function of trusteeship. Too often, boards defer and delay decision making so long that any decision looks good to their directors, and the question of whether the decision is any good becomes beside the point. Sometimes, board discussion goes on so far into the day or night that exhaustion sets in and directors will agree to anything, good or bad. Or the CEO may sometimes bring matters to the board so close to the time when action is needed that coherent discussion is impossible, thus yielding the decision that the CEO wanted. In each case, decision quality suffers.

Recruitment as an Ongoing Process

How do boards get the people they need? The first and most obvious step is for boards to determine the capabilities they need. Boards frequently do not have visions and missions that can help provide direction here. Then there is the simple issue of finding "live bodies." Developing interested, capable directors is always a problem.

Partly because of the difficulty of the task, boards often approach recruitment as a last-minute affair. People invited to join often have no real knowledge of the nonprofit organization; frequently, introductory material is not available. New directors say it can take a year or more before they know what is going on.

Boards cannot accomplish trusteeship if they are casual about recruiting. Visiting committees, advisory boards, or leadership circles are excellent places to begin recruiting, but boards should go beyond that. We recommend that boards keep recruitment files on an ongoing basis. Anyone can contribute to this file, and each board should assign one director—perhaps the nominating committee chair—the responsibility of keeping it updated.

When a person is nominated for directorship, the board, logically through its nominating committee, should conduct an initial interview with the candidate to determine his or her interest, time constraints, and so on, even if the potential for becoming a director is in the future. If the nominee's interest is positive, then the board can begin to gradually involve that person in the nonprofit organization's affairs, during which time, both nominee and organization mutually test their fit for one another. Directorship on the visiting committee should be an initial step toward directorship. A directorship should be the end of a process of involvement—it should not commence the process.

In the entire recruitment effort, the nominating committee plays a central role. That committee, one of great importance to the board, works closely with the CEO to establish a continuing list of candidates. The nominating committee continually assesses board functions and their performance to ensure a supply of interested, competent directors. Recruitment must be planned, not the quick fill-the-gap approach so common today. Thus, recruitment and preparation of directors becomes a necessary rather than a sufficient condition for successful trusteeship.

Conclusion

Nonprofit directors serve as trustees of civic purpose. This trust is complicated, because what the community wants is not always clear. But the nature and structure of the organization itself should be such that diverse and evolving areas of community concern can express themselves. In the next chapter, we will look at the articulation of specific visions, missions, and goals and the development of strategic and tactical approaches to accomplishing them. But without a trusteeship structure, decisions about these elements are likely to be warped and even self-serving.

Exercise 2

Try to define the concept of trusteeship for your board. What kind of job are you doing in the trusteeship role? What kind of job is the board doing as a whole?

1. Do you have one of the special kinds of boards mentioned?
   - Money board
   - Status or prestige board
   - Professional board
   - Stakeholder or client board
   - Trophy board
   - Sponsorship board[6]

2. How can you move toward a more "trusteeship" structure?

3. What steps does your board follow in spotting potential members? Can the process be improved?

Think of establishing a two-tier community representative system as a way to achieve better representation (a visiting committee, advisory board, or leadership circle). Could you do it? Why or why not? Do you already have something like this in place?

---

[6] A sponsorship board occurs where some organizations agree to form a new board to oversee common interests.

Chapter 6

Articulate Vision, Mission, and Goals

Introduction

The board is responsible for articulating a vision for the organization. Once the vision is complete, then the board can derive a more specific mission from it. Expressing a mission leads to a strategic plan and then to annual plans.

Vision and Mission

Vision embodies and expresses the hopes and aspirations that form the core of the organization's raison d'être—its reason for existing. It speaks of the longing for accomplishment, rather than accomplishment itself. An organizational vision is usually a short phrase: "helping teenage mothers" or "reducing domestic violence in the tri-county area." Organizations sometimes express their visions in their names and in logos or symbols (including colors) that identify and reinforce their overall missions. Organizations may also have mottos that seek to capture the essence of the agencies.

Involving everyone in creating visions, names, mottos, and logos can be exciting and motivational (Tropman & Morningstar, 1989). We urge some caution, however: Boards must anticipate and be prepared to manage conflict in partici¬pants' understanding of vision. Boards must also recognize that involving everyone calls for broad representation of all stakeholders, including staff, clients or customers, and the community in which or on whose behalf the organization operates. All should be part of this conversation.

Whereas the vision is a phrase, the mission statement is a paragraph, or at least a complete sentence, expressing in detail the areas in which the vision operates. Some sample vision and mission statements appear on the facing page.

Strategic Plan

Vision and mission are longer term, but not timeless. They remain current and endure over time, until the board decides to change them. The strategic plan, however, is time limited—usually two to five years—and stipulates the specific areas in which the nonprofit organization works and the programs it offers. Strategic plans are vital because each program should become a division or department of the nonprofit organization (and a committee of the board, as we will see in Chapter 9). Most agencies find 3 to 10 areas of service to be about right, 5 or 6 seem to be the average. Too few, and the nonprofit organization is monolithic, too many, and the nonprofit organization can't redirect what it is doing.

Boards have to encourage their own directors and the organizations they oversee when it comes to strategic planning. Many people say, "Plans are too rigid. Let's just play it by ear." A plan is just that—a plan. It doesn't have to be carved in stone, if the environment changes, so can the plan. Think of the process as dynamic and changing, not fixed (Mintzberg, 1994). Planning requires constant establishment and alteration of direction. In this dynamic context, strategic planning is helpful and necessary. The virtue of strategic planning is the thinking and exploration that goes into it.

Sample Visions and Missions

Organization 1
Name:　HELPMOM
Motto:　The Future of Kids Is Moms
Vision:　Functional Competent Families
Mission: Helping Teenage Mothers

Mission statement: HELPMOM works with pregnant teenagers around issues of their own health and the health of their babies, marital and partner relationships and arrangements, and housing.

Organization 2
Name:　SafeHome　　　　　　Logo:
Motto:　Conflict Kills—Peace Saves
Vision:　Community Without Abuse
Mission: Reducing Domestic Violence in the Tri-County Area

Mission statement: SafeHome advocates and trains to achieve non-violent mechanisms for managing conflict in the home and provides "cool houses" for individuals before they begin violent episodes. We also provide harbor homes for victims and their families.

Annual Plan
By outlining the nonprofit organization's goals and activities for the coming year, the annual plan further specifies the strategic plan: "This year we are going to do these things." Measurable goals are attached to each element.

Most boards do not think they approve an annual plan, when in fact almost all do. It is called "the budget." Unfortunately, many organizations discuss their goals by way of the budget or through arguing about allocations. In fact, discussion of the annual plan should come before the budget discussion. The budget discussion is just an instrument to accomplish goals. One might as well discuss goals directly.

57

Implementing Vision, Mission, and Planning

Developing these elements is one thing. Implementing them is another. Much of the rest of this book deals with how to accomplish implementation. It is important to say here, however, that implementation is greatly assisted by the "deliverables" that appear as goals in the annual plan and the strategic plan. This allows boards to check progress and make adjustments, if necessary.

Conclusion

Vision, mission, strategic plans, and annual plans represent important policy decisions by the board. This process is the first aspect of trusteeship through quality decisions. Quality decisions cannot be made in a haphazard, catch-as-catch-can manner. The board needs a coherent, understandable organizational plan for its mission; and the organizational structure and allocation of effort must then be broken down into components that achieve that mission. As crises arise, they can be considered within the framework of the organizational vision, mission, and strategic and annual plans.

Exercise 3

1. Does your nonprofit organization have
   - a vision statement?
   - a motto?
   - a logo?
   - a mission statement?
   - a strategic plan?
   - an annual plan?

2. If so, are they up to date?

3. If not, why not?

4. If not, what can your board do to get them under way?

Chapter 7

Make and Oversee Policy

Introduction

Policy making is the vehicle of board action. But making good policy is not an easy task. It is not always clear what level of decisions boards should focus upon. This leads to a consideration of the policy-administration dichotomy.

Policy and Administration

The role of the board extends beyond policymaking to overseeing policy implementation as well. The line dividing policy functions from administrative functions is always unclear. We prefer the idea of intersecting sets illustrated in Figure 2.

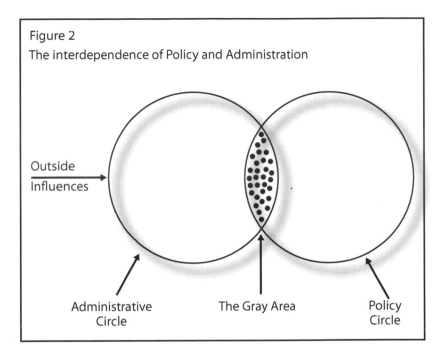

Figure 2
The interdependence of Policy and Administration

Outside
Influences

Administrative
Circle

The Gray Area

Policy
Circle

Differentiating policy from administration is never easy, and the separation will always be controversial. Directors should try to stay in the policy areas, however. Imperfect though the distinction may be, the following lists should help keep things straight.

Policy functions are generally those decisions that
- have broad scope and implication,
- commit the organization's personnel or resources in a substantial way,
- are precedent setting,
- have potential to impact the nonprofit organization's mission and purpose, and
- are in force over substantial periods of time or until changed.

Administrative functions are generally those decisions and actions that
- are relatively narrow in scope and implication,
- involve reversible commitments,

- tend toward the application of precedent rather than its establishment, and
- are in force over relatively shorter spans of time.

Clearly, while these elements can be hard to differentiate, these points provide a working basis for such activity. Sometimes organizations specify to some degree "hard" parameters. For example, the CEO can spend so much on her or his own authority, but over that board action is required, etc.

Precisely because of their longer-range implications, policy decisions require oversight. Many aspects of a major policy decision require other subsidiary decisions to put the intent of the policy into practice. Board involvement is necessary here, in cooperation with administration, to execute policy. Without understanding the need for board oversight, CEOs may well resent their boards; without understanding the need for CEO involvement, boards may in turn resent CEOs' intrusion into policy matters. There is no completely clear demarcation between policy and administration. Relationships between CEOs and boards are worked out to the satisfaction of both from organization to organization.

The gray area includes those issues that involve policy and administration at once or in which the amount of either is unclear. Typically, these issues become the province of the CEO committee and are hashed out there before being allocated to the board as a whole or to the CEO.

Review and Refurbishment

Boards should make decisions in the policy area. In addition to decision making, however, there is decision "remaking." This is not redundancy; rather it is a policy review and refurbishment. Every three to five years, the board should take in-depth looks at its mission, role, and articles of incorporation to ascertain whether changes in direction are necessary. Each year, the board should select one specific area of the nonprofit organization-board relationship for review and, hopefully, refurbishment and improvement. The overall quality of

61

policy decisions should be audited yearly. Thus, the board might scrutinize personnel policy one year, financial policy in another year, and so on. At the end of this three- to five-year cycle, the board will have reviewed all of the subparts of the organization. Frequent evaluation regarding satisfaction with board meetings, and yearly assessments of decision quality, when combined with policy review and refurbishment and supplemented with information from the program audits, provide a useful overview of the organization's activities. These reviews can be accomplished during an annual one- or two-day retreat or at a special meeting in which people can look at the nonprofit and, in doing so, reconsider their own roles in the organization.

Review and refurbishment is longer range than the yearly assessments. Perspective and point of view are multi-year. Simply taking yearly evaluations and then looking at everything at the end of a longer period is both too little and too much. Yearly evaluations combine with the more intensive "sector" analyses when one is looking at the overall nonprofit organization mission and role in the five- to seven-year review cycle. Chapter 8, on strategic change, introduces detailed information on the overall process of change.

There are two ways to look at what bylaws, policies, etc., need to be revised. The first is retrospective and examines those areas in which practice is not following the bylaw or policy. The second is prospective, and looks at by-laws, mission, visions, and strategies to see what in the environment has changed since the last time it was examined. Each approach should inform policy review and refurbishment.

The Budget

Approval of the budget is one of the most important elements of the board's action. Money and its care are at the heart of fiduciary responsibility. Through the budget, the board implements the annual plan—and, by implication, the strategic plan, the mission, and the vision statement—by assigning portions of the nonprofit organization's budgetary resources to its program¬matic components. The board decides approximately how much of organizational resources should go toward accomplishing particular objectives. Ideally, boards should make these assignments regardless of the revenue generated by particular components.

Consider, for example, a nonprofit organization with two central components—counseling and residential care. The board of directors might decide to spend 60% of resources on counseling and 40% on residential care. This decision permits budget makers and other policy people within the organization to draw up a budget consistent with that general directive. The income from counseling and the income from residential care may not match the proportions of effort the organization wishes to spend on them. Residential care may be generating more income than counseling, or counseling may bring in more revenue than what the board decides to budget for it. In that case, the amount of subsidy that one program requires and the other program provides is clear.

The degree of outside fundraising is also clear, and the extent to which support from outside sources must be channeled to one function or another becomes more apparent. One can simply extend this example to a nonprofit organization with four or five functions, and the budget proportion allocation gives the board an opportunity to look at the various functions, assess the way in which those functions are helpful to the organization, and assign proportions of effort represented in dollar amounts to the range of functions. The Index of Dissimilarity, discussed in Chapter 13, is a way to assess how close an organization is to where one wants it to be.

Operations Audit

Quality operations are hard to assess, but it is important that the board look at the nonprofit organization's operations at the end of the year. An operations audit simply examines the performance of the organization to see if the components of the annual plan have, in fact, been achieved, or, if not, why not. The board makes appropriate adjustments in the plans, targets, and goals— or personnel and other internal organizational elements—to more successfully accomplish those goals in the coming year.

The operations audit is good not only for what it does— review and adjustment—but also for what it signals. Employees of the organization are aware that, given a set of organizational missions and roles, and five-year and annual plans, there will be some accountability about the extent to which they have moved toward those goals. Particularly in the human service field, accountability is often lacking. Some techniques appear in Chapter 13, but a few points about cost and profit centers and program financing are worth mentioning here.

In the cost-and-profit-center concept, the board and CEO look at what areas of the nonprofit organization are making money (areas of profit) or losing money (areas of subsidy). There is nothing wrong with either—a sliding-scale fee-for-service program, for example, might well be in the red by design. The important thing is that board and CEO are aware of this.

Program financing often comes up in areas of subsidy (departments in the red) and with new proposed programs. In our experience, CEOs often give more planning thought to programs than to funding. This should not be surprising. Thinking up new ideas is often a lot more fun than thinking about ways to pay for them. And indeed, one wants to avoid bottom-line mentality, in which every new thing is initially judged against criteria that the new idea cannot meet simply because it is new. Hence, there may be good reasons why an organization should start or subsidize a program, and the board may not disagree. What may be at issue, however, is how to pay for it.

Decision Assessment

Evaluating policy decisions is a key policy action. Chapter 13 gives a range of techniques for approaching this, and we make a few overall comments here.

One of the most important initial steps in evaluating policy decisions and being accountable for them is to make decisions in the first place. All too often, when a problematic decision area arises, people are unaware that they made a particular decision, and upon scrutiny of the records, the method and the reason for the decision are unclear.

Most likely, the decision was not made at any one point but rather evolved at several points over time—as if one contracted separately with six architects to design a piece of a house that was then assembled by one builder. When you view the final house, you think, "My God, how did we get this?" At the end of the year, or whenever appropriate, one should be able to go back and not only answer the question, "What decisions did we make during the year?" but also review the impact, structure, and quality of those decisions overall.

Because it can be difficult to assess the impact of a decision immediately after the decision is made, such a retrospective assessment is essential to accountability. Sometimes, the wisdom or foolishness of a decision emerges only after the passage of time. An accountability review also takes into consideration the extent to which the information available at the time of the decision was sufficient and accurate. If an organization continually makes decisions that prove to be unsound, it should study very carefully how it gathers information and considers alternatives.

The decision audit or autopsy is a useful device. We detail the specific procedures for decision autopsies in Chapter 13. What we can share here, however, is that it is very useful to have a book of resolutions (decisions) running by date over the history of the nonprofit organization. It is often very difficult to find decisions in the minutes, and to do a decision audit or autopsy they need to be pulled out anyway. If a resolution/decision changes or cancels a previous one, then that previous one can be noted easily at the time the new resolution is added to the book. These actually can be kept in PDF format on the nonprofit organization's website. So everyone can see them easily.

The idea of a decision audit and autopsy implies a careful review of the decisions made and an assessment or judgment about whether they were successful. Clearly, those involved in decision making will quickly notice that the result of a successful decision requires two interrelated elements—a high-quality decision to begin with, and good implementation. An outstanding decision can be ruined by lousy implementation. An awful decision can be tempered, and even made to look good, by creative and brilliant implementation. In any review process, directors should look carefully at both of these aspects. They should never assume that because an outcome was positive, the decision was correct; or because the outcome was wrong, the decision was wrong. Rather, directors should look at the decision process separately from implementation.

Conclusion: The Policymaking Responsibility

Policy decisions are the central feature of the organization. Improving them is a key responsibility of directors. Essential to developing quality policy is an ongoing process of developing and reviewing goals. Without constant examination, organizational ennui quickly sets in. That is problematic in itself, as directors stop coming to meetings, and so on. It frequently leads to mission drift.

Exercise 4

1. Consider your boards recent decisions. Can you locate them here?
   - Policy matters
   - Policy-administration (gray area) matters
   - Administrative matters

2. Are you working in the proper areas? Why or why not? How can you improve?

3. Has your board developed a plan for policy review and refurbishment? If not, why not? How can the board begin one?

4. Has substantive program discussion preceded the budget discussion? Why or why not? How can you improve?

5. Do you have an operations audit in place? If not, how can one be set up?

6. Do you know where the cost and profit centers are in your nonprofit organization? If not, how can you begin to find them?

7. Do you evaluate your board's decisions? If not, how could you begin?

Chapter 8

Selection and Evaluation of the CEO

Introduction

Another key board responsibility, and one that is often problematic, is the search and evaluation process for the CEO. There are several common problems.

First, the search process doesn't happen very often. Many directors don't do "search and hire" in their daily lives as regularly as they do some of the other things their board roles require. Hence, their knowledge of the process is low.

Second, selecting one candidate from among many involves inherent interpersonal problems, as well as the problems of evaluation, which may in turn involve organizational criticism or redirection. No one likes to receive criticism, and most of us don't like to give it either. Yet the health of the board, the health of the organization, and the ability of the board and the organization to accomplish their goals depends on good hiring and the CEO's supervision.

Improving these functions requires attention to three areas. The first is the set of considerations and policies that deal with these matters. The second is the specific process that one goes through to hire a CEO—the search process. The last involves specific techniques for accomplishing the evaluation process. An overview of the search process appears subsequently.

Considerations and Policy in CEO Search

The whole process of CEO search and assessment can be simpler if directors attend to a few matters first. Among the more important is setting up a contractual period for which the CEO is to be hired[7]. Three to six years is a good range. If directors want a longer time period, then the board should undertake a specific major evaluation of the CEO midway through the contract period, and it should write this requirement into the contract. The board should already plan to evaluate the CEO annually, specifying the procedures in the contract. Being this specific is important—establishing positional procedures is always easier when no one is in the position yet. Candidates are then aware of these requirements as they interview for the position.

Directors must also be aware of legal requirements regarding the hiring of a new CEO. Some of these requirements may be specified in the organization's bylaws and may detail specific procedures for search and selection. Other laws may also govern the search process.

Agencies can often secure help with both search and assessment from national organizations or specialized search firms. For example, United Way of America and United Way of Canada both assist local United Way chapters in the search process; conferring with representatives of these central organizations may be useful before directors set about selecting a new CEO.

The Selection Process

The selection process itself is complex and has many steps. The process begins when the nonprofit organization determines it has a

---

[7] Actually relatively few organizations have a contract with the CEO. We recommend it for the protection of both parties and for the thinking that is required to actually develop it.

vacancy, and continues until it announces a final selection. Because organizations engage in this process so rarely, they often handle it poorly. They must take special care to proceed thoughtfully, rationally, and systematically.

The overall sequence of steps is straightforward—decide on the search criteria, advertise the position, narrow candidates to a short list, interview those on the short list, and make a final selection. Several specific difficulties are worth considering.

Steps in the Search Process:
1. Review mission and goals.
2. Reaffirm goals.
3. Establish search policy and protocol.
4. Establish staff, funding, and other necessary resources.
5. Appoint CEO assessment committee.
6. Post the position, based on review of mission and goals.
7. Network in the field, who are the go-to people, universities, etc.
8. Seek candidates as well as accept applications.
9. Review written materials; review references.
10. Prepare short list.
11. Notify people not on the short list, be careful to treat candidates recommended by board members, donors, etc., with some special consideration. A more personal letter being specific about how accomplished and skilled the individual is, but how the accomplishments and skill don't match what the committee is searching for.
12. Prepare the contract draft.
13. Interview, using questions based on search policy and protocol.
14. Rank candidates.
15. Make an offer; be open to negotiation.

Search policy

What are the criteria? What is the timeline for making a final selection? What is the salary range? How will the organization respond to secondary issues, such as the career of the spouse? Talk about all of this ahead of time, before announcing the position. A consultant can be very helpful.

Search committee. Who should be on the search committee? Should it be a committee of the whole, a specially elected committee of the board, the nominating committee, or the CEO committee? We recommend using an augmented CEO committee of five to seven members, drawn from the officers of the organization, the chairs of the other major committees, and possibly one or two directors specially elected at large. This gives breadth and depth to the selection process. The search committee chair should be someone other than the board president, because the president will have enough ongoing responsibilities. The board can hold a special election to fill any of these positions on the search committee. Political considerations also are handled here. What happens when a board member's friend's daughter wants the job and is somewhat qualified? Often the other board members just cave in. We have run into this in the past and find it difficult to gain acceptance of the idea of recusing oneself from consideration in such a case. Such issues are better handled up front and agreed to ahead of time.

The other process that is very useful is having the staff help with narrowing to a short list. It doesn't wear the board committee out and it gives the search staff a chance to have input at two levels: the first is removing the obvious bad candidates. The second level is when the interviews take place and the candidates are narrowed to three. Then have the staff interview and rate the candidates for the committee's final choice.

Staff assistance. What kind of person should the board select to provide the staff support mentioned above? It has to be someone with access to the organization's mechanical resources—such as word processors and the photocopier—as well as someone who is sufficiently knowledgeable about the organization. Sometimes, the outgoing CEO serves this role. Other times, the board may want to secure an outside person for this task or use a consultant or search firm. If there are internal candidates for the CEO's position, be careful that they do not exercise undue influence or are unduly neglected.

More and more organizations are using "head hunter" or search firms. These firms have several advantages. They often have specialists in the specific areas where agencies need assistance. Because their people make a lifetime of this kind of work, they bring a wealth of savvy to the task. But their experience does not come cheap.

Money for the search. Is this to be a national or a local search? Some considerations for making this decision are:

- Does this candidate need a local network to function well?
- How much can the outgoing CEO transfer in terms of connections and network?
- Does this candidate need relationships with local funders?

Generally local and regional organizations should look for local and regional candidates; national organizations should look for national candidates. Will the search committee bring in candidates from out of town for interviews, or will it conduct such interviews by telephone? Sometimes, the committee may want to visit candidates. The search committee will have to work out overall procedures and make arrangements with the organization for a special budget line so the committee knows with what it has to work.

Rewards for the candidate. The cost of the search itself is not the only budgetary item that needs consideration. What is the salary range of the job and its possible perquisites? For example, is the nonprofit organization willing to pay moving expenses for an out-of-town candidate, or provide a car? Boards often fail to consider such questions until candidates bring them up.

Vision and mission. Many search committees flounder immediately because someone says, "I can't look for anyone until I know exactly what we're going to ask that person to do." That sounds reasonable on the surface, but it has the seduction of a half-truth. Certainly it is important for the organization to have a set of general expectations for the new CEO. These expectations may even be written down in a job description. It is equally true, however, that most organizations hope that the CEO will assist in defining the mission and role of the organization and that he or she will give vigor and vitality to that process. In the back of people's minds is the notion that if the job is defined too specifically, the most interesting applicants won't take it. Who wants to simply carry out the detailed instructions of others? Hence, the board should develop a general statement, but it should be an "open statement"—not overly detailed, but something that will give candidates and the search committee a sense of the nonprofit organization's mission and interests. The statement should also convey the board's expectation that the candidate will contribute materially to the nonprofit organization's mission and vision.

Proactivity and reactivity. The search committee must be balanced between proactivity and reactivity, between invitation and response. Many committees take the view that they will post a job; interested candidates will apply; and, from that applicant pool, one will be selected. This view is only partly accurate. While the search committee is looking over the potential CEO, she or he is looking them over. The assessment and interview process is always a two-way street. Search committees must both assess and recruit the potential candidate. The archives of boards of directors are filled with sad stories about "the one who got away"—the perfect person who, in the final analysis, was not interested, often be¬cause of hostile treatment (sometimes called "tough questions") by the search committee. We do not mean to suggest that search committees should avoid asking "tough questions," rather that questioning not come off as antagonistic, off-putting, or unwelcoming.

At least initially, search committees should not be too rigid about who is and who is not a candidate. The committee may ask someone to apply, but that person may already have a good job and no initial interest in applying. The committee may have to "create" an interest. Too, the idea of "applying" makes some potential candidates feel like applicants, and they perceive themselves to be at a disadvantage. In such cases, the search committee may find it useful to invite those candidates to "explore possibilities" with the committee. This can be informal discussions in which the individual begins the process as a "consultant" to the organization—regarding the nonprofit organization's future, for example. During initial discussions, the search committee can scrutinize the extent of the candidate's abilities in a more tranquil atmosphere and explore the extent of the consultant's potential interest somewhat more diplomatically. The committee must be open to explore possibilities with a range of people and a range of positions, at least during the early stages of its search.

Look, look, look! Most search committees sit and wait for applicants to approach them. It is important to identify strong potential candidates and approach them—ask them about their interests, invite their applications or consultation—and produce a solid list of candidates. Veterans of the search process know to expect the unexpected. The best candidate, the candidate of choice, may drop out at the last minute for personal reasons. When that happens, the nonprofit organization, which has relied heavily on that candidate, has to start its search all over again.

Keep candidates informed. Maintaining an equitable and informative process is vital for both the candidates and the board. Once the board decides about its overall time schedule and search procedures and begins the process, it should keep candidates abreast of developments in the search. Candidates who are clearly not in contention should be told so quickly. A more difficult situation arises when the search committee develops its so-called short list, selecting three or four top candidates and then making a choice from among them. Often, the search committee will want to avoid rejecting the other two or three people on the short list until the first choice decides what he or she is going to do. There may be no good solution to this problem. Many committees hesitate to inform candidates that they are not the first choice, but leaving candidates without any information until some distant endpoint is not satisfactory either.

In the final analysis, the board and its search committee should remain in contact with all candidates throughout the search. Many times, candidates never learn the disposition of their applications.

Unbelievable as that may seem, once they make their selections, search committees forget about the other candidates. Few organizational activities rival the lack of courtesy that often attends the search process.

These points do not cover all of the difficult areas inherent in the search process, but they do touch upon some of the more common ones. Perhaps what is most important is for the search committee to put itself in the applicants' shoes. That will give the committee a more realistic idea of the nature and sequence of its questions and search procedures. And it suggests the kind of treatment that might be appropriate.

Review and Assessment

The search process can set the stage for the process of evaluation. Earlier, we suggested that an evaluation policy be in place specifying a contract period and requiring regular evaluations. Holding such evaluations annually may prove most useful, although other time periods may be more appropriate to particular organizations. The important point is for the board to sit down with its CEO and discuss accomplishments and failures during the year. This process is easier if there are two steps rather than one. However a board approaches the CEO evaluation process, it is good to keep several things in mind. First, all evaluations begin with goals. Without goals, evaluation is a meaningless and harmful exercise. Second, set up the procedures and expectations at the beginning of the process so both board and CEO know what to expect. Third, both board and CEO should participate in the process. Fourth, keep in mind that evaluation is fateful, has elements of power involved, is judgmental, and involves working to or above standard. This makes the process full of affect. Lastly, frequent feedback makes evaluation much easier.

A system that works well is for the board to begin the evaluation process by discussing with the CEO his or her organizational goals for the coming year. These should be operationalized or applied versions of the organization's larger mission statement and its annual goals and should represent agreed-upon directions and activities for the organization and the CEO. Often useful is for the president to ask the CEO to prepare a list of achievements that he or she hopes to accomplish in the coming year and to outline how they track with organizational problems and strengths. The board or its CEO committee should review this memorandum, accept it or revise it, and usually talk with the CEO about it. Out of that discussion should develop mutually agreed-upon activities for the year. This is important, because the CEO's accomplishments depend, in large part, on the actions of others, including the board itself. Hence, the board needs to be aware that insisting on some objectives for a CEO might require their involvement in a variety of ways, and they have to be prepared to commit those resources.

In any event, the board and the CEO agree on a document, which provides the basis for assessment at year's end. It is important to have "weights"—"proportions of effort" as well as areas of effort. Often there is agreement on areas and the weights are implicit, leading to trouble later on.

An evaluation meeting is scheduled, with prior input from the full board. Most often it is the executive committee which sits with the CEO. A written evaluation should proceed the group meeting. This process is a two-step one—with goals being set early, and mutually, with ongoing assessments throughout the year and then a second evaluation meeting at the end of the year.

Boards might use other approaches to evaluation, but this two-step process of establishing targets and measuring progress toward those targets is among the better ones. The point is to have a system and to use it annually.

Termination

The whole process of search and review is designed to prevent the need to terminate the CEO. Termination represents a failure of processes like those we have been discussing. Frequently in such cases, expectations and problems are not communicated. Sometimes, CEOs not only receive no feedback, the board lies to them: "Everything looks great." Privately, however, the board is upset and angry. The final result is termination.

Organizations can avoid such problems with thorough review and discussion. Regular, frequent meetings take the sting out of one big blockbuster session. CEOs do leave, but boards should work toward and help CEOs find a proper fit.

Firings sometimes should and do occur. At these times, feelings run high, alternatives seem few. The best course here is to use performance reviews and specific, attainable goals and rely on the written record. It is not a case of how someone feels, but what someone has done, or not done, that is important.

Regular reviews of the CEO mean that goals and objectives can be specified. Then, the board can talk with the CEO about whether those goals have been appropriate.

Conclusion

The hiring, evaluation, and termination processes are difficult. No amount of procedure, structure, or rules can make them easy or can remove the tension, uncertainty, and complexities that arise from them. Those difficulties can be minimized, however, and one of the board's more important roles is to handle these matters with dignity and dispatch.

Exercise 5

1. Review the system your board uses to evaluate the CEO.
   - Is there a system in place?
   - Is it satisfactory?
   - Does it conform to the ideas suggested here?
   - How could it be improved?

Chapter 9

Assure Financial Wellness and Integrity

Introduction

Agencies, on the one hand, worry about "mission creep," a situation in which they stray from their mission in pursuit of money, money which will only pay for **other** missions. In time, the nonprofit organization loses its focus altogether. On the other hand, there is truth in the saying "no money, no mission." So the question becomes, frequently, one of finding ways to assure health through ensuring financial support, without compromising basic principles. Successful work here requires both thought and skill.

Common Issues in Nonprofit Finance

Nonprofits have many "crazy" financials which make their life even more complicated. Clara Miller, in her interesting work "The Looking-Glass World of Nonprofit Money: Managing in For-Profits' Shadow Universe," (*Nonprofit Quarterly*, Spring, 2005 12,1) starts our thinking with a small quiz. Here it is:

Test Yourself First

In Nonprofits...

THE CONSUMER BUYS THE PRODUCT	TRUE FALSE
PRICE COVERS COST AND EVENTUALLY PRODUCES PROFITS, OR ELSE THE BUSINESS FOLDS	TRUE FALSE
CASH IS LIQUID	TRUE FALSE
PRICE IS DETERMINED BY PRODUCERS' SUPPLY AND CONSUMERS' ABILITY AND WILLINGNESS TO PAY	TRUE FALSE
ANY PROFITS WILL DROP TO THE BOTTOM LINE AND ARE THEN AVAILABLE FOR ENLARGING OR IMPROVING THE BUSINESS	TRUE FALSE
INVESTMENT IN INFRASTRUCTURE DURING GROWTH IS NECESSARY FOR EFFICIENCY AND PROFITABILITY	TRUE FALSE
OVERHEAD IS A REGULAR COST OF DOING BUSINESS, AND VARIES WITH BUSINESS TYPE AND STAGE OF DEVELOPMENT	TRUE FALSE

As you may or may not have known, each of these is false. Consumers do not buy the product typically; funders buy the product (remember the issue of "dual customer base" we discussed in the chapter on the differences between profits and nonprofits? Here is that issue specifically.) Price frequently does not cover cost. Many agencies run "subsidy business" for which subventions are regularly needed. They often never go out of business. Cash is not liquid; it is locked up by funders in special purpose accounts. Many profits (the "surplus" if readers recall our short intro on terminology) do not drop to the bottom line; they go back into funders' accounts and sometimes back to the funders; or they are used to give more of the funded service, which may be a poor strategic option for the nonprofit organization. Nonprofits typically have poor infrastructure because funders do not like to pay for it. Overhead is also not supported by funders. Contractors working with for-profit organizations appear to have a different mindset when executing contracts. They routinely allow for infrastructure and overhead; not so for the large number of nonprofit contracts, which often do not even pay the full cost of the product.

Regular Knowledge Is Not Quite Applicable

Because of these elements, and others, regular "business" knowledge does not directly apply to nonprofit financials. Perhaps this is one of the reasons why "businessmen" who seem to be a desired category of director, have not been very successful overall in bringing their "wisdom" to bear. And many nonprofit managers are not really attuned to their complexities either. No wonder it is hard to find CFOs.

Regular Knowledge Is Not Even Present in Proper Amounts

Not only is usual fiscal knowledge not a perfect fit for the non-profit financial scene, but regular financial knowledge may itself be in short supply. As mentioned in Chapter 2, CEOs are often undertrained in fiscal matters to begin with, though many do pick up a working knowledge over time. Standard accounting training does not typically address nonprofit issues (including complex reporting requirements for different funders, multiple manners in which funders demand costs and expenditures be prepared, etc.), so help is hard to come by. And directors typically do not receive training in this either.

Funder Exploitation of Nonprofits' Caring Impulses

Because all of the people working for the 1.9 million nonprofits care about the mission (or most do), they are sensitive to the fact that, when funders undercut their market, one result might be no service, no zoo, no international program, etc. So they accept, or feel forced to accept, subpar funding as "the lesser of two evils," thereby also perpetuating that evil.

By and large, subpar funding means that organizations are running a subsidy business, and have to expend organizational resources to raise the dollars for that subsidy. Raising such dollars can be very expensive. Nonprofits rarely perform a cost benefit analysis to see in detail what those subsidy dollars actually cost them.

Funders, as well, have unrealistic expectations about the cost of service. A common measure is the percent of overall budget which goes to "care" as opposed to "administration," as if "care" managed itself. Using such a measure implies that the closer one gets to 100% "in care," the "better" the nonprofit organization is, when it is actually more exploitative of staff.

Caring Impulses Cloud Judgment

Another element of the caring impulse is that directors become attached to various programs even as the financial climate and climate of needs change. This attachment issue frequently has a couple of problematic results. One is that programs which should be closed are maintained. The second is that programs which are actually dying are "saved at the last moment by some fiscal heroics." We call these "dysfunctional rescues" because the programs actually should have died.

The Role of the Board

The assurance function for financial health involves two functions. One is an "outside" function and one is "inside." Most finance committees attend to only part of the inside function.

Revenue—The Outside Function

Part of a board's responsibility is to look at the sources of current and future revenue and plan for its continuance and development. Most organizations have a fourfold set of income streams. One is grants and contracts, a second is fees, a third is charitable gifts, and the fourth is investment income.

Directors need to look at each of these income streams (and their subpart) from the perspective of their particular nonprofit organization and assess what makes sense, what is cost effective, and what is the proper mix. In addition, they need to look to the future to see what developments in each of these areas might be on the horizon, and position themselves accordingly.

Grants and contracts may be one way to go, but as states cut funding and foundations become ever more picky, directors may want to take a hard look at this source.

Fees—dollars actually paid by users—may be a potential area of growth in some instances. Unfortunately, those who need and those who can pay may be different groups, and therefore issues of mission come up quickly here. Sometimes agencies "chase" grant dollars that are "mission marginal." Other times agencies continue programs that they no longer need because they want the dollars.

Charitable gifts—the fund raiser—are a time-honored way to bring unrestricted (hopefully) cash into the organization. Many agencies require all board members to contribute—appropriate to their financial situation—as a *sine qua non* of effective fund development. There are many ways to mount the development function. University of Michigan Social Work graduate Terry Axelrod has developed one very successful program which you can read about at www.benevon.com.

Historically, investment income has been from "endowments," something which are highly prized by many agencies, and often a lot of energy goes into getting "endowments" something around which much energy is expended. Since standard rates of return suggest that one only gets 4%-5% of operating income from every dollar of endowment, seeking endowments may not really be a cost-effective way to proceed.

Many agencies are actually looking to start a for-profit investment subsidiary to assure unrestricted operating income.

Expenses—The Inside Function

The inside function has four parts. One is ongoing monitoring of expenses flow, something which directors usually do in terms of the monthly (or regular) financial reports. Typically, not only categories of expenses are considered, but expenses against revenues and budget.

This monthly review, however, done by the directors themselves, is not sufficient. Every organization should have a yearly audit, done by an outside firm, and the directors should have a private meeting with that auditor to look at the overall picture[8].

Thirdly, the directors should consider the infrastructure cost of the organization—what it actually costs to deliver a unit of outcome for each of their businesses (much like a retail outlet looks at cost and revenue per square foot for various merchandise bundles). This allows analysis rather than review, and can set the stage for future programmatic decision making. The Professional Unit Method of Analysis (PUMA) discussed in Chapter 13 can be a help here.

Finally, the directors need to take a serious look at the adequacy of their compensation and benefits program for workers. Human service agencies pay less than commercial organizations, sometimes seriously so. There is a grim acceptance of this situation (though usually CEOs do relatively better).

Consultation with compensation professionals can be of great assistance here. Directors, like many people, usually view "salary" as an "expense," and hence, seek to minimize it, as opposed to an investment, which, like all investments, needs to be managed. An ongoing program of adequacy of total compensation is appropriate here. Cash of course is always a point of focus. But also there are other forms of compensation that are useful to consider. Psychic income—opportunity to advance, opportunity to grow, quality of life, flexibility are among important areas. The outline of the 10 points in a total compensation package is discussed in John Tropman's book, *The Total Compensation Solution* (2001). Other ideas are developed in some detail in a book called *The Total Compensation Solution* by the first author of this volume (Tropman, 2002).

---

[8] Obviously very small organizations need to establish ways in which their financial integrity can be assured; it may, for the, not be an audit.

There is also a host of ideas in Bob Nelson's book, *1001 Ways to Reward Your Employees* (1994).

In terms of CEO compensation, The Charity Navigator(http://www.charitynavigator.org/index.cfm/bay/content.view/catid/68/cpid/304.htm) found that, in 2005, the average nonprofit CEO made around $148,000, which translated into about 3.4% of the organization's expenses. Specific salaries, however, vary by region, size, and mission.

At the moment, however (2008), there seems to be general agreement that CEO compensation is lagging further and further behind other arenas—meaning that it will be harder and harder to attract and retain executive leadership talent going forward.

This last part—adequacy of compensation—leads to the human resources function in general, a function we have already identified as very weak in the nonprofit and human services sector. It is important to understand that assuring financial resources is not the end of the line here; it involves assuring appropriate human resources equipped to do the job as well.

Conclusion

The fiscal responsibility of the directors looks to assuring and ensuring adequate revenue sources in an appropriate mix, sources that are adequate to sustain the human resources needed to do the job of nonprofit work. This task is more than simply reviewing monthly financials, as we mentioned, though that is a small piece of it. Rather, it involves analysis and strategy, as well, and sometimes the collaboration with other similar organizations to make a collective case for compensation equity to funders and the public.

Exercise 6

1. Does your board have the financial knowledge it needs to assure and ensure financial health?

2. If not, where are the weaknesses?

3. What might be done to address those weaknesses?

4. Is the board regularly doing the analytic tasks (inside, outside) suggested in this chapter?

5. If not, why not?

6. What remedies might be useful?

Chapter 10

Introduce Strategic Planning, Change, and Entrepreneurship

Introduction

Individuals involved in board work are often struck with the permanence, if not intransigence, of board habits, board behaviors, and board culture. Understanding good board behaviors is of limited use without the ability to introduce change into the board system. Obviously, many changes should be targeted to particular boards. Some general considerations are helpful, too.

The Benefits of Strategic Change

Many benefits accrue to the self-improving board, including a greater sense of board community, higher-quality decisions, and more involvement with community and staff. Directors often ask, "Why do we need to change?" There are many reasons (see Myers, Ufford, & McGill, 1988).

A broader organizational picture. Most non-profit boards are only marginally aware of what their organizations are actually doing when viewed as a whole. An overall assessment and strategic initiative by the board allows a more global and a more in-depth picture of the kinds of activities an organization is undertaking; and the costs and benefits of these activities by the board and employees.

A focus on facts. Many organizations are full of what the late Robert D. Vinter of the University of Michigan calls "lore." These are assertive and impressionistic statements about what the organization is or is not doing, has or has not done in the past, will or will not do in the future, and could or could not accomplish under a range of conditions. Such discussions are not based on a common foundation of facts. A strategic initiative process should develop a focus on facts.

Shared identification of problems. A process of strategic change focuses on a shared perception of problems among stakeholders. Such sharing comes from interaction rather than assertion, from consensus rather than command, and requires time and effort to develop the common points of view that lead to sharing.

Identification of additional resources. Strategic change not only points to problems to be solved but frequently uncovers new resources with which those problems can be addressed. As one example, an organization might be really good at some process that it could sell to other organizations—a source of income. A strategic planning process might surface this possibility, which has been otherwise overlooked.

Alternative solutions. The shared examination of problems and a focus on facts, combined with the broader organizational picture, allows the board to develop alternatives for every examined problem. Indeed, the options memo technique, discussed in Chapter 16, is a precise way of accomplishing this objective.

Team building. The common focus on board problems leads to a sense of team, rather than competing camps, within the organization. Frequently, too, a sense of excitement develops as old barriers to communication fall away. Boards need to develop a sense of "us-ness" or "we-ness" that, on the one hand, embraces the sense of overall collectivity, but, on the other hand, does not slip into "group think" or inauthentic agreement. High quality decisions require diversity of input.

Transferability. The process of strategic development within a board is really the development of a kind of thinking. We call it the "eightball principle." In pool (eightball) the strategic player does not take the easy close shot. That is a good shot. The best shot is one that sinks an opponent's ball AND POSITIONS THE CUE FOR THE NEXT SHOT. Comfort with "eightball thinking" can be transferred to many other settings (just like "thinking like a lawyer" or "thinking like a social worker" can be).

Shift to the future. Many discussions of strategic plans, particularly at the board level, focus on defending the past. Individual identifications and egos become involved with programs that were doubtless appropriate for the time in which they were initiated but, with environmental changes in the organizational environment, they now have become passé and, in some instances, even counterproductive. The ability to build from what is appropriate to the generalized view of the environment is key to future success. The ability to build on what is good right now, based on a generalized view of the environment, is key. The strategic process involves a revolution of expectations. These expectations reconfigure the interrelationships among community, nonprofit/human service organization, board, and task environment. They allow the opening of new avenues of work and effort, and perhaps the closing of some old ones. But this repositioning within the task environment is always essential to continued success. As the organization grows and changes, so too the task environment shifts and develops. Thus, what was a good fit at one time may be a relatively poorer fit now.

Requisites for Strategic Change

As directors begin to involve themselves in a process of strategic development, they face certain requisites and certain commitments that must be made from the beginning if the process is to succeed, first for the board itself, but ultimately for the whole organization.

Frame of mind. Directors must approach their tasks with a different frame of mind, a commitment to learning and being open to wherever the facts lead them. If they come into the room with a "show me" attitude, the process is almost doomed from the start. If, on the other hand, they come in with a notion that "this time we are really going to make whatever changes are in the interest of our organization and I, as a director, am going to be able to help in this process," the prognosis is much better.

Temporal commitment. Directors are extremely busy, and they often travel, so they are not always around as much as they thought they would be. CEOs and others planning a strategic change should begin by being upfront about the time required for the effort. Probably two or three days overall, including one day-long activity, will be necessary. Many might think this is too long, but it is modest when compared with the time lost through board rework, awful meetings, and similar horrors. If directors cannot make adequate time commitments from the beginning, the process starts with problems, and the board won't have the backup and investment necessary to accomplish the change.

Longer-range view. Many directors, especially under the press of time, will opt for quick fixes: "What's the problem? Let's do this, this, and this." The North American penchant for action supports the quick-fix solution. Yet, nearly every problem has causes or precipitating circumstances at multiple levels. One cause is the immediate precursor event; others might be more deeply rooted.

Consider, for example, the voluntary organization whose United Way allocation was not received this year or was substantially reduced. The quick fix would be for the organization to replace those lost dollars with other funding and go about its business. If this were the organization's sole conclusion and action, however, it would be making a sorry mistake. Obvious reasons exist (though we may not know them clearly at first) as to why the local United Way did not make its allocation to the organization and what that might portend. The solution must involve more than just replacing the lost funding; the organization must fully understand and act upon the predisposing causes before it can respond effectively. The board has to set aside the immediate focus of finding a new funding source in favor of the longer-term view.

Now we recognize that this statement would meet with disbelief and cause a credibility gap with nonprofit readers. Without a large chunk of funding the organization may not exist long enough to figure out the longer-term view. It is true that "no margin means no mission." Our point here is to put out the idea that boards, singly and severally (perhaps severally is more important), need to take action to stop supporting/accepting subpar funding.

Facts and focus. In the initial stage, common and conventional preconceptions should be set aside. Everything that "everyone knows" should be viewed, at least at first, as suspect. One can always return, of course, to business as usual; but, since business as usual is what we are often trying to escape through such strategic initiatives, we should first agree to some kind of intellectual independence and an openness to new thinking, which can be a freeing, inspiring, creative process.

Better ideas. Finally, the board needs to better recognize itself as a source of new ideas. All too often, we tip our hats in acknowledgment to groups, to the group process, and to strategic

91

decision-making, and then return to the old, individualistic, supposedly long-range approaches that have been so comfortable for us in the past. Whether they were truly long range, of course, is an open question.

How to Achieve Strategic Change

How do directors, CEOs, and the nonprofit organization's staff go about achieving the benefits of strategic change? One answer is leadership. Leadership involves developing a vision of where the organization might be. Leadership may come from anywhere within the organization. A typical mistake assumes that leadership comes only from the organization's president, CEO, or board chair. Fortunate is the organization that has leadership resources in each position. Often, however, leadership must come from other directors or from staff before the organization can undertake a strategic change.

Individuals who are interested in introducing strategic change into nonprofit organization must often wait for an event that precipitates a willingness to act. A driver education teacher once said, "An accident really focuses your attention on driving." All the injunctions about driving carefully really do not hit home until someone actually has been involved in an accident and experienced the trauma it can create. Hopefully, it is a small accident, and the benefits of learning far outweigh the inconveniences and difficulties.

A similar point applies to agencies and boards of directors. Frequently, a small leadership group within the organization sees the need for change. Despite their discussions with other directors and selected community leaders, they may be unable to generate an interest in and momentum for strategic change until a cataclysmic event occurs. That event might be the sudden departure or resignation of the CEO. It could involve severe criticism in the media about something that happened within the organization. Or it might be the failure to secure an expected piece of funding. The list could go on. The point is that although organizational readiness for strategic change requires leadership, leadership alone is not always successful. Sometimes, difficult, trou¬bling events must occur to create the kind of organizational concern necessary to move the process forward.

Once an organization is ready to change, how should it proceed? An on-site analysis is one approach (Myers, Ufford, & McGill, 1988). A consulting team arrives on site and orchestrates the process of strategic change. However, agencies can also, with strong leadership, move ahead on change itself using a "change team" drawn from current employees.

The SWOT Analysis

As an alternative, the organization may wish to engage its own staff/volunteers in a strategic change process using a technique known as a "SWOT analysis," followed by a "5-C conference." SWOT analyses are relatively common in the field of strategic planning. Had the organization contracted with an outside consultant, the consultant likely would have used this method.

A SWOT analysis involves examining the organization from four different perspectives: strengths, weaknesses, opportunities, and threats—hence the term SWOT.

Teams of directors, staff, and others who might be interested, review the nonprofit's position vis-à-vis these four variables, keeping in mind the injunctions mentioned earlier in this chapter (open mindedness, a desire to improve the organization, and an honest search for a better strategy and way of accomplishing its mission). Usually, these four teams are coordinated through the office of the CEO, for such reasons as budget or management. Having a planner or consultant assist in the process may also be helpful; sometimes that person may become a resource as well.

Strengths. One team reviews the organization's strengths. What are its strong points? What are the things for which it is known, today and in the past? How might these strengths be capitalized, extended, or converted to new purposes? The strength assessment group examines these and other related questions.

Weaknesses. Paralleling an organization's strengths are its weaknesses. A "weakness team" thinks about the problems the organization is facing. What are the points of difficulty? The areas of low quality? The areas of trouble? The weakness team must take particular care to be honest, open, and direct. Every organization, like every person, has strengths and weaknesses. Organizations, like people, tend to overstate their strengths and minimize their weaknesses. Indeed, listening to many individuals in an organization describe themselves, one would think that the organization's weaknesses were either infinitesimal or nonexistent. Clearly, personal and organizational defense mechanisms are at work here, and powerfully so. To obtain a fair and honest picture of what is really troubling an organization, these defense mechanisms must be set aside.

Opportunities. A third team looks at opportunities in the environment. What opportunities might be available for this particular organization? Are they being exploited now, or could they be exploited in the future? Is the environment changing so as to make new opportunities likely? For example, colleges and universities well know that, following a "baby boom" comes a "baby bust," with fewer students in the college-age bracket. Naturally, colleges and universities will seek to expand the proportion of college-age people who actually attend college. It is also possible, however, and even desirable, to redefine what "college age" means. Many universities are aggressively seeking older students—in their 30s, 40s, 5Os, and even 60s—who have a yearning for an education that they were not able to complete at an earlier age, or who simply seek to expand their knowledge. One must first see the opportunity in the older student, however, before one can pursue it.

Threats. Finally, a fourth team assesses threats to the organization. What in the environment might harm the organization? Have government allocations become increasingly uncertain? Has a particular residential treatment center, run by a nonprofit/human service organization, had a string of difficulties that have drawn the attention of accrediting groups? Is there an ominous decline in the number of people who are interested in working for it at the current wage rates? These and other questions represent an analysis of the threats facing the nonprofit/human service organization. Threats may link with weaknesses; in fact, if an unfortunate confluence of threats and weaknesses occurs—if threats seem to come in areas of weakness—then the organization is in a perilous state.

Putting them All Together. There is no special formula for carrying out these analyses, although the large amount of material available on strategic planning suggest a variety of ways to approach it. The main point is to "just do it." Once the analysis is complete, the organization's directors come together, often in a retreat format, to discuss the findings and to plot new directions. Presumably, new directions arise from a consideration of strengths and opportunities on the positive side and a scrutiny of threats and weaknesses on the negative side. The process seeks to neutralize threats and reduce the impact of weaknesses while augmenting strengths and seizing opportunities. This small exercise can really help an organization avoid trouble in the process of self-renewal.

The 5-C Conference

It is very difficult, however, and not really helpful, to undergo strategic planning every year. The process becomes tiresome and unproductive. The organization should therefore try to establish, on an annual basis, a 5-C retreat.

The 5 Cs are the characteristics and competencies of people; conditions of the organization; context, on the environment; and change. The board will probably find it most helpful to conduct a 5-C assay annually. A 5-C assay is similar to a SWOT analysis, but not as complex. It simply involves small groups of people—again, coordinated by the CEO's office—looking at the characteristics of individuals within, and served by, the organization, and those who serve on the board; the competencies of the staff and the directors; the conditions, structure, and culture of the organization; the contexts within which the organization operates; and the changes that are needed and that are under way. Findings are reported at an annual 5-C retreat, where the organization directors discuss the fit between and among characteristics, competencies, conditions, contexts, and change. The 5-C retreat allows an ongoing, less painful adjustment to shifts in the environment, in the mix of personal characteristics, in competencies or the need for certain competencies, and in changes in organizational conditions and contexts. The 5-C conference is less dramatic and volcanic than a SWOT analysis and, because it is done yearly, less threatening. Adjustments required as a result of the 5-C review are smaller.

The annual 5-C retreat does not circumvent the need for a SWOT analysis. Indeed, one might want to use a SWOT analysis as a basis for the five- to seven-year organizational renewal requirement, which we discussed in Chapter 5. If the environment is turbulent, however, the intervals between strategic assessments should be shortened! The 5-C review, however, does allow for an ongoing, regularized attempt for directors and staff to look at the organization and the tasks and problems it faces, and to make adjustments as necessary.

Getting Ready for Strategic Planning

As boards begin strategic planning, it is imperative that they think through what the process requires. The first step is to review the perspectives and requisites of strategic blending planning so that directors have a common understanding of the energies that will be required and a common agreement to set aside presuppositions, predefinitions, and simple solutions, and to adopt a readiness to explore new opportunities. This readiness must come before all else. The Professional Unit System and the Index of Dissimilarity—which we discuss in Chapter 13—are useful techniques for the strategic planning process. Without that original readiness, however, the tools one uses will not make much difference—progress will not occur.

Entrepreneurship—The Importance of Innovation and Invention

As the directors are looking over the SWOT analyses and putting elements together in a 5-C Conference, one thing that should not be forgotten is the need to innovate and invent. Innovation refers to improving the things you do—usually through some combination of "Faster, Better, Cheaper." Can we do this process more quickly? Can we do it at higher quality? Can we accomplish this goal at less cost? Successes in one, of course, require, at minimum, holding the others constant, and, if possible, improve each of them as well.

Invention, however, involves doing things the organization is not now doing. Agencies need to be attuned to both kinds of change and take steps to assure themselves that activity is ongoing in each area.

We mention this point specifically because directors often say, "Well, that happens everywhere all the time." Our experience suggests that what is asserted to happen "everywhere" usually happens nowhere. Innovations and inventions frequently rely on champions to get them going; however, a champion-based system has some flaws. One is that it requires champions to be present, champions who not only can innovate and invent but who also are willing to expend the energy to do so. Further, champions, the messengers of the new and the different, are frequently the victims of the "Shoot the Messenger" game because their innovations and inventions threaten convention and established customs, practices, and power. All change is in part destructive, and as such, champions need protection.

That said, directors should welcome and protect champions, but not place full reliance on their appearance. Rather, they should create an organization climate and culture which produces innovations and inventions on a regular basis, from everyone. A simple way to accomplish this task is to place a requirement for inventions and innovations as part of the job description of each staff person, from the janitor to the CEO. Hoping is one thing; requiring is something else. There will be lots of small, perhaps not relevant, things suggested, but there are usually some nuggets as well.

Exercise 7

1. Does your board or nonprofit organization have a strategic plan? How old is it? Does anyone use it?

2. Has the structure of the board been aligned with the strategic plan?

3. Plan a SWOT analysis for your board.

4. Plan a 5-C conference for your board.

5. What inventions and innovations are in your pipeline?

Part IV: How to Do It

Competencies—Board Organization, Development, and Evaluation

Overview

Knowing what to do is one thing. Being able to do it is something else. Those with whom we talked emphasized five requisite elements necessary for boards to function properly:

- Boards have to be organized properly and have the right committees.
- They must attest to the balance
  - between CEO and board, and
  - between internally and externally focused activities.
- Boards must train themselves so that they improve over time.
- Directors must know how to carry out their positions.
- Finally, they have to evaluate themselves, their decisions, and their processes.

Carrying out these major responsibilities is a daunting task. Boards must organize themselves to accomplish these purposes, and there are several areas to which they must a give attention:

Board organization. Boards cannot simply "meet." They must develop structures for attending to the various aspects of the business at hand. Directing a modern nonprofit agency in a complex organizational environment requires a structure that is proper for the task. Typically, such a structure requires the board to establish subgroups or committees that can deal with and engage special aspects of the problems facing the whole organization and make policy recommendations to the whole board.

Proper balance. There are two parts to proper balance. First, issues of policy and administration speak to the topic of balance between the CEO and the board.

The CEO has both administrative and policy roles in the organization. How the policy role is articulated is one question. In some organizations, CEOs are ex officio directors of the board; in others, they are full directors. In still others, the CEO has the title of president and is chair of the board. As we noted in Chapter 1, this is a time of transition for CEO and board responsibilities. Organizations must give careful attention to how they outline each, and they should consider cooperative templates where interests are shared.

The second half of this task entails maintaining a balance between internal and external matters. The board's internal focus involves oversight, which we have already mentioned. The external focus is attention to the environment in which it operates, to linkages and partnerships with other organizations, to changes and developments in its world. Too much looking inside results in tunnel vision—the board misses the forest of a world in change "out there" because of preoccupation with things "in here." On the other hand, looking "out there" all the time fails to address how things "in here" are actually going. Balance is the key.

Training and development. Boards are responsible for training individual directors—both new directors and continuing ones—as well as enhancing the development of the board as a team of policymakers. This need calls attention to the functions of: ethics, social and personal corporate behavior within the role of director, and the need to think systematically about what is appropriate social and personal behavior. Aspects of this question range from adequate preparation for meetings to the most serious questions of ethics and personal involvement. Boards are responsible for replacing departing directors, introducing new or incoming directors to the organization, training current directors, developing current directors' skills, and developing the board itself. The phrase, a sophisticated board, versus the phrase, an unsophisticated board, suggests something of the idea here. One seems knowledgeable and sure-footed in the tangle of decisions; the other lumbering and inappropriate.

Board positions. Directors have different positions on boards. Some are chairpersons; others hold such offices as treasurer, secretary, and so on; and some are simply board directors. Being clear about what is required of each position is vital. Contemporary boards often prepare job descriptions for each position as well as that of the director itself to improve understanding about what is involved.

Assessment and evaluation. The expectations for boards and individual directors fall into four main categories:
1. the individual behaviors of directors in their various positions;
2. the efficiency and effectiveness of the board as a team;
3. the quality of the decisions the board makes;
4. specific decisions regarding the organization's mission, and the need to continually look at that area to see if the mission is still relevant or, needs updating, and so on.
Each of these categories should be evaluated annually.

We urge evaluation of both the directors' performances in their various roles and the decision stream of the entire board. Funders, partners, and potential organizational members involved who look at these organizations are paying increased attention to the need for directors to look at strategic policy matters as opposed to becoming enmeshed in administrative concerns—though there is an overlap, to be sure, as we have already suggested in "the grey area."

1. Balance

The board needs to achieve a proper balance among its functions.

- Maintains proper board organization _____
- Achieves CEO-board balance _____
- Balances outward and inward focuses _____

2. Training, personality, and assessment

The board needs to develop proper positions, training, and evaluation.

- Conducts training and development _____
- Assumes proper positions for boardship _____
- Performs evaluations and assessments _____

Chapter 11

Establish Proper
Board Organization

Introduction

The board's functions are many and varied. Typically, an entire board cannot accomplish all of its functions as a "committee of the whole," so most boards break up into committees and subcommittees to address the different tasks.

Board consultants suggest—and our own investigations confirm—that approximately half of a board's time is wasted in unnecessary agenda items—for example, items for which there is insufficient information to allow the board to act. Board organization that can process items and bring options to the full board for consideration, therefore, is one of the most important elements of quality decision making. Without an appropriate committee structure, it is very difficult for the board to properly carry out its decision-making and oversight role.

103

In general, the makeup of most board committees should include at least one director from the board itself, but no more than three. Other committee directors come from the visiting committee, leadership circle, or advisory board, as we discussed in Chapter 3.

Committees and Subcommittees

The board should not approach its issues casually or in an offhand manner, but rather with sustained thought. Boards operate much better when working from the recommendations of committees. With rare exceptions, therefore, the board should assign upcoming tasks to committees, requesting that they study their assigned matters with appropriate staff, other directors of the organization, and the community at large to develop proposals for action with alternative considerations, and present their recommendations to the board. The board as a whole does not have to acquire or guess at the relevant information to make decisions. The board can deal with issues more effectively and efficiently with committee input.

Key committees fall into three groups: operating, strategic, and ad hoc.

Operating Committees

There are commonly seven key operating committees with important ongoing functions for most organizations. Their functions may be combined, however, within a smaller number of committees. Although, in many ways, the strate¬gic committees may be more important—for it is within the strategic committees that the organization's programmatic elements find expression. These operating functions, expressed within standing committees—the operating committees are essential to run the organization.

Executive Committee. The executive committee comprises the board president, its officers, the CEO, and the perhaps some others. The CEO Executive (or CEO) Committee can usually take action in emergency situations when the full board cannot meet, and it often sorts out those activities and proposals that need board approval. The Executive Committee usually meets ON BEHALF OF THE BOARD—when the board does not meet in a month, for example, and deals as well with "the grey area"—realms/issues where policy and administration mingle.

Budget/Finance Committee. The budget and finance committee generates the organizational budget and handles financial oversight, reviewing financial trajectories monthly, at least, and sometimes weekly. It works with the organization's chief budget or financial officer in preparing budgets, making proposals for new expenditures, and other such fiscal matters. The budget and finance committee should involve people from the financial community to facilitate access to banks and other local sources of financing when necessary, but this committee should involve others as well—it may be consumers, alumni, etc., from the "leadership circle." The budget and finance committee reports to the board on both overall budgetary strategy and specific budget proposals.

Resource Development Committee. The financial resource development committee develops financial resources for the organization. Its activities may involve seeking public contributions, planning fundraising events, securing grants, or developing contributions of property. All directors should have the opportunity to serve on this committee at some point in their tenure on the board. Because raising resources is such a difficult task, people can tire of it quickly and burn out. Regularly rotating directors on and off this committee can help keep its directors fresh and its work invigorated. Finally, actually raising the funds that one spends introduces a note of realism into the allocations process. This function is often merged with the Budget/Finance Committee and feels free to call upon all directors and advisory directors for assistance.

Audit Committee. New thinking in the finance area is suggesting a separate audit committee—one that can take an independent look at the finance picture. This may well make sense in large organizations but might be difficult to implement and costly in small ones. In smaller organizations an outside audit is often required, in such cases the Budget/Finance Committee should meet with the outside auditors to review the audit and understand any concerns the auditors may have. If an organization is sufficiently small so that it does not have an audit, some mechanisim for assuring fiscal integrity is appropriate.

Human Resources Committee. The human resource development committee oversees the organization's human resources. Traditionally, this body has been called the "personnel" committee, but that is too narrow a construct. The committee does, of course, develop the personnel policies for the organization, but its role is larger. It helps provide the resources necessary for the staff and board to do their jobs, through development and training. (With board activities, it works with the recruitment and training committee.) It stays in touch with staff and their concerns on the one hand, as well with as the broader human resources community on the other. Its purview can involve such issues as compensation, holidays, and employee burn out. The HR committee also typically handles grievances and the identification, interviewing, and review of top agency staff.

Public Relations Committee. The public relations committee enhances and improves the agency's image with the general public. It prepares annual reports, newsletters, press releases, and other pieces of public information and seeks favorable publicity about the agency. Sometimes the board may merge public relations and community relations into one committee, but the function of public relations tends to be focused more on media policy.

Community Relations Committee. The community relations committee focuses on the personal aspects of community involvement—for example, organizing tours of the agency, providing speakers for public functions, and interpreting the agency's mission and role to key people in the community. Whereas the public relations committee tends to concentrate on the media, the community relations committee focuses on people. Its role often relates to government, and this committee frequently cultivates relationships with political figures at the local, state, and national levels and seeks to develop political clout for the organization.

Board Recruitment and Training Committee. The board recruitment and training committee seeks to interest previously uninvolved individuals in the organization, its mission, and role. The recruitment and training committee may maintain a list of potential board directors—"good" people who might be interested in serving on the board. In recruitment, the committee meets with individuals, interprets the kind of job the agency is doing (how well they think the agency is carrying out its mission and vision), and promotes the candidate's involvement with the organization. The nominating function, which usually occurs annually to develop a slate of officers for the board, also may be the responsibility of this committee. But, whereas the nominating function moves people who have already participated in the organization (from the outer circle of the advisory or visiting committee) into full directorship and into officers' positions on the board, the role of recruitment is to secure people from outside the organization and bring them into this outer circle.

In training, this committee is responsible for preparing a board of directors' manual (see Chapter 11), conducting annual training sessions for the entire board, and providing additional training for individual directors if they so desire. In this task, it works with the human resources development committee.

Strategic Committees

These committees are driven by the mission, while their actions will be within the strategic plan. The strategic plan should identifies targets of emphasis—usually three on four things that constitute the organization's core activities. Each of these items should have its own committee for oversight and encouragement.

Strategic committees promote the structure and purpose for the mission and role of the agency itself. Agencies usually have somewhat general missions and roles that need concrete manifestations in the form of specific programs. Some activities need to be undertaken, and others stopped. All activities need monitoring and evaluation. A strategic committee often comprises professionals in the area of concern and lay people or volunteers interested in making program recommendations to the board. Strategic committees generally work closely (perhaps most closely) with staff.

Ad Hoc Committees

The board can form ad hoc committees for specific events on tasks. These committees are helpful because they are not permanent and can operate for the short term. Sometimes these are called task forces to denote limited mission focus within specified times. For example, a committee may be formed to put on a specific event for fundraising or community recognition of what the organization does.

Too Many Committees?

Boards can have too many committees. Some committee functions can and should be combined; we have broken them out here to carefully delineate all the functions which need committee attention. The point is to make the work of the board more efficient and effective. As we shall see in Chapters 15-17 on board meetings, each committees does not report at each meeting; a committee only reports when an issue requires discussion or a decision. Hence, the board avoids meeting clutter.

Board committee organization can be one of the most effective ways to position the board to carry out its functions. Organizations should pay careful attention to the way in which they set up their boards and the changes their individual board structures require.

Conclusion

Proper structure is essential to proper board functioning. All agencies will not use all of these committees. But using members of the "leadership circle" (page 50) can expand the person power available for board work, engage potential board members, and give them on the job training all at once.

Exercise 8
Board Organization

1. Does your board have a satisfactory structure?
   - Is there a way for the meeting agenda to include only items the board can deal with effectively?
   - Can the board deal with all its functions effectively?
   - Does it have appropriate committees?
   - Does it have both standing and ad hoc committees?

2. Is it about the right size?

3. Does it have appropriate committees?

4. Does it have both standing and ad hoc committees?

5. Considering some of the ideas in this chapter, how could your board's structure be improved?

Chapter 12

Balancing Inward and
Outward Focus

Boards play a range of internal and external roles in the process of carrying out their missions. Directors must understand the various roles and the issues surrounding them.

Individual directors and the board itself are responsible for acting appropriately within the context of their roles. We have discussed the individual requisites of those roles, particularly as they regard legal responsibilities and the avoidance of self-aggrandizement and self-profit. More importantly, we have stressed the positive aspects of one's personal role—acting as a trustee of civic purpose and taking a proactive, accomplishment-oriented posture. More detailed discussions of the roles of the board chair, director, CEO, and staff director can help flesh out these suggestions.

Society in the 21st century, however, is taking an increasingly closer look at the ethical behavior of civil and civic servants. Directors are more aware that simply wanting to "do good" is not good enough. In many ways, society holds those in the voluntary sector to higher standards than those elsewhere.

111

The Role of the Board

The way in which the board performs and presents its role—to itself and to the community—is very important. Both the board and its individual directors have certain functions to perform if the organization is to achieve its overall purpose. The board needs a structure so it can perform its internal and external functions. The directors need to work toward both board performance and appropriateness.

Distinguishing between decision making (generally an internal function) and advice giving (generally an external function) is especially important. Overall, the board's responsibilities typically involve three internal and four external functions.

Internal Functions

Policy Decisions. Policy decisions typically relate to the board as a whole and involve the board's formal legal authority as specified under the organization's articles of incorporation and state statute. Decisions made under this function are typically referred to as policy decisions, although other types of decisions may have policy impact as well. Crucial to this function are adequate information, time for review, feedback from appropriate parties, and reasonably prompt action consistent with the available information.

Directors should avoid "decisional prematurity" and "decisional postmaturity." Prematurity occurs when an item comes to a policy-deciding meeting without adequate information. Typically, the board spends a great deal of time on such issues; then postpones a decision. Decisional prematurity is one of the most significant causes of decisional postmaturity. Too often, a decision delayed is a decision denied. It is legitimate for a director to charge a board with undue delay. The question of what is undue, however, is a difficult one, and it generally answered by the common sense of the whole group. One good indicator is if opportunities are missed because decisions cannot be made in a timely fashion. External constraints, such as grant deadlines, fiscal year deadlines, and so on, often make the very best informed decision useless if it comes too late. Within the policy-deciding function, therefore, boards must balance information and decisional needs and pressures.

Policy Oversight. Policy oversight is typically accomplished through the committee structure. This function involves generating policy and reviewing components, as well as assessment and program audits. Policy oversight occurs once the board makes a formal decision. Oversight does not occur until the decision is made. Within the concept of policy oversight, however, is a certain amount of policy proactivity—the anticipation of upcoming events and the proposed adjustment of existing policies to take those new events into account. Directors of policy oversight groups must be clear about the scope and extent of the particular policies they are monitoring, and they should neither overextend their role to encompass tangential areas nor ignore or minimize the responsibilities that they do have. Essentially, oversight means occasional checking on the implementation, not "messing" with that implementation.

Policy Evaluation. The evaluation committee (or wherever that function is housed) is responsible for policy oversight. The purpose of this function is to provide feedback to the board on its decisions. Issues it must consider are timeliness of decisions, the quality of decisions, and whether they were made using defined board structure. In addition, policy oversight includes a review of the programs affected by policy decisions to insure they have enacted the board's wishes relative to functional changes in the organization. Policy oversight, in order to do its job well, must plan its actions based on not only what policies exist, but must anticipate what policies are likely to exist shortly. This anticipatory response allows them to move almost simultaneously with the actions of the board as a whole.

Policy administration. Sometimes, given unique situations, the board may establish a policy-administering committee. For example, in an agency crisis, the board may delegate power to a small group—along with appropriate financial resources, staff, and logistical support—to immediately handle, with the CEO, the particular situation. Most typically, fast-breaking situations require such a task force or ad hoc group. The task force dissolves when the situation is resolved.

Over the course of a year, a board will very typically perform all of these functions, plus the following external functions. The board must be sensitive to the different issues it will encounter in each of these areas.

External Functions

Boards of nonprofits have at least four external roles that are quite different from their internal roles. As agencies move into the interorganizational environment, they no longer have the imperative control given them by their charters and articles of incorporation. Rather, they move from a position based on authority to one based on cooperation, which involves networking and coalition building. In this environment, boards may play four external roles: policy sharing, policy advising, policy coordination, and policy implementation. Sometimes, boards may create other community committees that play these roles too.

Policy sharing. In this role, the board agrees to cooperate with other similar agencies so they may become acquainted with each other's ongoing programs. Such sharing does not imply any adjustment in either's programs, nor that any particular program is right on wrong, or appropriate or inappropriate. It simply reflects an agreement to get together and "show and tell" agency programs. This activity reflects a cooperative posture only.

Policy advising. Sometimes, a board may be asked for a collective opinion on a matter of community concern. The mayor, for example, may call and ask what the agency thinks about an issue. Simply letting the CEO write a quick recommendation is not sufficient, but often necessary, given the time the mayor has allowed for a response. Rather, the directors must discuss matter and prepare language that reflects the board's and agency's perspective. The recommendation must be approved by the board and entered into the minutes. The board may also make a statement in advance of any request as a statement on a community issue with instruction to the CEO to express that opinion should he/she be asked or even take a stand unasked if the board feels strongly enough – but this is a primary example of a decision that would in all likelihood come too late. The mayor is going to want a response within a week – the odds of a board meeting taking place within a week is less than 1 in 4 since many boards only meet once a quarter.

Policy coordination. Policy sharing sometimes leads to policy coordination. The board might be asked to approve a policy to share responsibility for a program with other agencies. For example, one agency might suggest to another, "We'll handle young children, and you handle older kids," or "We'll handle boys, and you handle girls." This kind of coordination requires agreement from the board. Organizational staff needs to be involved as well. Agency or organizational coordination requires joint planning and agreement. But again, this activity is mostly done at the CEO level. Partnerships on a certain level go to the board, but this level I would guess could even be made at the level of Program Director.

Policy implementation. Within the interorganizational system, the board of directors might become part of a team asked to implement a particular community-wide decision. Again, such an arrangement calls for delegated functions and those that require constant board oversight and approval. A director from an agency board who joins a community-wide group to coordinate and implement a community program does not carry any kind of board approval unless his or her board has specifically given such approval.

These are important functions for boards to play, and we strongly encourage boards to participate in policy sharing, policy coordination, and policy implementation at the community level. In such situations, however, the board might create a special committee or task force to handle the organization's relationship with the constellation of other organizations that are seeking to accomplish a larger social task.

Conclusion: Balancing Focus

Certainly, boards can play many other roles. These seven, however, divided between internal and external focus, are the most common and suggest some of the different dynamics that boards can expect to encounter.

Boards tend to be more inwardly focused, playing roles as corporate citizens in the collective community less and less frequently. Striking a balance between the inward and outward focuses is appropriate, but a balance dictates that boards spend some time in coordinating, implementing, sharing, and advisory roles.

Boards should pay more attention to the external roles than they have historically—particularly in the nonprofit community. Decision-making boards often find it difficult to play these external roles because they relinquish the authority they have with internal matters. This shift from an authoritative to a cooperative posture can be a challenge for a board, but one that the board must carry out.

Exercise 9

1. Consider the seven board policy roles:

Internal	**External**
Decision	Sharing
Oversight	Advising
Administration	Coordination
	Implementation

2. Has your board played all of these roles?

3. Which roles does it play best?

4. Which does it play worst?

5. Does the board adjust its behavior when its roles shift?

Chapter 13

Board Training, Development, Growth, and Learning

Introduction

Boards have a responsibility for training new and current directors. Several cases illustrate why this is necessary. For example, during the community development efforts in the United States in the 1960s, well-intentioned people aimed for the "maximum feasible participation" of low-income people. As Senator Daniel Patrick Moynihan (D-NY) [1969] put it, what came out was, mostly, "maximum feasible misunderstanding."

During that time, many people who lacked board experience were brought onto the governing bodies of nonprofit charitable organizations. Rarely did they receive any kind of orientation, yet they were often blamed for their own "failures." Other examples from both the profit and nonprofit sectors abound. We all know stories of boards acting too late or with too little energy, and the crises that often follow for those organizations.

The bad news is that boards have been insufficiently vigorous in the past. The good news is that they are waking up. The problem that is "waking up" creates further emphasizes the need to provide directors with training in boardship. Orientation is an absolute necessity for new directors; ongoing training is even more so for all directors.

The Board Manual

The first step in any training and development is to have the books. In this case, the book is a board manual. Every organized board should develop a manual for its directors.

Board Manual Section I

The board manual should open with a statement of the organization's mission, its purpose, and its *raison d'être*—its reason for existing—followed by a brief history of the organization. The manual should then detail the organization's legal responsibilities, referring the reader to the articles of incorporation in an appendix.

Following these opening sections, the manual should include a statement on the expected responsibilities of directorship, outlining the role of the typical director. This is a job description for the director, one that will be used for evaluation later on.

Board Manual Section II

The next section, which can be replaced regularly, should deal with the organization's current strategic plan and operating structure. Detail committees and their functions, as well as advisory committees and any important links; provide names, addresses, and telephone numbers of current and past directors; and describe plans for a training program for directors, retreat dates, and meeting schedules—all of the specific information that directors might need. Include the names and addresses of staff on a separate sheet that can be updated as necessary.

Board Manual Section III

Another section should contain a compilation of annual reports. This gives each director an opportunity to see what the organization has done over time and to consider what it is likely to do in the future. Future plans can also be listed here. In addition, a single summary sheet can give historical demographic facts about the organization, such as its annual budget or per capita expenditures on children.

Sample Table of Contents for a Board of Directors Manual

Directors' Manual
1. The Children's Center
2. Table of Contents
3. Mission and Purpose of the Organization
4. History
5. Philosophy
6. Legal Responsibilities
7. Legal Responsibilities in General, for All Board Directors
8. Legal Responsibilities in Particular, for This Particular Board
9. Responsibilities and Duties of Board Directorship
10. Current Operating Structure
11. Strategic Plan
12. Organizational Plan
13. Current and Past Directors, Names and Addresses
14. Committees & Functions
15. Financial Information
16. Program Plans, Schedules
17. Annual Reports
18. Future Plans
19. Appendix: Articles of Incorporation
20. Finally, include any pertinent reading material the board feels is essential to the director. These materials can include helpful copies of current articles, as well as a relevant bibliography if that's appropriate.

This is only a skeletal suggestion for a board manual. Some manuals are simple and direct; others are more complicated and intricate. What is vital is that the board itself develops its own manual.

Board Training

One of the most important board training activities is the training session for new director. If the board has used the two-tier process we described in Chapter 3—involving prospective directors in the organization by first inviting their service on a visiting committee, advisory board, or leadership circle—the new director will not begin from zero. This is too often the case, and it frequently takes six months to a year for the new director to become a useful participating director. In either case, whether the new director has participated in ancillary groups or is inexperienced, an orientation process should occur. It need not be long, but it should include two basic aspects.

The first deals with the organization's substantive elements—its purpose, mission, and commitment. New directors need to know what they are getting into before they can make substantial contributions.

The second part of this training should deal with the principles of good group decision making. Mutual education involving discussion, participation, and the acquisition of new knowledge is a very good way to establish the bonding between new directors and veterans that makes effective and efficient decision making possible.

The Annual Retreat

All boards should have an annual retreat for least one or two days. Attendance at that event should be part of the serving agreement, and non-attendance is only excused by a note from the director's pathologist. We have worked with many boards and directors facilitating retreats, and the sad thing is that, when push comes to shove, attendance is always lower than promised. We view this pattern as unacceptable, and suggest that, if a director cannot attend the annual event for whatever reason, she or he step back into the leadership circle. The reason we are taking a hard line here is to make the point that groups cannot function if their members do not show up, or if to schedule such an event becomes a major time issue for the CEO. Sports teams need to practice; orchestras and string quartets are the same. Boards are the same as well, though many directors do not seem to think so. Commitments are, well, commitments. All too often we excuse people from "volunteer" ones because they are a volunteer. We beg to differ. These are agreements that must be kept in order to have a healthy organization. A non-participating board member is worse than useless; they take up a space that could be filled by a dedicated director.

The importance of the annual retreat is two-fold. It is a time when a 5-C Conference can be held, though it is not necessary to do exactly that. Principally, the retreat is, as a cleric we knew once called it, "Pray and Play." It is, of course, mostly pray. Time is available for retrospective and prospective views of the organization. New ideas generated from the job description requirement can be discussed. Time can be spent refocusing on mission and assessing its current relevance; change and rededication are each options. It is a time to re-examine the mission and vision to see if it needs to be tweaked to better fit the environment. It is a time to review the strategy to make mid-course corrections (assuming, of course, this is not a year to revise it entirely), and, of course, it is a time to review the board's effectiveness and that of the CEO and top management. It is recommended that the retreat be done in a place that board members can reflect. The schedule should be such that members can enter each session with a fresh perspective.

Also, this is the time when new directors should be formally inducted. It provides a sustained time when they can step into board roles. Hopefully, through the leadership circle concept, they have already had the chance to participate in board work, so it will not be totally new to them.

Board Development

Although too few boards have proper training procedures for directors, even fewer have policies regarding the development of the board and individual directors. What's the difference? Board training is specific and focuses directly on the specific missions of the organization in question. Board and director development focuses on the education of the board and the director, toward a more general set of skills and competencies. The rationale for board development is the same that supports professional and staff development anywhere. Staff need training, of course, in the specifics of the agency, but they also need to experience development— the general education that comes from attending conferences and participating in seminars. The same expectation and benefit is due directors.

The board should provide for and establish an expectation of one development activity per director per year. Such an activity can be individual—a particular director going to a conference of interest to him or her—or it can be a collective effort, in which the board brings in someone to provide some educational component for the entire group. The important feature here is that directors have opportunities to grow during their tenure on the board. Our rule of thumb is to have one collective experience and one individual developmental experience per year. The annual retreat is a good time to build in group training. Given what we know about boards in general, financial matters, information technology, and human resources are good candidates for most board's development topics.

Networking

Some aspects of director training are costly and too difficult for one agency to conduct alone. Directors may wish to network with other organizations and create training and development opportunities in cooperation with other agencies—a "Saturday Seminar," for example. Or, the board may wish to work with a key community resource agency or local or state nonprofit assistance organization to sponsor and develop such sessions.

Growth and Learning

These activities, singly and severally, contribute to the important overall goal of growth and learning—both of individual directors and for the board as a functioning unit. Every director should ask the question of him or herself—"Am I, are we, learning and growing?" If the answer is not an enthusiastic "Yes!", then there is a problem that needs to be addressed.

Conclusion

The development of directors is one of the very deficient areas in contemporary nonprofit boards. Investment in director development pays large dividends. Boards should not wait for others to take the lead. Any board can be a leader in getting development activities of a developmental sort off the ground. Frequently, though, there are capacity-building organizations that can assist local nonprofits in their board development agendas.

Exercise 10

1. Review your board's training and development activities.

2. Are they adequate?

3. If not, why not?

4. Can you think of ways to improve them?

Chapter 14

Perform Board Roles
Appropriately

Introduction

Much of this book so far has focused on the more formal mechanical elements in directing and governing nonprofit organizations. Personal competencies (recall that competence = knowledge + skill) are involved as well, however. What does one actually do as the board chair or as a director on the board of a nonprofit organization? What specific activities and expectations do these roles involve? These questions deserve some attention, not only because they relate centrally to the performance of nonprofit directors, but also because directors often find themselves in board positions before they fully understand what the roles entail.

Board performance should be both efficient and effective. Efficiency refers to the economical use of time. If, through preparation, one can reduce the amount of time one spends on an activity, so much the better. The other goal is effectiveness—spending time on the right topics. Successful performance of one's role stresses both of these elements as interdependent and interlinked.

125

The Chair

The role of the board chair is one of the most complex in the nonprofit field. So many expectations and hopes rest with the chair—from being the custodian of the organization's tradition, to running efficient meetings, to providing leadership for new directions. Finding and developing committee chairs is a difficult enough task for the chair (in consultation with the CEO, of course). Finding and developing a good board chair is even more difficult.

Often, the experience of chairing the board is a trying one for the incumbent as well as for the other directors, and sometimes for the whole agency. Problems frequently occur because the new chair does not fully understand the roles of leadership and organizational development that devolve upon the chair and upon the board as a whole. Board chairs sometimes feel that, to do their jobs, they have to become deeply involved with their agencies' ongoing daily operations. They fail to realize that the leader's job focuses much more on creating expectations than on action—that doing more is not as important as expecting more. We sometimes attribute a chairperson's poor performance to his or her own personal characteristics. There is no question that some people are, for example, power hungry, abrasive, or indecisive. More likely, however, is that the chairperson's poor performance results from his or her lack of knowledge of the roles the chair should play and the kinds of actions he or she should take—and the chair often receives little help in preparing for the role.

Preparation for the Chair's Role

There is much wisdom in avoiding a direct move into the roll of chair before performing a subsidiary or related role within the organization. Often, people—particularly those who have performed a range of civic leadership functions—get tapped for organizational roles simply because of their personal prestige and status and the skills they demonstrated in those other roles. The appeals are often seductive: The recruiting agent flatters the ego of the potential chairperson while minimizing—and possibly not sharing at all—

some of the problems and difficulties it might be experiencing.

Thus, a key guideline for anyone who is considering an offer to chair a nonprofit board—and a key requirement of any organization seeking to recruit a new chair—should be for that person to have at least one year's experience with the organization's board before assuming a formal leadership position. Many agencies have incorporated this piece of wisdom into their bylaws; they move people up the organizational hierarchy through a series of positions: second vice chair, then first vice chair, leading to the position of chair. Of course, although this is sensible for organizations that have candidates in abundance, many organizations would find this approach problematic since they do not have enough people to fill these positions. The idea behind this policy is still a good one, however. Not only should individuals avoid taking formal leadership positions without prior experience, but organizations should avoid proposing such appointments. The work of the nominating committee, men¬tioned in Chapter 3 as an important activity, should help prevent some of these difficulties.

This is the usual route. Sometimes, however, an organization may deliberately bring in a new chair that is not acquainted with the agency, often to shake things up. That person must receive special orientation.

Pre-acceptance Activities

Let's assume that one is contemplating the chair's position because of personal interest, an invitation from the board, or a combination of the two. What tasks should one accomplish before assuming the role?

The statesperson perspective—The person moving into the role of the chair must assume the perspective of a statesman—a "statesperson," to be gender neutral—rather than of a partisan. The typical director may have specific interests, programs, and ideas that he or she wishes to pursue, promoting them vigorously in board meetings. This desire is fine—indeed, directors should introduce and fight for ideas. The board chair, however, must set aside the perspective of promoting her or his personal agenda. ("Now that I'm the chair, I can push what I want"). Certainly, the chairperson will have ideas and will provide leadership for ideas. The hallmark of the chair's role, however, is much more the blending and orchestrating of others' ideas. The chair becomes a statesperson.

The situation is much like that of a first violinist who becomes conductor of the orchestra. Taking to heart the perspectives and problems of the entire orchestra, the new conductor must schedule musical compositions that reflect and showcase the range of talent present in the orchestra, not just the strings. Statespersonnship is perhaps the most important of the pre-acceptance tasks, or 'prework," that potential board chairs must undertake.

Assess the other directors—The second piece of prework is a detailed assessment of the other directors on the board. We often work with people in organizational settings without knowing much about them. The board chair has to understand the other directors motivations. Why did they join the board? What do they hope to gain from involvement? What ideas, skills, and interests might they contribute? Answering these and other questions gives the new chair a better understanding of the people with whom he or she will be working. Even though the board chair may work with other directors over long periods of time, such an association does not mean that the chair knows the interests and motivations of those individuals in any depth.

One way to explore the interests of other directors is to schedule short meetings with the others—a phone call or coffee. The chair can explore the interests and commitments of each director; this can provide lots of information that can inform committee assignments, special assignments, and other duties. This method may be time-consuming, but it's useful.

Conditions of appointment—The third piece of prework the chair-to-be should undertake is to negotiate any resources, special help, and particular undertakings of interest that are conditions of appointment. As with any job, there is a period of negotiation when one agrees to fill the position of board chair. Those negotiations are very difficult to recapture once one has accepted and is in office. Not all chairpersons may have such special demands, but one should explore one's own interests to see if any exist. A discussion with the other directors—"I'll be happy to be chair, but I would like the board to develop a strategic plan as a condition for my acceptance"—is perfectly legitimate. Of course, the chair-to-be may not get all of his or her wishes, but the chances are greater at the early negotiating window than after acceptance. Many a chair has sadly lamented, "Well, I assumed that when I took over the chair we would be doing...."

Self-assessment—Finally, the chair must do some self-assessment. The appointment of a chair is a signal to other directors, the CEO, and agency staff. The chairperson-to-be must understand how others may regard him or her, even if that reading is somewhat inaccurate. For example, if the new chair is an accountant or someone from the financial community, some may take the appointment as an indication of financial tightening and a focus on financial matters. If the new chair is from the human relations field, then some might assume that a human relations focus is coming. These assumptions may not be accurate, but they inform the behavior of others and, hence, must be taken into account.

If all of these elements can be satisfied, then the chair-to-be should feel free to undertake the responsibility. Going through these steps may seem problematic and time-consuming, but the problems that new board chairs have experienced over the years suggest that undertaking these steps can enhance success. Of course, we have to correct for realism. It's not likely that everyone can do all of these things. If there are too many prerequisites, no one will ever get to be chair. But these prework tasks are a good place to start.

After Acceptance—The chairperson has now assumed the formal chair position. After accepting the chair, what roles does the chair play? How, specifically, can the chair carry out his or her responsibilities as chair during the course of regular board meetings? Overall, the chair's responsibilities fall into three broad areas:

1) Operational responsibilities or working with the CEO. These responsibilities deal with running the place; they also include running meetings and appearing on behalf of the organization.

2) Intellectual responsibilities or developing ideas. These aspects of the chair's roles involve generating, supporting, and managing ideas. Without leadership from the chair, new ideas are not likely to surface, and old ideas are not likely to receive careful review and rethinking, resulting in either premature or "postmature" decisions based on inadequate or "overadequate" information. Chairs have to help groups consider topics and reach decisions.

3) Interpersonal responsibilities, or developing people. This involves the "people part"—enhancing participation, involving those who hang back, and dealing diplomatically with troublesome and difficult individuals.

Let's consider each in more detail.

Operational responsibilities

The board chair and the organization's CEO work hand in hand to provide a central leadership team. As part of the preparatory discussions, the chair-to-be should have an opportunity to consider a range of issues with the CEO so as to avoid any surprises on either side. The CEO is frequently involved in recruiting the chair because every CEO knows that the chair's leadership is crucial to the ultimate success of the organization in general and to the CEO's career in particular. The CEO and the chair should map out areas of agreement between them of both substance and process.

On the substantive side, the chair and CEO should in general agree in advance on the goals they want to emphasize and the strategic matters that will influence the overall direction of the organization in the coming year. This should not preclude other directors on the board raising issues or putting fresh items on the agenda; but, at the very least, the CEO and the chair should have some understanding of where they are going and what they would like to do. Difficulty or disagreement between the chair and the CEO can bring the organization to a standstill.

On the procedural side, the chair and the CEO should agree on how they will carry out their respective positions and roles. Some chairs like to give CEOs a great deal of latitude; others want CEOs to keep them more directly informed. Typically, new chairs like to receive more information at first, a practice that often diminishes as the working relationship between the CEO and the chair grows.

The CEO and the chair should discuss differences in their styles frankly and honestly before the new chair takes office. What participation does the CEO want to have in meetings? How does the new chair feel about this level of participation? Does the new chair want the CEO to work toward any particular style? The two leaders should iron out these issues and others as fully as possible so that they each understand the other's wishes. Human relationships being what they are, disagreements will always arise, but such a prior discussion will help minimize the problems.

The chair should meet regularly with the CEO or president to review agency matters, plan meetings, and think through issues. Little can substitute for these regular meetings. This means that the chair has at least three sets of regular meetings to attend—the meeting with the CEO, the CEO committee meeting, and the regular full board meeting.

Typically, as well, the chair "chairs" the board meetings. It is her or his responsibility to see that these meetings provide accomplishment for the participants and the agency. Subsequent sections on meeting management and decision crystallization (discussed below and in Chapter 18) should be very helpful here.

Intellectual responsibilities

The chair has responsibilities for processing and developing ideas and for improving and refurbishing the general policies of the organization. The chair must undertake several activities in this regard.

Every new chair should establish a policy agenda for the coming year. This policy agenda comes from the strategic plan, which, presumably, the organization has put together to cover the agency's direction for the next two or three years. If there is no strategic plan, one of the chair's earliest jobs is to get the organizational process under way and produce a strategic plan within a year or so.

Assuming a strategic plan does exist, however, the chair identifies key areas of policy work for the coming year. The board may have already chosen some items for its policy agenda, because the strategic plan may necessitate that some activities be undertaken within specified time frames. Or the plan may be more general than that, giving the new chair an opportunity to set some areas of his or her own interests as policy priorities—after discussion, of course, with other directors, the CEO, and agency staff via the CEO.

Additionally, the board should undertake an annual policy review and refurbishment, as we discussed in Chapter 5. If controversy and conflict arise over a particular policy area, the policy review may occur sooner than once a year, of course. Agency conflict often results, however, in the absence of such a review. Policies become outdated, provide insufficient guidance, or become a source of crisis and difficulty for the agency. Revisitation and review can help avoid such problems to some extent.

A second major activity for the new chair is decision crystallization. We discuss this challeng¬ing process in greater detail in Chapter 18. Basically, however, the process involves breaking big issues into smaller pieces, helping the group to discuss them piece by piece, "crystallizing" decisions by suggesting action, and working with the group to reach a decision. If the chair models this behavior, others will pick it up.

Preparation and timing are especially important for decision crystallization. If boards do not have adequate time to consider issues, then they will likely be forced into conservative, "Let's do it as we've done" procedures, practices, and decisions. Providing enough time to consider issues is an important first step toward changing and improving the board.

Interpersonal responsibilities

Although some of the responsibilities of the chair involve the development of ideas, others involve the development of people. There are several aspects to this role.

The first step is for the chair to understand that he or she has a development responsibility at all. Development of people means that the chair initiates programs and activities that, among other things, enable staff, the CEO, and other directors to grow and improve, become more capable in their jobs, or take on more responsibilities. Being the chair is not just minding the store. It is improving the store.

Chairpersons recognize this aspect of their leadership responsibilities differently. But without the growth and development of the agency's human capital, new programs will not have the talent and energy necessary for them to succeed. Energetic, developing people are prerequisites for energetic, developing programs. Each stimulates and is a requirement for the other.

The specifics of developing staff and directors are myriad. We discussed this role in Chapter 11. Which programs are in place is not as important as whether programs are in place. Whatever else the agency is, it should be a teaching institution, sharing vital new ideas and approaches and valid older ideas and approaches to all those who fall within its compass. Not only will the teaching role be helpful in and of itself, but the culture it creates will add quality to all agency programs.

The responsibilities of the chair do not end with this kind of leadership. Other interpersonal tasks are involved as well. The chair should assist in developing a fun atmosphere within the agency and board. When the interpersonal climate is fun, people like to work with you, and you in turn gain a more productive staff and board.

Additionally, the chair seeks to support specific directors in and out of board meetings. The chair protects those who are "underparticipating" and maintains some control over those who are "overparticipating," for a while at least. If they do not tone up, then they should return to the leadership circle. The chair sets the stage for evenhanded treatment of directors in and out of meetings. Overall, the chain tries to make the climate of the board meetings and the agency itself one of interpersonal value and strength. The goal is the development of the agency's human capital.

The Director (Board Member)

We have undertaken considerable discussion about the role of the chair because of the uncertainty and anxiety it generates. One cannot be a good chair, however, without having good directors as members of the board. This seemingly innocuous role of director is the heart of the board. If the chair is the orchestra conductor, then the other board directors represent the orchestra itself. Thus, there are at least three tasks that the director should plan to perform well:

Review, review, review. Conduct a review of the agency, its mission, and purpose before accepting a nomination to the board. As is the case with the chair, people often accept invitations to serve as directors with little understanding of the nature of the enterprise in question, its stresses and strains, its history, or its potential conflicts. Indeed, to attract distinguished directors, boards often minimize and occasionally even misrepresent such matters to potential directors. Only later, after the new director has actually joined the board, does he or she realize that the situation is not quite as originally presented. Thus, a certain amount of background is absolutely essential. Securing such background includes a great deal of reading, as well as participating with the board in several joint projects. Consider the two-tier directorship plan suggested in Chapter 3. Join a visiting committee, leadership circle, or advisory board for a year or so and see whether the nature of the organization, its mission and purpose, its operating style, and its policies, procedures, and practices suit your taste as a potential director.

Establish or update vision and mission. Look with some care at the existence or absence of a mission statement and strategic plan. Decision making—which is the essential job of boards—is difficult unless one has some overall sense of mission, purpose, and the strategic direction in which the organization is moving. The new director, or any director, needn't agree with a particular strategic plan. Strategic plans can be changed, and frequently are. The absence of a plan, however, suggests a potential lack of thoughtfulness in an organization's decision making and a likelihood of ad hoc decisions based on constantly shifting forces. Potential directors should assure themselves that the organization has a decision-making framework in place.

It is important to see if the framework actually works in practice. Does the agency have good decision-making systems? Explore the reasonableness and thoroughness of decision-making procedures. Not only are mission statements and strategic plans necessary, but the appropriate mechanics for decision making must be in place or the organization will not be able to achieve its goals. (For example, avoiding the premature and postmature decisions, keeping track of decisions, [a resolutions book is good here], preparing for meetings in ways that weed out those things that could be handled offline or by committees, etc.)

If the director-to-be has sufficient experience with the organization and is satisfied that the agency is on a desirable track, she or he can feel comfortable accepting the board position.

Once on the board, the director should observe at least five rules of thumb:

1) **Do your homework.** And do not lie about or misrepresent the extent to which you have actually done your homework. Quality decision making requires preparation. Without it, the discussion will not be of high quality, and the decision is not likely to be as good. If you are not prepared, keep a low profile at the meeting. Too frequently, directors who are unprepared to discuss particular issues will introduce extraneous matters into the board meeting, thus diverting the. board's attention from a discussion for which everyone else has organized themselves.

2) **Don't dump on the group.** This occurs when the director raises a problem for which he or she does not offer a possible solution. Try, in all instances, to offer a solution to the problem you have raised. Even if you do not believe that yours should be the final

135

solution, it can help get the discussion rolling. If you see a problem but cannot think of a particular solution, share that uncertainty with the group.

3) **Aid the chair.** Directors frequently blame the chair for rotten board meetings. Often, when the chair asks for input, directors avert their eyes or are hesitant to speak. Then, when the meeting breaks and everyone leaves for coffee, loud discussion occurs, almost as if by magic. Aiding the chair means chipping in occasionally when the chair asks; helping the chair control "overparticipators"; and, on occasion, inviting those who have not spoken to share their views. Too frequently after a board meeting, one director might say to a fellow director, "I know you have some great ideas on the topic. Why didn't you speak up?" Who knows? Perhaps the person was shy or needed to be encouraged. In any event, the time for that director to share his or her wisdom has passed. Aiding the chair means helping the chairperson make the meeting go well while the meeting is in progress.

4) **Use supportive communication.** Being a director involves open and supportive communication within the board context. At one level, this means controlling one's body language, especially indications of disfavor. Observers at board meetings frequently report looks of disgust, head shaking, and whispering to others as proposals are discussed. This indirect communication often fails, because no one is quite sure how to read it. Nonetheless, it creates a negative atmosphere and discourages other directors from making suggestions and proposals for fear of the scorn that may be indirectly heaped upon them. More direct, straight-forward statements of agreement or disagreement are more effective and can clear the air.

5) **Be loyal to the board.** Directors frequently differ on policy matters. Individuals win and lose on policies that are important to them. Sometimes, one loses on a policy proposal that later turns out to have been the correct road the board should have taken. Keep discussions and criticisms of the group within the group's boundaries, particularly within the boundaries of the board meetings. No

one likes people who seek to establish their own presence by criticizing board decisions to others. Although critics may believe they are enhancing their own status, they're really only diminishing their status in the eyes of their fellow directors and saying that the board is not up to snuff reduces the image of the board more than it raises one's personal status.

With these behaviors in mind, the director's role should be a productive one. While these are difficult tasks, understanding them is a good first step.

The CEO

The CEO or president of the organization is often an ex officio member of the board. This *ex officio* status was clearer when agencies used the title CEO almost exclusively. In that case, a lay board of citizen volunteers founded or supervised some kind of helpful enterprise called a social agency. They hired an administrator—the CEO—to do the administrative work and to participate, by ex officio status, in forming the agency's policy. The CEO was—and, for the most part, remains—a nonvoting director of the board, although he or she may have had substantial informal influence through personal contacts and participation at meetings. In corporate parlance, CEOs of human service organizations were "outside directors."

In addition to being, as we have said, a nonvoting director of the board (although this practice may vary in some specific context), the CEO today provides a number of important services for the board of directors.

First, she or he acts in an administrative function by staffing the board; orchestrating the preparation of agenda materials for meetings; assisting the board, its CEO committee, and the other committees in carrying out their functions; synthesizing and organizing materials; and, on occasion, assisting committees in actually writing documents. The board should establish guidelines to avoid using the CEO's time capriciously.

The CEO performs a substantive function for the board as well. Typically, a CEO is hired because of his or her substantive expertise in the areas of the agency's mission. The CEO can apprise the board regularly about developments in the field. In a sense, the CEO serves an educational function for the board, both collectively and individually. Again, the board may choose to delegate some aspects of these tasks, lest they become too time consuming, considering there is only one CEO but frequently many directors.

As we said in Chapter 10, a delicate balance must be maintained between the board and the CEO. Typically, one thinks of the board as responsible for policy and the CEO for administration, but obviously there is an important gray area where these two realms intersect. Most central is the relationship between the CEO and the board chair. They are, respectively, the organization's chief paid administrative and volunteer lay officials. Their relationship is critical, and they should meet with each other regularly, sharing perspectives and views, not only about specific proposals under consideration, but also about the organization's general philosophy and orientation.

Evaluation of the CEO occurs under the guidance of the chair. CEOs frequently lament that they just get a new chair "broken in" when that person leaves and a new one takes over. Although it may seem overly formal, an early meeting between the CEO and the chair, even going so far as establishing a written memo of agreement about areas of interest and activity, can go far toward preventing conflicts that can threaten the organization's productivity and morale.

Conclusion: Ultimate Responsibility

When all is said and done, the final responsibility for the organization ultimately rests with the board of directors. This is an important truth, even though the CEOs surely devotes much time and energy toward developing particular services and orientations and may hold strong opinions about specific matters before the board. Indeed, the board may not always accept the CEO's recommendations, and that may sometimes mean that the board makes incorrect decisions. Nonetheless, the overall wisdom in the field is that, in the long run, an independent, volunteer board of directors produces the best decisions.

This view has been supported in recent years. Consider the many examples of the relatively self-serving conduct by corporate boards. The organizational interests of inside directors did not give them sufficient breadth of view and independence of perspective to take the necessary actions that could have prevented many sectors of American industry from becoming deeply troubled. There is also research on decision making that suggests that a group of non-experts will usually make better decisions in the long run than a single "expert." An excellent book here is *The Wisdom of Crowds* by James Surowiecki (2004). What is required for this result to obtain is that the group be properly managed—and the material further on meeting and decision management will be very helpful in this regard.

Exercise 11

In this exercise, you can create a total for each role. Scores run from 4 for "yes/often" to 1 for "Don't Know."

Assessment of Board Roles

Area of Responsibility   **Assessment**

CHAIR	Yes Often	Somewhat Sometimes	Not a Great Deal Hardly Ever	Don't Know
Is prepared for chair role				
Preacceptance Has statesperson perspective				
Has assessed other directors				
Has negotiated conditions for appointment				

Area of Responsibility   **Assessment**

CHAIR continued	Yes Often	Somewhat Sometimes	Not a Great Deal Hardly Ever	Don't Know
Has performed self-assessment				
Operational responsibilities				
Clarifies expectations with CEO				
Agrees with CEO on overall strategy and goals				
Establishes working relationship with CEO				
Meets regularly with CEO				
Intellectual responsibilities				
Establishes policy agenda				
Helps to crystallize decisions				
Uses discussion				
Uses decrystallization to prevent premature closure				
Interpersonal responsibilities				
Recognizes role of developing people				
Helps others to grow				
Develops fun atmosphere				
Provides support for directors				

Area of Responsibility   Assessment

DIRECTOR	Yes Often	Somewhat Sometimes	Not a Great Deal Hardly Ever	Don't Know
Assessed agency background before acceptance				
Checks strategic planning				
Reviews decision-making procedures				
Does homework				
Doesn't dump on group				
Aids the chair				
Participates openly				
Is loyal to the board				

Area of Responsibility   Assessment

CEO	Yes Often	Somewhat Sometimes	Not a Great Deal Hardly Ever	Don't Know
Clear definition of role established				
Staffs the board				
Provides the board with substantive knowledge				
Has good working relationship with chair				
Recognizes board has final responsibility for the organization				
TOTAL				

141

Chapter 15

Undertake Regular Assessment and Evaluation

Introduction

Assessment helps the board work well. Before one can improve something, one must first assess its current condition. Individual directors, board decisions, and indeed the direction of the entire organization should be assessed. But evaluation is always uncomfortable, and for that reason people resist it.

When considering evaluation, bear in mind that assessment and evaluation do not seek to assign blame. Evaluation is like watching game films. The team must continually assess its progress.

Improvement is a process—a journey—and assessment is where that journey begins. Individuals and groups alike are nearly always interested in improving themselves, and evaluation should become as much a part of the organization's culture as improvement.

Organizations should try different approaches to evaluation—individual, group, organizational, programmatic, and others. Many measures are better than one.

All evaluations and assessments begin with goals. Without expectations to serve as benchmarks, no assessment is possible. This means the organization must have such items as a strategic plan, job descriptions for its directors, and explicit annual plans for the CEO, among others. Evaluation is the first step toward development. If the organization does not know where it is, it cannot plan how to get where it wants to go.

Assessing Directors[9]

Each individual director serving on the board should receive an annual evaluation. This idea runs counter to some thinking; after all, volunteers are not paid, and, besides, the prospect of an evaluation might discourage one from volunteering in the first place. But, a director, like any volunteer, commits to the role. A volunteer's commitment is no less important than any other. Hence, evaluation of how the director performs in that role is necessary. Why is evaluation of directors important?

It emphasizes the seriousness of the director's role. The roles that no one looks at are the ones that no one cares about, paid or unpaid. Far from making the director's role less attractive, the very fact of evaluation emphasizes its importance.

Evaluation helps get the job done. When we know we will be evaluated, we are more likely to do the job than if no one ever looks or asks. Hence, the very presence of evaluation, regardless of the method, is an incentive to complete assigned tasks.

Evaluation of individual directors becomes a vehicle for overall organizational assessment. The information, when compiled, provides the organization as a whole a sense of its decision-making performance.

Staff often believe that directors do whatever directors want and that no one holds directors accountable, while the staff does the real work of the agency and are always under scrutiny. Evaluating directors sends a message to staff that all directors of the team are, in fact, accountable.

Directors' performance, then, along with overall board performance and the performance of other personnel, should be evalu-

---

[9] Doms point on terms because of poor evaluation.

ated regularly as part of an organizational assessment system. We have already introduced some ideas about evaluation and assessment in Chapter 12. As we have said repeatedly throughout this book, an assessment system must begin with developing job descriptions and descriptions of goals and missions. Without that initial step, at the individual or organizational level, examining performance is meaningless.

Am I a Good Director? Reflect on how you have contributed to the board. Consider such things as:
- regularity of attendance
- preparation for meetings
- willingness to play "task" roles (pushing for goal achievement)
- willingness to play "process" roles (encouraging and soothing others)
- ability and willingness to support change
- ability and willingness to support innovation

If the board desires, it can assign a numeric scale to these items so they can be scored.

Write a paragraph critiquing your own board performance, and propose specific ways in which you plan to improve. Share this with other directors.

Who should perform the evaluation? Organizations could follow a couple of different approaches. One, of course, is self-evaluation; the example above can be used in this way. Self-serving self-reports are a possibility, however. The very best method is a three-way approach:

Each individual director completes the "Am I a Good Director?" worksheet, but the CEO and the directors also use this form to evaluate each other. The board can assign numeric scales to the evaluation so that each area can be scored. These scores are averaged and presented to all directors at a board meeting. A consultant could do the averaging to ensure anonymity when directors are evaluating each other. This three-way approach gives directors a feel for the views of their board colleagues, as well as their own.

Evaluating Decisions

Boards of directors have products—their decisions. Boards must ask themselves, "Are our products—the decisions we make—any good?" Without evaluation, the board is not likely to have the feedback necessary to sustain quality decisions. Evaluating the board's decision making requires two tools: decision audits and decision autopsies.

The Decision Audit

The board appoints a committee of three directors to review and grade its decisions. The auditing committee extracts a year's worth of decisions from the board's minutes. This information will be easily available if the board follows the Rule of Minutes detailed in Chapter 16. The most recent decision should have occurred about six months prior to the decision audit to allow the auditing committee to make fair observations as to how good the decision was[10]. Each auditor grades the decisions according to a scale:

A. The A decision is one in which, in the judgment of the auditors, all parties to the decision were winners. This is an "all-win" or a "win-win" decision: Everyone affected by the decision must have come out ahead—although everyone does not have to come out equally ahead.

B. The B decision is one in which there were some winners and some losers. It is a "some-win" decision; but, on balance, the outcome is positive.

C. The C decision results in some winners and losers, but the win-lose balance is about equal. The C decision is a "win-lose" decision—there are both losses and gains, but they tend to cancel each other out.

D. The D decision is the opposite of a B—some wins, some losses; but, on balance, more losses than gains.

---

[10] We need to keep in mind that R=D+E (Results = Decision + Execution [or implementation]). Great decisions can collapse through poor execution; brilliant execution can "save" rotten decisions. Here we are only looking at the decision portion.

146

F. The F decision might also be called the "no-win" or "nuclear win" decision. No one wins, and all are further behind after the decision than they were before.

When grading decisions based on their outcomes, auditors should give special attention to and differentiate between the decision process and the implementation process. Poor outcomes could result from either, but the changes necessary would be different.

The auditors compare their individual ratings for patterns and areas of agreement or disagreement among themselves. Decisions that all three grade as As or as Ds or Fs should be set aside for decision autopsies. Patterns of divergent grading for the same decision—for example, if one auditor gives a decision an A and another gives the same decision a C—most likely reveal that the auditors are using different bases to assess the decisions. The discrepancy itself should become a subject for the board to consider.

The Decision Autopsy[11]

Before reporting their findings to the board, the auditors should conduct a decision autopsy. This is simply an intensive examination of one pair of decisions, one graded as an A and the other as a D or F. Naturally, when one does something right, as in an A decision, one should analyze the decision and how it can be repeated. Similarly, but more painfully, in the case of a bad decision, one should find out what went wrong and how it can be prevented.

Reporting to the board on the good work behind an A decision has the added benefit of praising directors for their efforts. Auditors should bear in mind, however, that, on the downside, the board is likely to be defensive toward a review of poor or failed decisions. This defensiveness is blunted in part—but only in part—by praise for the A decision.

Decision autopsies in which we have been involved have revealed common patterns of difficulty among D and F decisions. Some of the most frequent causes of bad board decisions include:

---

[11] If all the board's income comes from contracts alone, the board's abilities are limited in terms of control, except over acceptance or not.

- The board was under pressure to make a decision quickly, as in a crisis.
- The board had inadequate information to make its decision.
- The board was intolerant of independent or different views when making its decision.
- The decision was the result of coercion or group-think (see Chapter 14) or premature or improper agreement on a restricted set of alternative decisions.

These are among the most common reasons why bad decisions happen; we offer more reasons and examples in the next chapter.

Once the decision-auditing committee completes both its audit and the decision autopsy, it is ready to report to the board on the grading of the board's decisions in the last year; the board should discuss divergent areas in the auditors' grading, and the results of the decision autopsy.

Execution Assessment

Once decisions are made, the agency needs to execute that decision. As noted a moment ago, good decisions plus flawless execution makes for a great agency. Impaired decision-making most always leads to wobbly and flawed execution.

John Spence, an organizational consultant, asked executives the following question:

What percentage of the time do you feel companies that know what they are supposed to be doing (have a solid strategic plan, clear goals, specific measurable outcomes)—actually do what they are supposed to be doing?

"The answers I most often get are… 20% or less! That is absolutely shocking. It means that many companies are losing as much as 80% of their productivity (at staggering direct and indirect costs) simply because their employees do not effectively implement current plans."(http://excellencetree.net/journal/24)

Spence, whose firm, Excellence University assists organizations in this area, has the following assessment protocol:

C = Clarity

Has a plan been clearly communicated to all key stakeholders in a consistent and easy to understand way? Are people truly clear on what they are supposed to be doing? Although most executives will argue that they have done a very good job communicating their vision, plans and goals; our experience is that managers and employees are often quite unclear about what they are supposed to be doing on a daily basis. Even after leaders report "talking this stuff into the ground," it is often surprising for many of them to learn how infrequently their goals and objectives make their way into the "to-do" lists of their managers and employees in clear ways.

A = Alignment

Are all of the various departments and people aligned for successful achievement of the plan, or are there situations where key goals are at odds? Are people told to do one thing, but rewarded for the opposite? Are there systems, processes and policies in place that are in direct conflict with achieving key goals? Does the plan call for bold risk-taking, yet the culture in the company is completely risk-averse? These are difficult and extremely complex issues, but always remember: the more alignment you have across individual, departmental, and organizational goals, the more purposeful execution you can expect. Without consistent alignment of organizational goals, there is little chance for successful implementation of any plan.

C = Consensus

Do people agree with the plan and are they committed to making the business plan... a business reality. Much like alignment, the more individual support you have within your organization for the implementation of plans, the higher the chances you have for consistent excellence within your organization. Without high levels of consensus, there is little hope that even the best ideas will be successful. And remember: consensus does not always need to mean 100% agreement with everything that happens within an organization, it simply means that a high percentage of your employees support your goals and believe that your goals are aligned with each other. The more consensus you have throughout your organization, the stronger your chances are for high levels of execution.

E = Execution

Once you have Clarity, Alignment and Consensus for organizational plans, the final—and most challenging—part of the process is to get to work on implementation of those plans. This takes us to the final area of focus in the CACE Assessment: Execution. So often leaders mistake execution with "motivation" ("my people don't execute—they must need motivation training"). We have actually found that motivation is only ONE PIECE of the execution puzzle. The other four-fifths of the puzzle are:

1. time perception for goal-pursuit
2. accessibility of materials needed for success
3. a certain amount of passion or enjoyment for the work
4. properly aligned social support—from leadership, management, and co-workers.

There are lots of discussions about "organizational execution" on Google. This one is especially on point. Boards will find it helpful to ask that question: "Given that the policies are in place, do we actually DO it?"

Operations Assessment

Boards must also evaluate the economy and appropriateness of their agencies' operations (as distinct from execution.). This first requires that the board establish the total resources, in terms of personnel and money, available to carry out the organization's tasks. With this as a base, the board can look at how the agency's resources are allocated. One way to approach this task is through the professional unit method of analysis. This method works well for agencies and their boards in strategic planning efforts, as well as for CEOs in terms of developing materials and staff assignments (see Tropman & Tropman, 1995).

To conduct a professional unit analysis, the board must first develop a professional unit of service that is simple enough to allow all directors to understand the process, yet complete enough to be useful. This unit is the worker week. The analysis then proceeds as follows:

The CEO, and perhaps a small committee of directors, calculates the number of direct service workers available to the agency. Consider only those who perform the actual work of the agency; do not include those who do administration, supervision, janitorial work, clerical tasks, or similar duties. In a clinical service agency, this would be the number of clinicians, up to and including fractional amounts (for example, one-third of so-and-so's job relates to clinical work). In a planning agency, it would be the number of junior and senior planners. These are direct service workers; other workers are support staff. Even the CEO, unless she or he sees clients or spends some time reviewing planning reports or policy documents, is considered support staff. For the purposes of our example, we will assume the agency has 10 direct service staff.

Calculate the number of weeks of work available to the direct service staff to perform the agency's work. In calculations we have done in trials, the approximate number turns out to be around 45 or 46 weeks out of the total 52 in a year. This accounts for such things as holidays, vacation, and sick leave. To simplify the multiplication in our example, let's assume the agency CEO and board has 50 weeks of staff time per worker for whatever tasks the agency undertakes.

Multiply the number of workers by the total number of weeks. In our example, the agency ends up with 500 worker weeks for all agency programs and activities.

Then divide the number of worker weeks into the total agency budget. This gives the total dollar amount per worker week. If we assume our agency budget is $500,000, then the total amount of money per worker week is $1,000.

The board and the CEO can now use this material in any number of analyses. For example, dividing the total dollar amount per worker week by the number of the agency's programs, the CEO can review with directors agency's priorities. Human service agencies, as well as other organizations, commonly experience organizational "drift," wherein agency allocations, personnel, and resources move slowly from desired goals to other objectives. One can measure this drift using staff time records. If kept accurately, these records can reveal much about time allocation.

Organizational drift is the rule rather than the exception. A variety of informal and historical factors can cause organizational drift, and it frequently goes unnoticed. A strategic assessment would note such a reallocation and allow the agency to correct or redirect its course. Too, the agency may be doing exactly what it is supposed to be doing according to its goals and objectives, but, upon review, the agency determines that its goals and objectives are inappropriate to the needs of the community. Here again, the professional unit method of analysis allows the board to see the overall allocation of effort more clearly, in terms of both personnel and dollars.

The professional unit method of analysis fuses dollars and people into a single, easily comprehensible unit. Boards think more in terms of people than money, but much of their planning and decision making is often done in terms of disembodied monetary units, removing it from the reality of human services. The professional unit method of analysis allows a crisper, cleaner approach to strategic thinking. After all, once an organization determines its objectives, it has to begin allocating staff and budgetary resources. The professional unit method of analysis offers a clear view of what the organization is doing and what it might be doing, and a factual basis for determining whether its activities correspond with its objectives.

Strategic Drift and Strategic Centering

Lastly, the agency needs to look at strategic drift and strategic centering. Is it placing its resources where its goals are? To answer this question, the agency must compare what it is really doing with what it would like to be doing or what it is supposed to be doing.

Here, the drift index, or index of dissimilarity, is useful. It provides a numerical value measuring the difference between the organization's actual activities and assignment of staff on one hand and its desired activities and assignments on the other. The agency can conduct this assessment in a variety of ways, but the index is a relatively quick yet sophisticated measure that provides lots of information for minimum effort. It builds on the professional unit method of analysis.

Once the CEO or a planning committee has developed a professional unit analysis, the directors fill out a small questionnaire. The questionnaire is simply a list of the major organizational activities or programs. Directors are asked to allocate the percentage of organizational time they feel should go to each activity. The questionnaire also includes several blank lines that allows them to propose activities that the organization does not currently undertake.

The planning committee or CEO averages the directors' allocations for these activities and inserts the averages in Column A, on the Drift Index Worksheet (shown on page 154). The percentages of time for what the agency is actually doing, derived from professional unit analysis, go in Column B. Thus, Column A represents the ideal, Column B the reality. Column C represents the difference, subtracting B from A (disregarding the sign, or converting negative amounts to positives). The percentage differences in Column C are then added and divided by two. The resulting number is the drift index, or index of dissimilarity, and quantifies the difference between what the organization is actually doing and what it wants to do.

The index provides terrific factual information that the board can use to refocus, redirect, and reinspire the organization. The percentages are easily converted back into professional units, so directors can quickly see what their percent of effort means in terms of percent of budget allocation. Indeed, instead of professional units, the drift index worksheet can also use actual budget fractions in Columns A and B.

Percentage allocations clarify the choice process. Directors don't always have a broad sense of organizational allocations. They often talk in terms of placing more emphasis on one area and less on another. Forcing the choice by use of a percentage mechanism pinpoints differences in approach and emphasis.

The drift index quickly reveals one deficiency of most organizations. Many allocate nothing for innovation, new programs, or experimental work. Absolutely everything is consumed by operating programs. It is tough to become an entrepreneurial board if there are no resources at all for new and innovative programs. We suggested a guideline in Chapter 7 that 15% of the organization's resources be targeted toward innovation. This item and percent are fixed in the examples in this chapter. This goal may take three years to reach if the board is not presently targeting any resources toward innovation.

The drift index is extremely flexible. The CEO can use it with staff to compare the CEO's assignment of work load with the staff's actual percentage allocations. As the beginning of a strategic process, either at the board level or within the organization, the technique is a good start.

Drift Index Worksheet

Percentage Use of Time, Budget, or Professional Units

Operational Goals or Activities	Column A Ideal %	Column B Actual %	Column C Difference A-B*
1. Residential Treatment	50	40	10
2. Counseling	15	30	15
3. Home Care	10	10	0
4. Unique Item	—	—	—
5. Innovation	15	0	15
6. Misc.	10	20	10
TOTALS	100	100	50
Sum of Column	C÷2	50/2	
Drift Index	25%		

Conclusion: The Key to Success

Assessment and evaluation are crucial to the successful board. For the excellent board, evaluation becomes second nature to its operation. Assessment and evaluation must take place in four areas: the performance of individual directors, the board's policy decisions, the organization's operations, and the possibility of mission drift. Of these, evaluating the board's decision making may be the most critical. Because policy decisions are the central product of the board, improving them is a central feature of the directors' responsibilities.

Exercise 12

1. Does your board have an evaluation policy?

2. If so, can it be improved?

3. If not, can one be developed?

4. Complete the Drift Index Exercise.

Drift Index Exercise

Write down your organization's mission statement.

Now list, in priority order, a set of operational goals derived from the strategic plan. Insert these on Lines 1-6 of the worksheet. If you have more, adapt this worksheet as necessary. Using the sample Drift Index Worksheet on page 154 as an example, complete this worksheet for your organization.

Operational Goals or Activities	Column A Ideal %	Column B Actual %	Column C Difference A-B*
1.			
2.			

155

3.

4.

5.

6.

   Innovation   15

TOTALS   100

Sum of Column   C÷2   x/2

Drift Index

The number you get from the procedure (SumC/2) is the drift index, also called the index of difference. It tells you how far away from your goals you actually might be. One implication of the word "drift" implies that your goals are fine, and that your implementation/execution has "strayed." And that might indeed be the case, and often is the case. Sometimes the phrase "mission creep" is used to talk about this process. We are firm and right about our mission, but we have allowed the day-to-day events push us away from a focus on that mission. Reasons for mission creep can include attractive funding from arguably "close" activities, preferences of staff, lack of mission-focused execution and operations, among other reasons.

But sometimes it is the goals that are unrealistic. In our enthusiasm at the retreat or in the board meeting we propose commitments that, realistically, could never be kept. Every January 1 millions of refrigerators have such "resolutions" stuck to them, to be forgotten within weeks, if not days.

The bottom line ... both policy and practice need to be evaluated.

Part V: How to Do It

The Board Meeting

Overview

As we mentioned in the Preface, knowing what to do and actually doing it are two different things. As we look to the competent director and competent board, we are thinking—as we have also mentioned—that competence equals knowledge PLUS execution.

Part V: We have arrived at the point "where the rubber hits the road—the "on the ground" application of this knowledge in the setting where it all happens—the board meeting. Everything we have discussed will, or will not, happen within the meeting context. All the knowledge one has will not help if the meeting is poor to awful. Board meetings are just a subpart of general meeting malaise within American society. The fact that boards are, actually, responsible for 1 trillion dollars of assets (not counting an additional $250 billion+ of volunteer time) makes one aghast.

Available evidence points to the widespread awfulness of board meetings. There are the jokes—A board is a group that takes minutes to waste hours; or A camel is a horse assembled by a board of directors. Then one can consider the cartoons—check out the New Yorker cartoons on boards of directors and meetings (cartoonbank. com). Page after page details the ineptitude, indeed silliness, of the typical board.

Then there is the evidence from our own interviews and participant observation. Finally, there is the evidence from the many nonprofit executives who find themselves derailed, flaming out, or in calamity or supercalamity situations. (Tropman and Schaefer, 2004). One question that repeatedly comes up as executives disgrace themselves and their careers, their families, their agencies, and their sector is: "Where was the Board?" "What WERE they thinking?" Usually when we ask that latter question—"What WERE they thinking?" the unfortunate answer is—"They were not thinking at all." Rarely when an executive is dismissed for bad behavior does the board dismiss itself. When William Aramony exited the United Way of America (Glasser, 1996), the board did not hold itself accountable and step aside. The very board which could not manage one executive then appointed another—a person who had no experience whatever with the United Way!

The five chapters in this section are designed to provide the skills—or at least the recipe—for helping things go right. We begin by inviting readers to think of decisions as an organization product. We already introduced this idea when we talked about grading the decisions as part of assessment and evaluation. We then continue (Chapters 16 and 17) with principles and rules for building great meetings. Chapter 18 looks at meeting roles, and Chapter 19 addresses issues of "decision management" in the very best sense of the term.

Chapter 16

Making High-Quality Decisions

Introduction

The board of directors as a group, and directors as individuals, cannot accomplish the tasks we have discussed in this manual unless the board meetings, and the processes surrounding the development of board meetings, are effective and efficient. A casual meeting that approximates a social gathering and does not attend to the items at hand in a serious way will not only produce decisions of inferior quality, but may also leave the board's decisions open for judicial review. This applies to committee meetings as well, as they, too, are part of the overall process. What are some common problems of board meetings?

What Goes Wrong

Board meetings have many potential pitfalls. They often start late, can go on too long, and frequently accomplish little on nothing. You may have your own list of problems. Much has been written about group decision making, and experts have identified some common decision problems and pitfalls.

Decision avoidance occurs when agencies put off necessary decisions until the very last minute, or even after the last minute. One form of this malady is the "non-decision." A decision may appear to have been made, but it really has not been. Things go along very much as they have. Over time, this pattern of non-decision can lead to the "boiled frog phenomenon" (Tichy & Devanna, 1990). As we explained before, if one puts a frog in a Petri dish filled with water and slowly heats the water over a Bunsen burner, the frog will not jump out, and it eventually boils to death. Why does it not leave? Apparently, the just-noticeable difference in the temperature is never enough to cause action. This just-noticeable difference phenomenon is an important source of non-decision in organizations. Directors see things pretty much as they were, so they never see a need to act.

Decision randomness, or the "garbage can model," is a second problem. Cohen, March, and Olsen (1972) argue that organizations and their boards usually include four types of personalities: problem knowers (people who know the difficulties the organization faces); solution providers (people who can provide solutions but do not know the problems); resource controllers (people who do not know the problems and do not have solutions but control the allocation of people and money in the organization); and decision makers looking for work (those who are ready for decision opportunities). For effective decision making, all four elements must be in the same room at the same time. In reality, most organizations combine them at random, as if tossing them into a garbage can. No wonder bad decisions result.

Decision deflection, or the "Abilene Paradox," (Harvey 1974) is another scenario of bad decision making. A group of people are outside the town of Abilene, Texas, with nothing to do. Somehow, they wind up going into town—a hot, dusty drive of many miles with no air conditioning—to have a very bad meal. On the way back, the "search for guilty parties" begins as the group tries to figure out whose idea it was to undertake this wholly unsatisfying road trip. The Abilene Paradox has come to refer to group actions undertaken with no real decision to do so.

Decision coercion, also known as groupthink, is yet another well-known decision problem (Janis 1972, 1983). In groupthink, board decisions capitulate to power. One kind of power is group cohesion. In very cohesive groups, there is a coming together—not an agreement on the issues, but rather a strong wish to maintain the cohesion of the group. This commitment to the group sometimes means that no one really explores alternatives or considers options, because that might cause differences within the group, potentially harming cohesion. Decisions, therefore, are made too quickly. A second kind of decision coercion involves a powerful director, chair, or CEO. When such a leader says, "We're all agreed then," most at the table say, "Aye." Only later, in the hallway, when the real discussions occur, do problems surface.

To achieve more effective board meetings, we first must understand why things go wrong.

Why Things Go Wrong

Meetings go wrong for lots of reasons. We stress here some key ones, as they may not leap immediately to mind. Since many individual directors have lots of meetings in other aspects of their lives, they think they "know" about meetings. In all likelihood, they are really not aware of some key problems.

Contrary values. Boards and committees, as examples of group life, tend to be contrary to American values. Zander (1982) says it best:

Readers face a dilemma...[we] are not all that interested in explaining or improving group life.... Individuals feel that the organization should help them; it is not the individual's prime job to help the organization.... Basic values.... foster the formation of groups that put the good of the individual before the good of the group. In Japan, in contrast, important values foster interdependence among persons, courtesy, obligation to others, listening, empathy, self-denial, and support of one's group. [p. xi]

We like to do things individually, improving group decision making requires extra effort.

Hidden functions. Another reason for why things go wrong relates to a number of hidden functions that boards and committees perform—such as representing the community or providing a voice for those whose voices cannot be heard otherwise. Hidden functions flow from expectations that people have about boards. Some believe boards should 'represent" all of the positions and groups in the community. Some see boards as vehicles for social justice and social action, while others see them in more narrow, organizational terms. These expectations often surface around decisions, processes, procedures, and outcomes, causing conflict and decision delay.

Lack of training. Because of the problems of group life in general and in board and committee life in particular, group directors tend not to be prepared for group roles. Group directors often suffer from a simple lack of knowing what to do. Remedies, such as this manual, are all too rare.

Lack of preparation. Finally, for all of the above reasons, directors tend not to prepare themselves well for meetings, taking instead a casual, "let the chips fall where they may" approach. Material is often late and either inadequate or over adequate. Directors tend to not attend meetings regularly, and they do not always read the material when they do attend. To counter this trend, the board often reviews material at the meeting, which offends those who have prepared, and so it goes. Meetings become one disappointment after another; for this reason, many directors consider any investment in preparation to be a waste of time.

Self-fulfilling prophecy. These four reasons combine to create self-fulfilling prophecy that almost ensures board meetings of poor quality. Since group directors don't believe in meetings; since groups often perform a range of obscure and hidden functions; and since directors have neither the training nor take the time to prepare for meetings, group meetings are likely to go badly. This experience results in an inappropriate generalization about meetings. We come to believe that something inherent about meetings makes them go badly. The evidence of rotten meetings only reinforces the original presupposition. This reinforcement, in turn, convinces directors that efforts to improve meetings are a waste of time. And this conclusion virtually ensures increased difficulty in the meeting itself. Once this cycle starts, the meeting quality spirals downward.

A Recipe for Improvement

The problems with meetings are more than mere annoyances. They lead to bad decisions that can result in poor service to those in need, make the agency an awful place to work, and ultimately cause the agency's demise.

Discussing why things go wrong sets the stage for a recipe that can help make things go right. As with all recipes, the ingredients must be applied promptly and together. One can't sprinkle a little bit here and there and expect things to come out in a good fashion. What this means for the board of directors is a systematic and planned approach to improving meeting quality. The next chapter shows you how.

Exercise 13

Grade your board meetings (A = Excellent, B = Good, C = Average, D = Poor, F = Failure). To get an A, your meetings have to have three features: Decisions are made in a timely fashion, decisions are of high quality, and people have fun and enjoy themselves.

Consider some problems with your board meetings. List them here.

Chapter 17

Seven Key Principles for Effective Board Meetings

Introduction

How can we make things go better in meetings? Many of the people we interviewed about governance shared some of the approaches they use. We called these people "meeting masters," and their board meetings share three characteristics:

1. decisions get made;
2. decisions are of high quality; and
3. directors have "fun"; that is, they have a sense of authentic participation and the secure knowledge that the board meeting they are in is the real meeting, not a fake one.

How they managed to accomplish this, we detail here. Their techniques can be applied to any meeting, not just board meetings.

If board meetings are to be improved—and they can and should be—then we need principles for a new kind of meeting structure. These principles form an important base for thinking about how meetings can be improved.

The Orchestra Principle

Board meetings should be like an orchestra performance: They should be at the end of a process of development and preparation rather than at its beginning. No decent orchestra would simply stroll onstage and begin playing. Rather, the orchestra chooses its musical selections, holds rehearsals, and procures the proper soloists and accompanists. An orchestra would look very funny performing a piano concerto with no pianist. It would be even funnier if the conductor said, "Ladies and gentlemen, please excuse me, but the oboist has to leave early tonight. We know you'll understand. Unfortunately, the last piece on our program has an oboe solo in it. Therefore, we're going to ask the oboist to play those notes right now. Then, if you could kindly remember them when we get to the oboe section of the last piece, it would be a favor to us all. Thank you."

How often is this scene repeated in board meetings? The chair gets up and says, "Excuse me, but Sheila has to leave early. Therefore, we'd like to go directly to her business," regardless of the nature or complexity of that business or its position in the structure of the meeting itself. If directions can think of the meeting like an orchestra performance and apply the rules of quality and structure that one would apply to such a performance, we are already moving toward improved board meetings.

The "No More Reports" Principle

Reports have become the enemy of many board meetings. Frequently, boards have numerous standing committees, each of which is invited to report at every board meeting, regardless of whether the committee has any actual pending business. Board meetings have become oral newsletters—and thus the minutes have turned into actual newsletters. Under the Three Characters Principle, below, all reports are culled in advance as information, action, or discussion items. These items are then scheduled at appropriate places on the meeting agenda.

The "No More Reports" Principle thus contains two interrelated but crucial elements. First, unless the committee has specific

business, no report is scheduled. Rather, an announcement of committee activity is attached to the meeting announcement. Second,
and perhaps more importantly, reports are disaggregated into their
parts. Rather than having a treasurer's report, for example, which
may contain items for decision, some for discussion, and still others
for information, those items are distributed in appropriate places on
the agenda. The treasurer, therefore, may appear three times on the
agenda, once during the announcement stage, second during the
decision stage, and finally during the discussion stage.

Does this kind of structure seem odd? Applying the orchestra
principle, it's certainly no odder than having the oboist appear at
several points where the oboe is called for. No one would seriously recommend that a particular instrument get up and play all the
notes for that instrument at one particular point during the performance simply for the convenience of the performer. Yet we routinely schedule for the treasurer or some other committee chair a large
batch of unrelated items merely for his on her convenience.

Of course, the items are not totally unrelated; in the case of the
treasurer, for example, they all apply to money. What is important
here is not only their substantive link, but also their action imperatives—announcement, discussion, or decision.

The "No New Business" Principle

New business is another enemy of board meetings. This may
come as a shock and surprise. Board chairs frequently tell us, "We
don't know what the directors want to talk about until they get to
the meeting, do we?" Well, not unless we ask them. And indeed, that
is one of the most important rules for running effective meetings.
Finding out in advance what items are coming up for discussion is
imperative, because only in that way can one be sure that the information and people germane to that discussion are present. Without
adequate information, people tend to substitute stereotypic information: "What we all know is true." Discussions around new business are typically the most unprofitable in any board meeting. We

are usually ignorant of new business items, but our ignorance does not keep us from participating in the discussion. Rather, it seems to increase our desire to say something—anything—regardless of how ridiculous it may appear in retrospect.

The Principle of Proactivity

New business is often introduced under a cloud of pressure. A CEO or board chair will come into a meeting and indicate that an item is up for discussion and decision but that action must be taken immediately because of one pressure or another. Without question, pressure is the enemy of high-quality decisions. Under pressure, clarity and quality of thought seem to decrease, evidence becomes sparse, emotion and table pounding replace the absent evidence, and the board takes a series of problematic decision-making steps.

Retrospective analyses of decisions that have gone terribly sour almost always indicate that an early step was made under conditions of great pressure. This kind of decision is reactive in nature. Major outlines of what must be done are already in place—put there by the environment, or outside funders, or similar forces. Directors in this situation have very limited options, and these limitations are usually the source of the pressure, which in turn leads to rotten decisions. But it is imperative to understand that the pressure is not an "Act of God." Rather, it was created by problematic process management of a reactive sort.

We need to move toward proactive decisions and a decision-making style that anticipates environmental developments and tries to deal with them at an appropriate distance—not too far away, because then the issue seems unreal, nor too close, because then pressure makes solutions too difficult. A midpoint of distance works best for proactivity.

The Three Characters Principle

Only three kinds of business occur in board meetings—announcements, decisions, and discussion. Nothing else goes on. But we often schedule these items in disregard of their character, thus whipping the directors from an announcement to a decision then to another announcement, then to a discussion, and so on. The board becomes hopelessly lost. And, frequently, the exact character of the item is not identified, so some directors think they are hearing about it, others want to decide it, and still others want to discuss but not decide. Of course, this confusion among the directors means there is confusion in the meeting, if not chaos.

Under the Three Characters Principle, the agenda items are identified in advance as

1) announcements
2) decision items, or action items
3) matters requiring discussion or brainstorming.

All items of a similar character should be handled at the same time in the meeting, and in this order:

1) announcements
2) decisions, with discussion, and
3) brainstorming items.

This facilitates group interaction and allows for orderly progression from one type of item to another. The Rule of Two-Thirds and the Rule of the Agenda Bell, in Chapter 17, build on the Three Characters Principle.

The Role Principle

We often hear that a board's problems are the result of the personality or personalities of one or more directors. People have spoken to us about "getting rid" of certain "troublesome" directors. Directors have told us that the reason their board meetings are bad is because of the "mental illness" of individual directors and offer as evidence ample illustrations of "crazy behavior" by the directors in question. Individual directors are often typed or characterized by aspects of their personalities Arthur Angry, Tillie Talk-a-Lot, and Sam Stall all make frequent appearances on boards of directors.

Such diagnoses are a result of our individualistic pre-suppositions. As a society, we tend to view deficits in procedures and functions in terms of the characteristics and personalities of the individuals performing those procedures and functions. This book, however, has stressed the importance of examining the roles themselves, rather than the people filling the roles, in strengthening and improving functions, procedures, and rules. These repairs alone will make a substantial difference in the quality of meetings and will enable us to rethink our diagnoses of insanity on the part of individual directors.

More often than not, the person is playing a role scripted by the norms of the group. Consider "Jim," for example.

As a new director, Jim applied his habit of arriving on time for meetings. But he soon noticed that this board started meetings very late; before long, he was coming late as well. Older directors started to comment, "It's too bad about Jim. We hoped he would come on time, but he's just like the rest of us!" Talk about blaming the victim! These seven new principles, the 10 new rules we propose in Chapter 17, and the three new roles outlined in Chapter 18, will help re-script board meetings.

The Principle of Quality Decisions

In the final analysis, boards of directors are after decisions of high quality. Quality decisions do not just happen, any more than excellence in any kind of performance—sports, acting, music— simply occurs. When we observe such outstanding or excellent performances, they often appear to be flawless, easy, and even simplistic. Yet anyone who has ever tried to saw his or her way through a violin concerto, or sink a 20-foot putt, or cast a fishing fly in exactly the right place understands the months and years of practice that go into such flawless performances. Board decisions must be approached with care, not casualness. When approached with care, the decision, as a "performance," is not only likely to be of high quality in and of itself, but is also likely to be part of a pattern of high-quality decisions, which in turn result from a decision-making system of high quality.

Conclusion

Board meetings are the central engine through which boards conduct business. Preparation is necessary, of course; materials have to be developed for the meeting. But if the meeting is not well-run, then all the preparation and commitments of the volunteers—the directors—are wasted. The first step is a paradigm shift, to start thinking differently about the basic structure of board meetings. That is what these new principles do. Chapter 16 offers a recipe for planning board meetings, and Chapter 17 discusses the positions and roles in board meetings.

Chapter 18

Ten Key Rules for Effective Board Meetings

Introduction

Boards of directors must think long and hard about how to improve their meeting process—a prescription that applies, as well, to meetings within the organization itself and meetings in which the organization joins with others in community efforts. The rules here are driven by information. Without that information, it's hard to make good decisions. The cumulative focus of these 10 rules, therefore, is to follow up on items that need information, focus the information required for any decision items on the meeting agenda, and transmit that information to the board in an understandable, timely fashion so the board can act on it.

The Rule of Halves

The first rule is a simple agenda matter. It asserts that all items for an upcoming meeting must be in the hands of the agenda scheduler one-half of the time between meetings. Thus, for a monthly board meeting, the agenda scheduler should receive all agenda items two weeks before the next meeting. All directors should have an opportunity to contribute to the agenda to ensure that the agenda is built from the concerns of the directors, not issued as some standard template.

The agenda scheduler is usually the CEO or the chair; sometimes, the two work together. A frequent pattern is for the CEO to put together a draft agenda, then check it with the chair. This arrangement is fine, as long as the CEO examines all of the items closely, screens out those that could be handled outside of the board meeting, sifts through them for items that are too big and should be broken down or too small and should be packaged with other items, and assesses the items with respect to the availability of information. There is very little point in scheduling an item if the information required for a decision is not available. Sometimes the CEO needs to check with directors and staff directors who are working on or otherwise involved with issues that show up as potential agenda items. Checking with them in advance is a courtesy as well as a help.

The Rule of Sixths

Once the agenda scheduler—let's assume that it is the CEO—has assembled a list of potential agenda items, they should be reviewed from the perspective of the Rule of Sixths, which we first discussed in Chapter 7: About one-sixth of the agenda items should be from the past, what we used to call old business, about four-sixths, or two-thirds, should be from the "here and now"—current issues that are no older and no further in the future than one or two months.

The final sixth is the most important for entrepreneurial boards. These should be "blue sky" items—items of an anticipatory nature looking ahead six months, a year, a year-and-a-half. These items represent the fun part of board meetings, when directors have the opportunity to look ahead, to influence the future, to structure their options. Here is where the Principle of Proactivity is really enforced. Although every meeting might not contain such items, most should because it allows for a certain amount of psychological rehearsal. CEOs and other agenda schedulers have to anticipate the kinds of possibilities that may be coming up and take the board through a series of "what ifs." This not only permits the board to look ahead, it forces meeting planners, CEOs, and board chairs to look ahead and do a bit of scenario constructing.

It is amazing how beneficial this technique is. An advanced discussion of "what if" often permits the board to develop alternatives that no one has thought of before, introduces perspectives that previously have been concealed, and generally improves the quality of the eventual decision. Individual board chairs often tell us, "We don't have the time to do this." In our long experience with boards and the analysis of board decisions, this is just an excuse. Of course, emergencies occur from time to time, but if the board's whole life is a series of emergencies, then it is imperative that the board look at its decision-making system and try to anticipate issues and deal with them before they become emergencies.

The Rule of Three-Quarters

If the board is following the Rule of Halves, and the agenda scheduler receives all potential agenda items at the halfway point between meetings, then the Rule of Three-Quarters should be possible: An agenda with appropriate attachments should be distributed at the three-quarter point in time between meetings. For the board meeting monthly, that means three weeks after the last meeting and one week before the next.

CEOs and other agenda schedulers usually have to work very hard during the "third quarter" between meetings. During this time, information necessary for the board to discuss agenda items is pulled together, presenters must be lined up, needed reports are copied, and so on. The Rule of Three-Quarters ensures that directors get information at just the right time before a meeting—not so late as to prevent them from reading it, and not so early as to invite them to put it aside.

This rule is one of the toughest to implement because lots of norms support handing out items at the meeting. Resist that temptation, get stuff out ahead of time, and expect people to read it!

The Rule of Two-Thirds

In the last chapter, we talked about the Three Characters Principle—all business in board meetings falls into one of three categories: announcements, decisions, and discussion. Following this principle, the Rule of Two-Thirds divides a meeting into three parts. The first third is the beginning or opening, where the announcements take place. The middle third is where the greatest amount of work is done, where the board makes decisions. The last third is a time for discussion and decompression. The two-thirds point is a good time for agenda schedulers to locate a break—a sort of seventh-inning stretch after the hard work is done and before winding down with discussion.

The Agenda Bell

Middle third has qualities of
- psychological focus
- physiological alertness
- attention
- attendance

The Rule of the Agenda Bell

Following the Principle of Three Characters and the Rule of Two-Thirds, the agenda bell illustrates the ideal organization and flow of a board meeting. Assuming the agenda scheduler has received all potential agenda items according to the Rule of Halves, and has screened them using the Rule of Sixths, the scheduler should outline all agenda items in an ascending-descending order of difficulty, beginning the meeting with relatively easy, noncontroversial items; building to the most difficult items in the middle of the meeting; and tapering off to the easiest items, those for discussion, at the end of the meeting.

With a seven-item agenda, the flow of the board meeting might look something like the agenda bell illustrated in Figure 3 on page 177. Item 1 might be approval of the minutes from the previous board meeting (assuming the presence of a quorum) and should take no more than 10 minutes. Item 2 consists of a few brief, noncontroversial

Figure 3

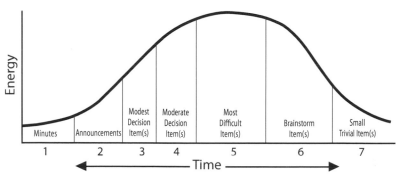

announcements and should take no more than 15 minutes. Item 3, of modest difficulty, typically lies within the first portion of the meeting and begins the process of inviting people to make decisions. The time for Item 3 is about 15 minutes, bringing the total time for the first third of the meeting to 40 minutes. For many boards, this item (or items, 3a, 3b, etc.) is called the "consent" agenda.

The difficult decision items come in the middle third of the meeting. Of modest difficulty, Item 4 may involve some controversy, but not great controversy. Time about 15 minutes. Item 5 is of the greatest difficulty and could take 25-40 minutes to complete. The most difficult items are best scheduled to fall at the peak of the agenda bell. This is the point by which most latecomers have arrived, early leavers have not as yet slipped out. Attention, at this point, is sharpest, and the psychological and physiological energy necessary to deal with the complexities of the tough items are highest.

Item 5 completes the first two-thirds of the meeting agenda, which should take about 40-55 minutes total. This is a good time to schedule that seventh-inning stretch. After the break, the agenda shifts to discussion only and Item 6. Items scheduled for this final third of the meeting do not require decisions, issues can be discussed and thought through. Item 6, which should involve 15-30 minutes of discussion, should allow the board to begin the process

177

of de-intensification and winding down, which is necessary for decision-making groups. The final item is always very easy and should take no more than 10 minutes to complete; its purpose is to put an end to the discussion in Item 6 and to end the meeting on a note of agreement (Item 7). Even though the agreement may be trivial, it is still important for group bonding. Total time for the final third of the meeting: 25-40 minutes.

Following the agenda bell, the entire meeting of seven items takes no more than two hours and 15 minutes. The agenda bell makes it possible to structure the meeting consonant with the flow of energy and within the time available for group decision making.

The Agenda Rule

The actual written agenda should be a clean, crisp document that is instructive and helpful. Its language reflects the decision and discussion aspects of the scheduled items, signaling directors in advance about each item's particular focus. The agenda should contain the following elements:

The agenda is like a restaurant menu. The wording for each agenda item should be as specific as that for items on a menu. Avoid general wording. That would be like saying, "Meat," on a restaurant menu instead of "Roast Chicken."

Following the menu concept, beneath each item write a brief statement concerning the essence of the item, just like restaurants do with their offerings.

Beside each item, in parentheses, insert one of three character words: action, discussion, or information. Directors need to know the context of consideration as well as the actual substance.

On the right-hand side of the "menu," in lieu of price, place a running clock, giving times for each item. The sample agenda below organized according to the agenda bell.

The Rule of Reports

Most reports are too long and do not contain the essential information necessary for quality decisions. The Rule of Reports argues for a CEO summary-type of report—an options memo—divided into three parts

1) a statement of the problem
2) a list of possible solutions
3) an outline of which option seems most reasonable and is recommended by the person or committee preparing the report

This three-part CEO summary-style of report is not only briefer than the typical long report, but it also gives the board some tools with which to work. Placing the recommended solution following the other options allows decision makers to consider options previously unrecognized, possibly combine them with the recommended option, and come up with a stronger, better-quality decision.

Although the reporting individual or group may strongly support the recommended solution, they should resist any temptation to eliminate options other than the recommendation. Removing the options takes away from the decision-making group one of its most powerful tools and creates a rubber-stamp situation for the recommendations.

A sample options memo follows.

Options Memo
Memorandum
To: Board of Directors, Child Help America
From: Training Committee
Re: Board Training Proposal

The Problem

The Children's Center is more than 30 years old. A recent visit from our outside consulting firm has raised some serious questions about the vigor and responsibility of the board. The consultant's report suggested that the board has let the CEO take too much initiative and that the board needs "invigoration," to use the consultant's phrase. The matter was turned over to the CEO Committee, which created a Training Committee to make a proposal to the board.

Options

We have several directions to consider:
- doing nothing, in spite of the criticism
- beginning a planned improvement of board activity
- and involvement in decision making—a one-day training session;
- working to improve selected areas of board activity.

Recommendation

The committee recommends Option 2. We feel that doing nothing is not acceptable, and if one group raises this question, others cannot be far behind. Too, the CEO feels that a bit more is needed than just an overall program of board improvement, and that piecemeal activities should be part of that overall plan. We recognize that several directors feel this is a waste of time, but hope that discussion of this proposal will lead to its approval. The committee has some ideas about the possible content of the day-long training session, once the board gives its approval in principle.

Board Meeting Agenda

Call to Order .... 7:00 P.M.
1. Minutes (Action) 7:00-7:10
2. Announcements (Information) 7:10-7:25
   a. Holiday schedules for staff
   b. Holiday open house needs board directors present through-out the day.
   c. Installation of new smoke alarms
   d. Other matters
3. Approval of Grant Submission to
   Youth Services (Action) 7:25-7:40
   Money to support discharged youth is requested from Youth Services Bureau. (Program Committee)
4. Mileage Rebate Change (Action) 7:40-7:55
   We wish to increase the mileage allowance to $.505.
   18¢ to 24¢ per mile. (Finance Committee)
5. Board Training (Action) 7:55-8:35
   A day-long plan for board training is proposed.
   A copy of the proposal is attached.
   (Training Committee)

6. Board Manual (Discussion) 8:35-8:55
    Should we have a directors' manual? What should it contain? A preliminary outline, for discussion only, is attached. (Training Committee)
7. Approval of Official Letter of Thanks to Della Furlong (Action) 8:55-9:00
    Ms. Furlong reached her 25th anniversary with the agency this year.
    Adjourn .... 9:00 P.M.

The Rule of Minutes

The Rule of Minutes calls for agenda-relevant content minutes rather than process minutes. Content minutes outline each topic on the agenda, provide a brief summary of the issue and the various points of view, and then, in different type, state the decision. Done properly, content minutes can handle most issues in a paragraph or two. Directors will find this system more comprehensible and intelligible than other systems of minute-taking, especially process minutes, which have endless streams of "he said" or "she said."

Agenda relevance simply means that the numbering system in the minutes should parallel that of the agenda, making it easy for readers to find the minutes in reference to particular items. This system prevents the minutes from simply rehashing last month's meeting. Sample minutes prepared according to this rule appear later in the chapter.

It is also good to have a book of resolutions—key policy decisions—available for easy references.

The Rule of Agenda Integrity

To maintain agenda integrity, the chair, directors, CEO, and agency staff must ensure that all items on the agenda are discussed and that items not on the agenda are not discussed. If directors are expected to invest their time reading materials in preparation for the meetings, then that investment must pay off in the discussion within

181

the meeting. When issues on the agenda, and for which directors have prepared, are not discussed in the meeting, or when items not on the agenda, and for which directors have not been allowed to prepare, are interjected into the meeting, directors conclude that preparation is not a good investment of their time, and they start avoiding the task altogether.

Sample Board Minutes

Board Minutes

1. Previous Minutes

   Minutes of the last meeting were approved as submitted.

2. Announcements

   a. Staff holiday schedules were announced.

   b. The board was reminded that the Holiday Open House needs directors present throughout the day.

   c. New smoke alarms are being installed.

3. Grant to Youth Services Board

   The board approved submission of an $8,000 grant request to the Youth Services Board for follow-up studies. One director was reluctant, noting that too much time was going into research.

4. Mileage Rate

   The Finance Committee's proposal to increase mileage reimbursement be updated to $.505.

5. Board Training Plan

   Board training plan was approved in principle. There was considerable discussion of the idea of board "training." Several directors took exception to that language. Two directors abstained. The Training Committee was instructed to prepare a day-long schedule for final approval.

6. Discussion of Directors' Manual

   There was considerable discussion of the Directors' Manual. Directors felt the outline was helpful and will provide suggestions to the Training Committee by October 1.

7. Letter of Thanks

   An official letter of appreciation to Della Furlong, acknowledging her 25th anniversary with the agency, was approved and signed by all directors.

The Rule of Temporal Integrity

Temporal integrity means to watch the clock. Begin the meeting on time, end on time, and follow the rough time estimates suggested by the agenda bell.

Posting times next to the items on the agenda, as suggested by the Agenda Rule, is helpful because it gives people a rough idea of how long the agenda scheduler feels is appropriate to spend on each particular item. This rule is especially important for minor items that tend to balloon and take inordinate amounts of time. The sample agenda on page 182 uses this system. By starting with more modest items—minutes and announcements—if people are a bit late, not a great deal is lost.

Starting on time is the best way to get people to come on time; and the meeting should always end on time, even if it gets to a bit of a late start. Ending board meetings on time is crucial.

Conclusion: Planning Sets the Stage

These rules involve setting the stage for the meeting. The kind of meeting planning we discuss here makes it possible to complete the board's business within allotted times. The dynamic aspect of board meetings—role playing and using decision rules—requires attention as well. These topics are covered in the next chapter.

One might think that focusing on "meetings" would be trivial. Nothing could be farther from the truth. Many great inventions come from making improvements on things that are in common use. One example—packaging water. Who would have thought it would become a billion dollar industry?

Chapter 19

Three Key Roles for Effective Board Meetings

Introduction

We have previously discussed the overall roles of the chair, the individual director, and the CEO. We examine here the specific roles that these three positions play in the board meeting itself. As the saying goes, this is where the rubber hits the road, especially for board chairs and directors.

The Chair

The chairperson must assume a stance in board meetings that considers the range of alternatives and does not argue against individuals within the group. Indeed, the chair supports both individual directors in their sharing of ideas and the ideas themselves. Even if a director's idea is not the greatest, it may inspire someone else to suggest just what is needed.

The chair models behavior for directors. If the chair attacks a proposal, then others are sure to follow. Instead, the chair should demonstrate through behavior, courtesy, attentive listening, and interest.

Nor does the chair advance pet ideas. That is not leadership. Rather, the chair promotes a blending of others' ideas, putting together components from the ideas of several people. The chair provides vision and overall direction, but it is not appropriate for the chair to use the role as a vehicle for implementing only one's own ideas. Part of the chair's role is to facilitate the accomplishment of assigned tasks by all directors of the group. The chair should not be a jack- (or "Jacquelyn") of-all-trades, trying to do it all himself or herself; that's not the appropriate role of the chair. If the chairperson is doing everything, then he or she has to start working on delegation skills.

Part of the chair's role also involves overseeing the preparation and organization of the physical meeting space, being sure that tables and chairs are in their proper order, cleaning up after groups that have not been so courteous, and leaving the meeting room in such a condition that others can use it after the meeting ends. This is a difficult and onerous task, and one that many directors often pass to clerical staff and others. But the chair doesn't have to do all this alone. Recruiting staff directors and other directors in this task is appropriate. This kind of involvement is precisely what the chair should seek to accomplish. But it is the chair's responsibility to see that these tasks are completed. That's what we mean by delegation.

The chair also acts as an administrator in working with the CEO to ensure that all necessary materials for the meeting are ready and available and, following the Rule of Three-Quarters, are sent to the directors under the appropriate time guidelines. Although an agenda scheduler may be assigned this task, the chair is ultimately responsible for ensuring that the task is completed. The chair has no business complaining that directors don't come prepared for the meetings if the chair doesn't see to it that the appropriate materials go out on time.

When the meeting starts, the chair has to be prepared for the issues under discussion as well as the attitudes, values, and points of view of the individual directors. The Rule of Halves, and the discussion that occurs while putting the agenda together under the Rule of Halves, helps the chair to prepare for the meeting in this way. Sometimes, as we discuss later in this chapter, the CEO helps prepare the chairperson by briefing her or him on what individual directors think and what their positions might be on particular issues. This kind of information is important and appropriate for the chair to have. Walking into a meeting without it leaves the chair open to criticism.

The chair has to be balanced. For example, the chair's presentation of an issue must clearly take into account all sides. Slighting one side, making snide remarks, or using body language to convey disagreement with a particular position is not acceptable behavior. Similar constraints apply to relationships with the public at large and the media.

As the meeting progresses, the chair tries to ensure that all directors have equal access to the floor. All groups have directors who are eager to participate and those who are shy or reluctant to participate. To get the full range of views on the floor, however, the chair must control the "overparticipator" and encourage the "underparticipator." Those who are slighted by the more aggressive participants in the meeting are frequently among those who complain after the meeting.

As we discuss in some detail in the next chapter, the chair must take the lead in summarizing and crystallizing issues for action. If the chair does not take leadership in decision, summary, and crystallization, the board simply spins its wheels, going round and round on the same issue.

Finally, the chair should follow Robert's Rules of Order or some other form of orderly procedure that facilitates decision making. There is no magic in Robert's Rules of Order. Indeed, Henry M. Robert was an Army officer, so his views on how meetings should run may be overly formal. What is important is that the chair follow some set of rules to maintain order and keep the meeting running smoothly. The "play it by ear" approach often slights people and can leave a lot of resentment.

The Director

The director's responsibilities mirror those of the chair in many ways. First, the director must come to meetings well-prepared and must encourage others to do the same. The second half of this responsibility may seem a bit odd to some directors. Good examples are the social legitimacy of asking the passengers in one's car to use their seat belts, or the new acceptability of asking one's guests not to smoke. It used to be very intemperate to say anything, regardless of one's own feelings. Today, however, it is quite acceptable to ask, "Excuse me, but would you mind putting on your seat belt?" or "Would you mind terribly not smoking in the house?" That one's colleagues on the board come to meetings prepared is a similarly legitimate expectation. Asking others to undertake certain responsibilities should be encouraged within meetings. If a director is making comments on material that he or she has clearly not read, it should be legitimate to ask that person to look at the material.

Directors should take initiative to participate in the board's discussions. The "Silent Sam" or "Quiet Kate" technique is rapidly falling out of favor with directors.

Certainly, some people are more shy than others and find it more difficult to participate in groups. Individuals should not leave it up to the chair, however, to always ask them to participate. Rather, each director should take that initiative and join in the discussions, at least often enough so that he or she doesn't become known as "that quiet person."

Conversely, directors should temper any tendency to over participate, instead matching the amount of their participation to that of their colleagues in the group. Obviously, this may not always be the case. On some issues, one will feel more exercised and passionate than with others. Rather, directors should be alert to patterns of over- or under-participation.

Directors should also be alert to those issues that occur outside the board's framework but would be of interest to the board, and bring them to the board's attention. Each director is part of the board's intelligence network. Sometimes, this involves simply alerting the board about items in the local press on issues of interest to the board. Other times, it involves reporting conversations and the like.

Directors should contribute proactively to the board's intelligence system.

Directors should follow through with assignments and requests for work. In Chapter 13, we talked about evaluating individual directors, and part of this evaluation takes into account whether directors are indeed following through. Of course, people forget and get sidetracked. The Rule of Halves, however, enables the chairperson or the CEO to remind directors about agreed-upon responsibilities. Directors, collectively with the chair, try to ensure a fair division of labor in which everyone chips in.

Finally, directors refrain from criticizing the board to others outside the boardroom. The director is a director of the group, even if a decision made by the group is one with which the director disagrees. To share those disappointments with others is a violation of basic ethical norms.

The CEO

With the board chair, the CEO is responsible for the mechanical and substantive functioning of the board meeting and for meetings of board committees. As a practical matter, and as the only regularly paid participant at the board meeting, the CEO usually is the person who "puts it all together." Typically, the CEO is an *ex officio* director and, as such, has the right to participate as a full director but does not have a vote. When the CEO works with the board in this way, it is often called "staffing" the board.

On the mechanical side, the CEO often plays the role of agenda scheduler, as discussed in Chapter 16. That involves getting the items for the meeting from relevant parties and organizing them (using the Rule of the Agenda Bell) for the upcoming meeting. Also involved here is the organization of any reports. Following the Rule of Three-Quarters, the CEO sends out materials for the next monthly meeting about one week before the meeting is scheduled.

The CEO provides or supervises vital editorial support and recordkeeping by documenting the proceedings of board meetings and taking notes that are later transcribed into minutes. Working with the chair, the CEO also prepares communications from the board to other organizations, such as letters, drafts, reports, and memos.

The CEO also acts as a researcher, gathering information at the board's request from libraries, books, journals, memos, minutes, and other organizations to help the board carry out its function. The CEO compiles and interprets research data, offering recommendations as to how it applies to the particular area of investigation. This is what happens when the CEO prepares a report to the board under the Rule of Reports. It does not do the board much good to simply collect a bunch of information and dump it, via the copy machine, on the directors. Rather, the CEO needs to collate, compile, organize, and process the information so that directors receive a comprehensible, intelligible report on the research. This report typically includes a statement of the problem, options, and recommendations, as indicated in the Rule of Reports.

This function of gathering and compiling data and making recommendations raises an important point. To make quality decisions, the board needs all appropriate information on a particular issue, as well as a full outline of the available options. Sometimes, that information and those options may run counter to the CEO's own views; but, as a professional, the CEO must be able to set aside his or her own views when they differ with the data or the recommendations. The professional is assessing a situation and bringing the news to the board for discussion and review—just as an attorney, for example, will bring precedents to the attention of a client, even if they do not support that client's case, so that the client may consider them.

Similarly, the CEO should participate only moderately in board discussions. Boards frequently give up their deliberations too easily and too quickly, turning to the CEO and saying, "Let's just do what the pros think." As tempting as it might be for the CEO to share his or her professional views strongly, our advice is to approach the situation in a balanced fashion. Board decision making is not always enhanced when professionals take over and give their views.

The CEO recognizes and points out ambiguous data to the board. Not all data will fall into neat piles of pros and cons. Indeed, data may be unavailable or of dubious quality, and the board must rely on the CEO to point out what is certain and what is less than certain. Obviously, the directors and board chair will make some of these judgments on their own, but they are guided by the CEO's professionalism in these considerations.

If the CEO has been in place for some time, he or she can be a great resource in terms of institutional memory. Directors and board chairs come and go, but the CEO may know the history of an issue and the trajectory of approaches toward a particular problem, both within the agency itself and among others. Simply getting information from the library, though important, is not always sufficient. There may be programmatic lore and culture that bear upon the board's consideration of an issue within this particular agency context. A Jewish agency, a Catholic agency, an African American agency, a Latino agency may each have its own particular view on certain matters, and these should be brought to the board's attention as it considers the issue or problem. Similarly, the CEO may offer a political assessment as well. Knowing how powerful people feel about the issues in question can be very helpful to the board. What is the political lay of the land? Although such analyses may not always make a difference, sometimes they may be very important to the board's deliberations.

"Across the Board" Application

This discussion of the dynamics of board meetings and the roles of the chair, director, and CEO applies, as well, to meetings within the board's committee structure and within the agency itself. Performing these roles is immensely complex. In fact, proper role performance is more difficult and complex than proper rule performance. Rule performance is methodical and mechanical: The Rule of Halves, the Rules of Sixths, and so on, do not involve great difficulties in implementation, although they may involve a certain amount of discipline. Once one gets into role performance, however, one's life is immediately filled with complexity and nuance. In implementing these role prescriptions, therefore, one should expect a certain amount of uncertainty at first. Only in time will the roles become smooth, seamless, and, ultimately, flawless.

No set of rules can guarantee perfect meetings; directors with a lot of meeting experience certainly know this. It's also true, however, that, for many reasons—lack of training and lack of preparation, especially—we tend to approach board meetings casually and with a relaxed sense of mission. To a certain extent, of course, this is good. One should not take these things too seriously. On the other hand, considering the important range of activities for which directors are responsible and the potential legal liabilities that they may suffer if they do their job poorly, a systematic and planful approach to decision making is certainly a good place to start.

As the central vehicle through which effective directorship takes place, the board meeting is the crucial tool. There are simple ways—outlined in Chapters 15-17—to make board meetings a source of surprise and delight. Evaluation is a key step, and the following exercise is customized to the material in these chapters to facilitate such assessment.

Implementation

As can be seen from the material discussed here, and will be experienced as one implements these practices, there really ARE better ways to run meetings. But there is a problem. Never underestimate people's devotion to rotten practices. We have worked with literally hundreds of boards, committees, task forces, and other groups around mastering meetings. Those who have adopted this system are seriously enthusiastic about its impact on their time and the quality of their group decisions, as well as the sense of accomplishment their whole group derives from participating in those meetings and decisions. Additionally, they take some delight in using an empirically based system, not just someone's idea. Sadly, though, it has been a minority of those with whom we have worked. The majority have a bouquet of reasons why it will not work, it cannot work, it might work other places but not here, it takes too much time, etc. The litany goes on.

We would like to share a couple comments on this resistance.

First, change is always destructive, because it takes away something from which people feel gratification. As all of us know, even the ill person experiences "secondary gain" in terms of the attention and role expectation forgiveness that s/he enjoys while being ill. Wellness requires those exceptions to be forgone. Boards do get satisfaction from bad practices, though it is not the satisfaction they should be getting.

In terms of time we can say that, yes, meeting prep does take time. But one hour in prep seems to save about 2-5 hours downstream, in terms of the absence of rework. That is why those in the quality movement say that "Quality is Free" (and even profitable) because of the rework hassles it saves.

That said, it is still good to think strategically about introducing a new system to your board. A good place to start is to get a buddy or two. Change, like exercise, is better undertaken with partners.

Second, build out from the group. You can use the KSS (KEEP, STOP, START) evaluation tool we have already discussed. Just ask the group what is good about the board meetings they would like to keep; what would be good to phase out (stop); and what would be good to initiate that the board is not now doing (start.) Then build your change suggestions out of the collective pattern of responses.

Finally, any change effort will face some common problems. These have been well described by the Nobel Laureate Herbert Simon, late of Carnegie Mellon University. In his book (with Smithburg and Thompson, 1951, 1971), he talks about the five "costs of change." These are as follows:

193

1) Inertia Costs—getting things moving
2) Cultural Costs—commitments to the old way
3) Personal Costs—directors personally have to expend energy to learn new patterns
4) Rationality Costs—directors need to understand deeply the need for change and
5) Subordination Costs—directors need to be involved in the change

He also suggests some ways to address these issues:
1) Inertia Costs—getting things moving
      Make compliance easy
      Make noncompliance difficult
2) Cultural Costs—commitments to the old way
      Link the change with valued symbols
      Don't trash the past
3) Personal Costs—directors personally have to expend energy to learn new patterns
      Find ways to provide compensation for the expended energy
4) Rationality Costs—directors need to understand deeply the need for change
      Overcommunicate and
5) Subordination Costs—directors need to be involved in the change
      Involve the board (KSS is a way to do this)

Conclusion

Discussing "role requisites" is a tricky endeavor, because role performance is frequently thought to be a completely unique, personal thing, done, as Frank Sinatra would have it, "MY Way." And there is truth to the need to have role authenticity, to play the role in a way that fits with the person of the chairperson, the individual director, and the CEO. On the other hand, as with musical performance, the performer adds her or his own "take" to any performance, on the one hand, but on the other hand, there is a score, and one needs to be playing the piece on the page. Achieving a balance is a work in progress.

Exercise 14

Now that we have discussed the principles, rules, and roles necessary for effective board meetings, as well as how to analyze the board's decision making, we offer here a model for assessing your meetings to determine the strengths and weaknesses in your board's decision-making process. Your board can use the feedback obtained here to improve its effectiveness. Boards should conduct this evaluation periodically—we recommend every six months.

Any committee director or board director can use this instrument; chairs can make especially good use of it.

The model should enable the group to examine its method of conducting meetings; that analysis, in turn, can provide information to help the group change and improve its performance. Unless the board analyzes the results of this evaluation, however, and implements recommendations based on these results, the effort here will be wasted.

Instructions

The evaluator should begin by observing five meetings of the board or committee being assessed. After five meetings, the evaluator completes the assessment form, indicating at how many of the meetings each rule was followed or task accomplished.

In evaluating directors or committee directors, the evaluator may, upon the board's recommendation, apply the questions to each individual director of the group, or rate the directorship as a whole. In the latter case, rather than answer "Yes" or "No" for each item, the evaluator should use three response categories: None to One-Third (in compliance), One-Third to Two-Thirds, and Two-Thirds to All.

Responses to individual items can be scored as percentages. For example, tasks completed in one meeting out of five would receive a 20% score; in two meetings, 40%; three meetings, 60%; and so on. Similarly, answers regarding board roles, individually or collectively, can be averaged to obtain percentage scores.

The evaluator can use the instrument as a discussion guide, involving all directors of the group in the assessment.

Assessing Board Meetings

Out of five meetings observed, in how many was each rule followed or each task completed? Indicate 0 to 5.

AGENDA SCHEDULING RULES

☐ Rule of Halves
Items for next meeting must be in the hands of the agenda scheduler one-half of time between meetings.

☐ Rule of Sixths
One-sixth of agenda items relate to past issues; one-sixth are future issues. Remaining four-sixths are current issues.

☐ Rule of Three-Quarters
Agenda scheduler sends out packets of material for next meeting at the three-quarter point between meetings.

☐ Rule of Two-Thirds
Meeting divided into three parts: start-up period (announcements), period of heavy work (decisions), and period of discussion and decompression.

Out of five meetings observed, in how many was each rule followed or each task completed? Indicate 0 to 5.

AGENDA BELL RULE

☐ Item 1, Minutes
Simple, straightforward.
Read and ratified (if quorum is present).

☐ Item 2, Announcements
Brief, noncontroversial, few in number.

☐ Item 3, Easy Item(s)
Items need action, decision but are relatively non-controversial.

☐   Item 4, Moderate Difficulty
        Items potentially controversial, fairly complex.

☐   Item 5, Hardest Item(s)
        Major decisions, highly controversial and complex.

☐   Break
        Seventh-inning stretch

☐   Item 6, Discussion Item(s)
        Discussion only of items to be decided at future meetings.

☐   Item 7, Easiest Item(s)
        Small decisions of no great importance that serve to unify the group.

MEETING RULES

☐   Agenda Rule
        Agenda written in inviting, clear manner.
        One-sentence summary and estimated time follows each agenda item.

☐   Rule of Reports
        CEO summaries and option memos are primary sources for decision making within meeting.

☐   Rule of Minutes
        Minutes correspond to agenda, are content-relevant, and focus on decisions.

AGENDA INTEGRITY RULE

☐   All items on agenda are discussed.

☐   Items not on agenda are not discussed.

TEMPORAL INTEGRITY RULE

☐   Meeting begins and ends on time and generally adheres to projected time estimates for agenda items.

Assessing Board Roles

THE CHAIR	% of Time in 5 Meetings	Comments
Leads group to consider alternatives. Supports directors both in sharing of ideas and in ideas themselves.		
Models appropriate board behavior to other directors of the group.		
Works to synthesize ideas rather than promote pet ideas and projects.		
Facilitates task accomplishment by all directors of group rather than doing it all him or herself.		
Acts administratively to see that meeting area is prepared for meeting and cleaned afterward and that all required materials are ready and available.		
Researches both issues and attitudes of directors in preparation for meeting.		
Presents balanced representation of the board to the outside, avoiding one-sided, intemperate statements to the public and the media.		
Presents balanced representation of the board to the outside, avoiding one-sided, intemperate statements to the public and the media.		

Assessing Board Roles (continued)

THE CHAIR (continued)	% of Time in 5 Meetings	Comments
Ensures all directors have equal opportunity to be heard on any issue.		
Allows more time during meeting for large issues, less time for smaller issues.		
Summarizes, crystallizes, and focuses discussion once everyone has a chance to speak on an issue.		
Follows Robert's Rules of Order or some other orderly procedure.		
THE CEO	% of Time in 5 Meetings	Comments
Acts as researcher, gathering information at board's request.		
Compiles and interprets researched data; makes recommendations as to how data apply to issues before board.		
Recognizes and points out ambiguous data to board.		
Includes necessary, appropriate information, even if it runs counter to his or her own views.		
Refrains from presenting slanted or purposefully unclear views to board.		

Assessing Board Roles (continued)

THE CEO (continued)	% of Time in 5 Meetings	Comments
Presents written documentation but avoids influencing discussion. Participates in discussion professionally.		
Source of institutional history— how board has handled similar issues in the past, how organization differs today from when previous decisions were made etc.		
Source of political information— such as views of those in positions of power within and outside the organization and in government.		
Sees that proceedings are documented.		
Prepares communications from board on request.		
Working with chair, prepares drafts of memos and reports for board review and revision.		
Assists chair when necessary to ensure meeting requirements are met, meeting space is prepared, and cleanup and follow-through are accomplished.		
Checks potential agenda items at halfway point between meetings.		
Makes sure directors receive agenda by three-quarters point between meetings.		

Assessing Board Roles (continued)

THE CEO (continued)	% of Time in 5 Meetings	Comments
Confirms day, date, time, and location of meeting with directors, making necessary adjustments to accommodate special individual and group needs.		
INDIVIDUAL DIRECTOR, COMMITTEE DIRECTOR	% of Time in 5 Meetings	Comments
Comes to meetings well-prepared, encourages others to do the same.		
Participates without prodding to take part in discussion.		
Tempers tendency to overparticipate.		
Overall participation about the same as that of other group directors.		
Alert to and pursues outside information and perspectives that may be of use to the board.		
Follows through with assignments and requests.		
Portrays board as decision-making body rather than a group of individuals; speaks of board decisions or policies, not internal dessent.		

Assessing Board Roles (continued)

DIRECTORS, COMMITTEE DIRECTORS AS A GROUP	0 - 1/3 of group	1/3 - 2/3 of group	2/3 - All of group
Come to meetings well-prepared, encourage others to do the same.	•	•	•
Participate without prodding to take part in discussions.	•	•	•
Tempers tendency to overparticipate.	•	•	•
Overall participation about the same as that of other group directors.	•	•	•
Alert to and pursues outside information and perspectives that may be of use to the board.	•	•	•
Follows through with assignments and requests.	•	•	•
Portray board as decision-making body rather than group of individuals; speak of board decisions or policies, not internal dissent.	•	•	•

Comments

Summary

1. What things are we doing well that should be continued?

2. What are we doing less well that should phased out or stopped?

3. What are we not now doing but should begin?

Comments

202

Chapter 20

Decision Management

Introduction

Decision building in any group-boards or families for that matter—require two dimensions. Most involved in decision building are only vaguely aware of them, but when they are spelled out, as they are here, they are instantly recognizable. One has to do with decision relevant information, and the other has to do with the deep structure of decision building process.

We use the phrase "decision building" rather than decision "making" because in our observations of decision processes in groups, decisions were really built—larger decisions constructed from smaller ones. The idea of "managing" a decision does not mean that a decision manager manipulates to get her or his way. Rather, it means that, as with all management, the decision manager sees that the right information is presented in the right order, using proper processes, so that a high quality result can emerge.

Decision Relevant Information

To make high quality decisions, decision builders need relevant information. The most useful outline of relevance categories, to us, comes from the work of Edward DeBono in his book, *The Six Thinking Hats*. DeBono uses hat colors to represent different kinds of information that need to be brought into play within the decision making process. He has five information types, and one manager type:

- The Blue Hat is the decision manager. The blue hat manages the sequence of information, seeing to it that everyone is talking about the same kind of information at the same time.
- The Green Hat represents positive information and perspectives. Here, the focus is on strengths and what is good about the proposal under consideration.
- The Yellow Hat is for creative approaches and enhancements to the proposal under consideration; possibly it might even involve a totally new way of looking at it.
- The White Hat refers to logical and analytic information. Facts, figures, estimate, budgetary requirements are placed here.
- The Red Hat addresses feelings and emotions with respect to the proposal.
- Finally, the Black Hat addresses problems and deep concerns people have with the approach.

It is important for the decision manager to address each category of information. Do not skip any. It is also important, as noted above, to have the whole group focused on the same kind of information at the same time.

And finally, it is important to follow the order suggested here. Negativity especially—the Black Hat—is about six times more powerful than Positivity. If one begins with negativity, it is almost certain to make for a very difficult and long discussion and negativity usually wins the day. We do not wish to ignore it, but we do need to structure it.

The Deep Structure of Decision Building Process

Eight Crucial Elements

How are decisions actually made in boards—or in meetings anywhere, for that matter? A very common answer is "consensus." But defining consensus turns out to be a daunting task, and most people have no actual definition at all. They wind up saying things such as, "Well, it's a decision everyone can live with." In this chapter we will explore some observations about what boards (and other decision making groups) actually take into consideration when they go about decision building.

Understanding this material takes us into the "deep structure" of decision making. Our research (from the Meeting Masters Research Project at the University of Michigan) suggests that decisions can be better understood, and hence managed, if seven concepts are well understood.

We should say a word about how these perspectives emerged. As the Michigan Researchers (principally Tropman) observed meeting masters to understand their skills in meeting management, it also became clear that better meetings led to better decisions. Or so we thought. It turned out that, while better meetings are more fun, they are a necessary, but not sufficient, condition for better decisions. Bad meetings almost certainly "produce" bad decisions (though good ones do emerge, by chance, now and then). And we did see lots of "excellent" meetings process-wise which did not, in the end, do good work. So while the meeting masters were/are a subset of the total meeting population, a subset of THEM were even more elite—the decision masters. They not only managed the meeting, they managed the decision process as well. The decision masters had an additional skill set, because they were working in real time (in the meeting itself), were using the material at hand (the comments and materials available at the meeting), were sensitive to timing, were thinking up ideas and suggestions on the spot, and were, in a sense, **building** (as opposed to making) decisions.

205

Our research reveals eight crucial elements vital to managing and executing decision making:

1. **Decision Rules**
2. **Decision Culture**
3. **Decision Mosaic**
4. **Decision Elements**
5. **Decision Element Dominance Hierarchy**
6. **Rounds Of Discussion**
7. **Decision Crystallization**
8. **Decision Sculpting**

1. Decision Rules. Good decisions are made on the basis of decision rules. Decision rules are norms from our larger life and culture that make decisions "ok" and legitimate. There are at least five decision rules used by groups in any given meeting. Each rule is one we all know and believe in. Each conflicts and competes with the others, in the sense that using any one individually would advance certain interests and ignore others.

The five are as follows:
1. Breadth
2. Depth
3. Involvement
4. Expertise
5. Power

Breadth. The breadth decision rule, or the voting rule, is the one most commonly used by boards of directors in their public actions and is frequently written into organization bylaws. This rule, which has a long tradition in North American society, states that each person has a single vote. It is a measure of a group's preference.

Important as this rule is, however, it fails to take into account other important interests. For example, the breadth decision rule deals with neither the intensity of one's opinions on an issue, nor the level of one's involvement in particular matters under consideration. Thus, other decision rules come into play, often informally.

Depth. The intensity decision rule gives weight to those who feel strongly about an issue. Boards that use this rule usually try to probe for depth of feeling among their voting directors. It protects minority interests. If you were the only vegetarian in a group, you might never call for a vote on the dinner menu if you knew you were going to be outvoted by the non-vegetarians every time.

Involvement. The involvement decision rule considers the preferences of those who might have to carry out a decision. If the board is voting on a particular action that an individual director has to carry out, that director is much more involved and may have a greater interest in the outcome than her or his colleagues. After all, they don't have to do it. Thus, the involvement decision rule gives weight to those with greater involvement. Frequently in board meetings, when someone says something like, "I'd like to hear what Sheila has to say because, after all, she has to do it," the involvement decision rule is being applied. This rule gives the CEO great influence, since he or she is often the one who carries out board policies.

Expertise. The expert decision rule takes account of one's specialized knowledge in a particular issue before the board. Some people know more than others. Attorneys on boards, for example, frequently receive great respect when legal matters come up. Similarly, boards often defer to physicians when medical matters come up. Boards often take into strong account one's expertise in a particular area of decision making when an issue reaches a vote. Evidence and science also play important roles here.

Power. The power decision rule. None of these rules deal with social or political power and influence. That is where the power decision rule comes in. Corporations frequently phrase this decision rule as: "What does the boss want?" This rule gives individuals of high organizational authority—the board chair or the CEO, for example—greater weight. It also gives people of great social status, such as physicians or attorneys, influence beyond their technical expertise that extends into matters of which they have no greater knowledge than anyone else. The board listens to and heeds them, however, because of their social power.

2. Decision Culture

As we noted, the application of each rule privileges one set of interests over another. Nothing is "neutral"; nothing is "fair." Everything has to do with preference. Participants "prefer" those rules through the application of which they are likely to win or secure their preferences/outcomes. Hence, much of the subtext of "discussion" that goes on in decision making situations is actually about the rules to be used and their weight, while ostensibly about "the issue at hand." Decision masters were acutely sensitive to this part of the decision process. The underlying question is always what rules should the board use at this point and what should their weights actually be. There are formal and informal answers to this question at the board level.

That said, most groups use most of the rules; it is the weights that really differ. As you think about your board (or any decision group, for that matter), think about what rules are used most of the time, and what their weight is. That is your decision culture. Know that a decision cultures privileges some participants over others, and one needs to be aware of that fact.

3. The Decision Mosaic

Though the word "decision" sounds like a single thing, it is actually a composite of many small things—put together into a pattern like a mosaic of tiles. Most of what we think of as a decision really comprise smaller decision elements that are assembled into such a decision mosaic. Consider a simple board decision, such as whether to have a board retreat. One might expect the issue to require only a simple yes or no vote. In fact, however, the decision represents a composite of smaller decisions—about time and location, about the facilitator, about who should organize it, and so on. Each of these is a decision element. Effective board chairs facilitate and lead the development of an overall decision mosaic. They build the decision, so to speak, element by element, until the mosaic is assembled. Then, the chair helps the group engage in decision sculpting, in which the overall decision is examined and its elements adjusted to create a higher-quality decision.

4. Decision Elements

Decision elements are all the small parts of the decision that need to be addressed. Consider an annual meeting for the agency. There are literally dozens of elements that need to be in the mix. Decision masters were excellent at having a pretty full sense of all the elements (or most of them) and the ones that needed board attention.

5. Decision Element Dominance Hierarchy

Not only does one need to understand most of the elements in the decision mosaic, one also needs to understand their structure. They fall into a dominance hierarchy, called a Guttman Scale. This scale is one that has the properties such that for items a...i, a impacts b through i, b impacts c through i but not a, and so on. This means for decision makers that it is important to start with "a" if at all possible. Starting with d, and then going forward, very likely means that when the group does get to a, and does b, and c the decision on d **will have to be changed**. Revisiting and re-deciding items that have already been addressed because of improper ordering (Sally has to leave, so lets .....etc.) is called REWORK. Rework occupies as much as 50%+ of the time of many boards.

The job of the board chair, therefore, is to identify the elements to be considered in the decision mosaic. Simply put, that means breaking the decision into reasonable elements that the group can consider. Without this step, a typical scenario develops, in which the chair asks, "What should we discuss at the board retreat?" From around the table come individual shouts of, "Programs," "Let's have good food," "How about meeting at a nice location?" and "Let's eat earlier than last year." Each contribution is important and appropriate by itself. Unfortunately, since one does not follow from the other, the decision-building process is very difficult. Instead, the chair should identify the initial topic to discuss—perhaps the retreat program—and then proceed, element by element, to build a mosaic.

6. Rounds of Discussion

Decision making is like freeway driving. There are only certain points at which one can "exit" and if that exit is missed, one needs to go to the next exit (or attempt the occasionally seen "berm backup" approach!) Those exits are at the end of a "round of discussion." A round ends when everyone has said one thing, or everyone who wants to has said one thing. At that psychological moment the chair (or decision manager) needs to be ready to move into decision crystallization mode.

7. Decision Crystallization

Decision building occurs via rounds of discussion in which each director who so desires has a chance to offer one opinion once. When the chair asks, "Anyone else have a view?" and no additional views are forthcoming, it's time for the chair to begin the process of decision crystallization for that particular decision element. The chair does not have to be the only person who undertakes decision crystallization, but unless the chair models both the procedure and the willingness to undertake the risk of rejection involved in proposing action, no one else will be willing to undertake it.

Decision crystallization is a four-part process. The first step is summative reflection. At the end of a round of discussion, the chair, who has been listening to and pulling together the different elements of the discussion, summarizes for the group what has been said. Groups do not actually know what individual group directors think until the directors have had a chance to share their views. A neutral, factual pulling together of the views expressed in the group is the first step towards decision crystallization. For example, the chair might say, "Okay, what I'm hearing is a general agreement that a training retreat for the board is a good idea.

Summative Reflection. There are some concerns about scheduling the retreat around other agency events, and some opposition to the notion that directors who have served on the board for some time should have to go through "training." Two good sites for the retreat have been suggested.

Action Suggestion. The second step is the decision suggestion or action hypothesis. Based on the views expressed in the summary, the chair risks suggesting action, but frequently uses the collective pronoun (we could) and/or the passive voice. The chair is working on behalf of the group here. "Perhaps we could agree that the board start planning a directors' retreat to be held in July at North Lake State Park, after the agency's anniversary celebration. The content of the retreat should take into account that the board has several experienced directors as well as a number of new directors."

It is extremely important that action or decision be suggested at this juncture. Groups often do not know whether they want to do something until someone actually makes a proposal. A familiar example is the age-old question, "Where should we go to dinner tonight?" Often, colleagues or family directors say, "Gee, I don't know," or "It doesn't matter to me," until someone suggests, "Let's have Chinese." At that point, under the threat of action, preferences become highlighted. Thus, decisions and actions offered in the decision suggestion or action hypotheses stage are fre¬quently rejected: "July's not a good time," "What about a local hotel instead of the state park?" "I'm still concerned about the content." That's fine; it's supposed to be that way. It's one way in which the group explores what it does and does not want. Over time, of course, as the chair becomes more skilled at understanding the underlying commonalties and uniformities of group life, the proposed action or decision will be more on the mark. Some people always seem to get their suggestions accepted. One wonders what special skills they possess. Frequently, they simply listen carefully and extract the common themes from among ostensibly diverse suggestions.

Action Legitimation. The third step, legitimization, follows directly from decision suggestion and provides for the board the reasons why the proposal is okay. These reasons articulate the decision rules. So, the chairperson might summarize views about the retreat and then say, "It seems that a retreat is a good idea [the decision suggestion is vocalized] because [here comes the legitimization] most of us think it is okay [breadth rule] and there is no strong opposition [intensity rule]. Sheila, who has to do much of the planning, thinks its fine [involvement rule], and Tropman and Tropman recommend it [expert rule]. Looks like the retreat's a go!"

Action Refocus. Let's assume for a moment that, with nods and murmurs of agreement, the group directors signal their acceptance of the chair's decision suggestion. At this point, the chair moves to the fourth stage, discussion refocus. Once the group reaches a tentative agreement on one element, the chair directs the group toward the next element up for discussion, targeting the group's attention and discussion and avoiding divergent, digressing, or conflicting topics.

Board decision making thus proceeds, element by element, building to the final mosaic. When the group has assembled all the pieces of a particular decision mosaic, and all of the relevant elements have been tentatively decided, the chair then invites the group to step back and look at the total package. Do all of the elements fit together in a synchronous and harmonious way? Should the board adjust earlier decisions in the mosaic because of the nature of later decisions? If, for example, in decorating an office, it turns out that inadvertently all of the colors chosen were beige, then one might wish to modify some of the colors. This question is difficult to approach, however, until the directors have reviewed all the elements of the decision. This overall review is called decision sculpting.

Glitches in the Decision-building Process. Suppose, however, that in the decision suggestion stage, a proposed direction is not accepted. That is, indeed, a very likely result. At that juncture, the chair should back off from the offering or proposal. The original purpose of the suggestion was not to ensure acceptance of that particular direction, but rather to help the group in its discussion and consideration of the decision. So if someone turns out to have a negative view about holding the retreat in our example—some issue or question that is now known because its possibility has been stated—then the chair proposes another round of discussion but seeks to ratchet down the alternatives in a couple of ways.

One way would be for the chair to remove the option of a retreat from the table. A second way might be to propose some other minor options for the board's consideration—such as holding longer meetings or a series of special meetings—as well as new ideas. Thus, the next round of discussion on the same element occurs with a reduced and refocused number of alternatives. The board can go through two or three rounds of discussion, each time narrowing and refocusing until it achieves a tentative decision on an element in the mosaic.

This process of decision crystallization is one of the central aids to high-quality decision making in boards. Where it occurs, decisions are likely to be viable and reflective of a range of input. Where it is not used, decisions are likely to be haphazard, 'by guess and by gosh," and very likely to be of poor quality. Although board decision making certainly has creative aspects, which should not be set aside, it also has very focused, very deliberate, almost mechanical procedures, which, if used, can be of great help to the group. Indeed, as in many other areas of life—such as driving or perfecting one's golf swing or tennis serve—the initial rules will eventually fade from consciousness and the group will proceed through them almost automatically.

The focus, so far, has been on the chairperson as the decision crystallizer. Indeed, as we noted above, if the chair models this behavior, others will pick it up. Sometimes, however, a situation arises in which the chair must reverse the procedure and de-crystallize a decision, which we first discussed in Chapter 12. Typically, boards have difficulty reaching quality decisions in a timely manner. Hence, the emphasis in board deliberations is often on decision facilitation. Boards sometimes come to decisions too quickly, without a thoughtful, reflective approach to the subject matter. Sometimes, as we discussed in Chapter 7, decisions may be conservative or overboard, therefore of questionable quality. In this event, the chair or others might interrupt the decision crystallization process. This involves broadening, rather than narrowing, the field of alternatives for consideration. In the case of premature closure, for example, when a board comes together and quickly says, "Let's do this," decrystallization introduces a range of other alternatives and raises questions about the implications and potential costs of those alternatives. Hopefully, these interventions create enough uncertainty within some directors of the group to move agreement from a critical mass to a marginal mass, and then open the entire subject for more detailed, thoughtful consideration.

Agenda item preparation and agenda timing are extremely important to decision crystallization. That is the primary reason for the Rule of Halves in Chapter 16. If the board does not have adequate time to consider issues, then it will likely be forced either into making a decision too quickly or toward conservative, "Let's do it as we've done" procedures and decisions. Providing enough time to consider issues is an important first step toward changing and improving the board.

8. Decision Sculpting

One important thing to consider in the "decision building" approach is that there is, at the end of the process, the need to look at the completed decision. This view is "big picture" and seeks to gain a perspective on the overall mosaic. Continuing the mosaic metaphor, it may be that there is too much of one color, or the design is skewed here or there. This point is the place where overall adjustments are made where the board can revisit aspects of the decision that no longer seem to fit and adjust them.

Conclusion

Our suggestion here is not to "use" any of this material right away, as opposed to the meeting material in the previous chapter which you can begin to implement right away.

Quality board decision making depends on several factors, being aware of the backgrounds of individual directors and staff, following the correct rules and procedures for group meetings, and understanding the dynamics and roles in the decision process.

Group directors and chairs need an additional perspective; however, that focuses on the decision rules. This little known but very important element of group decision making can make or break the board's decision strategy.

The decision-making process is complex and involves not only substance, but rules. Outstanding proposals often do not get the support necessary for their implementation because chairs and other directors fail to understand the need to consider expertise, power, depth of involvement, and breadth of support when the decision is made. Board deliberations can often reach a stalemate when group directors invoke competing rules, and chairs and directors do not know how to proceed. The likelihood of high-quality board decisions is greatly enhanced when directors are aware of, understand, and follow these decision rules.

Exercise 15

Which decision rules does your board use, and how often (in percentage of time)? On a scale of 1 to 5 (1 being the highest and 5 being the lowest), what weight does your board place on each rule?

Rules	Use	Frequency	Weights
Breadth Decision Rule (Voting Rule)			
Intensity Decision Rule			
Involvement Decision Rule			
Expert Decision Rule			
Power Decision Rule			

Are you satisfied with the way your board uses these rules?

Should the weights be changed?

Chapter 21

Toward a Better Board

Our dicussion of boards would be incomplete without some attention to common problems. The issues here focus on moving toward a "better board."

As must be clear from this manual, boards today face a host of problems. Many of these difficulties can be traced to a lack of preparation and serious concern on the part of the directors, the board's overreliance on the CEO, a lack of training and preparation for board roles, poorly developed information bases upon which to make decisions, and excessive fault finding among directors. Boards need a systematic plan of transition.

Transitioning to a Better Board

How does an organization move toward having a better board? Certainly not by simply asserting that things should be "better." Begin by viewing the board as you would any decision-making group, and work to improve the meeting and group decision process. Consider a training session, with a specific training curriculum. As your board's meeting processes improve, directors will be more receptive to spending some time on their specific roles as directors. A follow-up training session on board responsibilities would be appropriate. Developing a manual for board directors could assist the transition. This plan sounds straightforward, but it is really complex and requires a lot of work. Knowing that board meetings can and will improve can sustain and motivate the transition from an administration board to a policy board.

The Problems of Transition

Many a human service organization has been founded by a group of interested citizens who initially get together and are the agency. As time passes, the agency may acquire federal or state moneys. As more stable funding becomes available, the agency hires an CEO and perhaps a secretary. The organization begins to move from a very informal, non-bureaucratic, personal organization to one that is more formal and bureaucratic, with a board of directors legally chartered under the laws of the state. The transition often leaves agency founders feeling left out and like they need to move on.

Founding directors tend to be very involved in all aspects of the agency's life. Because they were involved in the organization's founding, they tend to believe and act as if they have special knowledge and wisdom about the direction that the agency should take, the strategic orientation it should demonstrate to the community, and how the agency should operate itself. Further, and again because of their founding roles, they tend to believe that their views should have more weight, that their preferences should dominate. The field of business enterprise is littered with the carcasses of firms and individuals who were unable to make the transition from what Flamholtz (1986) calls an "entrepreneurial" status to a "professional" status.

Because power and influence are not easily given up, new directors recruited to work with founding directors often find the job frustrating. Not infrequently, they believe that their own perspectives are not heeded, that board decisions are overturned or sabotaged indirectly, and that initiatives are undertaken without appropriate board consideration. Sometimes, a founding director or directors, along with other directors, will hire an CEO, hoping to "professionalize" the administration of the agency. Not infrequently, conflict soon breaks out between the founding directors and the CEO. In one case we know of, a new CEO entered his office and discovered a founding director sitting at the new CEO's desk, using the new CEO's phone. Adding insult to injury, the founding director asked the new CEO to wait outside for a few minutes while the founding director finished some business. Such behavior, and the assumptions behind them, is often the source of trouble and difficulty as the organization grows. Hence, preparation for transition, including a discussion of these very issues, is well advised. One should not expect, however, that this discussion will solve all the problems, but it certainly is a start.

Tom Harvey likes to call this issue "solving the authority problem." Trust has to be developed and nurtured so that those with authority can actually act, but those with authority need to act taking into account the needs of others.

Further Motivation for Change

There is another motivation for board improvement, however, that is more practical than improvement for improvement's sake. The goal of board improvement is better-quality decisions, not just pleasant meetings in which decisions are made. Increasingly, because of pressures for accountability and responsibility, boards are assessed in terms of the quality of their decisions and the processes they use to arrive at those decisions. This trend is beginning now with nonprofit community boards in a number of fields. External reviewers from national agencies, accrediting bodies, funders, and other groups are including board assessments in their review processes. While still not widespread, it is a trend of significant proportions and one that should serve as an important additional stimulus for boards to improve their functioning and the quality of their decisions.

Putting These Tools to Use

Many boards in the nonprofit sector seem to have difficulty carrying out their tasks (Schmid, Dodd, & Tropman, 1987). For this reason, constant review and refurbishment—of board decisions and decision-making processes, of how the board carries out its responsibilities, of how directors of the group fulfill their roles, and of how the board conducts its meetings—are necessary. This manual has offered a number of tools that will assist the board in rejuvenating, refurbishing, and redirecting the organization for which it is a trustee.

Appendix 1

The New Climate for Nonprofit Boards

In Appendix 1 we provide some technical information and discussion about legal issues that are affecting nonprofits. They include two discussions of legal issues, some overall thoughts on the strengths and limitations of the "Carver Model" of governance which has become very popular in recent years, and a discussion of issues in mergers and acquisitions. The section concludes with the presentation of a set of proposed new principles offered by The Independent Sector (Independent Sector.org) and a brief discussion of them.

Appendix 1.1

Legal Issues for Nonprofit Directors and Managers

For many years the role of the "charitable board member" or, today, the nonprofit director or human services director was not attended to in any rigorous way. Indeed, as Tom Croxton points out, such directors were actually protected by the doctrine of charitable immunity. For the most part, if one was "doing good" you were not liable if you "did it badly," except in extreme cases. Within the past 25 years, and especially within the recent past, there has been an enormous attention paid to the role of nonprofits, their accountability, and the actions of their directors. Some of this attention has developed because of questions about director behavior in famous cases of organizational collapse, such as Enron, but the nonprofit sector has made its own contribution to increased scrutiny, as in the United Way Scandal of the early 1990s (Glasser, 1994). In order to address these issues we are presenting two authorities on nonprofit issues here. Tom Croxton, an attorney and social worker and Professor Emeritus at the University of Michigan, has updated his material from the first edition on the legal background of nonprofit/ human service work, with special attention to the use of volunteer labor and attendant liability potential. Lloyd Hitoshi Mayer, from the faculty of law at Notre Dame University, provides detailed analyses of some of the legal issues surrounding this work.

Liability and Risk Management in Organizational Governance

Tom A. Croxton, MSW, JD[12]

Charitable Immunity

Throughout most of the history of nonprofit, charitable institutions, the doctrine of charitable immunity protected nonprofit organizations from most law suits. When matters related to civil wrongs came up, such as negligence or personal injury, the charity could hide behind the immunity doctrine to escape liability for wrongful acts.

If our legal system still adhered to the doctrine of charitable immunity, little consideration might be afforded to matters related to liability and risk management in a text on nonprofit boards. In large part, however, the immunity of charitable organizations from law suits has been abolished. Although many reasons exist for the demise of this doctrine, including the growth and development of both charities and the insurance industry, the principal rationale was provided by courts of law, which opined that when an innocent victim suffers harm as a result of the conduct of agency personnel, whether they be paid employees or volunteers, the innocent party should not have to bear the monetary burden of the injury.

An important point is that the charitable-immunity doctrine protected organizations, not individuals. Although the organization might have been protected from liability by the charitable-immunity doctrine, individuals who worked for the charity, employees and volunteers alike, were not. Ironically, the party with the most resources, the organization, was immune from suit, whereas the parties with the least resources, volunteers, were left with no protection.

---

[12] Tom A. Croxton, MSW, JD, is a professor emeritus at the School of Social Work, University of Michigan. Special thanks to John F. Tropman, who was heavily involved in an early version of this appendix.

Equally ironic is that as judges have abolished charitable immunity for organizations, they have not moved to provide immunity to volunteers, who offer their considerable energies in promoting organizational goals and serving clients free of charge. In other words, the courts did not substitute organizational liability for individual liability. While, as a society, we extol the virtues of volunteerism, encouraging individuals to participate in solving an array of social problems, we provide a considerable disincentive by asking volunteers to open themselves to the risk of personal liability for their conduct. The resulting policy question, quite simply, is: How do we expect people to volunteer services if, in doing so, they put themselves in jeopardy of being sued?

At the State Level

Some states have answered this question in limited ways. Alabama holds a volunteer who performs services for a nonprofit organization immune from civil liability for good faith acts within the scope of the volunteer's official functions and duties (Code of Alabama, 1993). As in other states, willful and wanton misconduct by a volunteer forms an exception. Colorado has adopted similar language and provides broad immunity to directors acting within the scope of their duties. The Colorado statute makes clear, however, that such immunity does not "diminish or abrogate any duties that the director...has to the nonprofit organization" (Colorado, 1996). Delaware allows an agency's certificate of incorporation to contain or limit the director's personal liability, except for breach of loyalty; acts or omissions not in good faith; intentional misconduct; a knowing violation of the law, or any transaction from which the director derives an improper personal benefit (Delaware, 1996). Some states, like Massachusetts, New Hampshire, South Carolina, and Texas, place absolute dollar limitations on suits against certain nonprofit corporations. These may be as low as $20,000 in Massachusetts to as high as $1 million in Texas (Nonprofit Risk Management Center, 1993, 1995).

But state legislation often comes in bits and pieces, without attention to more comprehensive policies. Some states provide fairly comprehensive protections for charities, while others provide fairly limited immunity. Some states may provide no protective shield. In considering such matters, each organization and each volunteer director must examine the laws of the state in which the nonprofit is incorporated and where it conducts its activities. The best way to discover applicable laws is for the organization to retain an attorney experienced in the law of charitable organizations. The Nonprofit Risk Management Center in Washington, DC, (http://www.nonprofitrisk.org) publishes an updated compendium of state liability laws for charitable organizations and volunteers.[13] The Council on Foundations in Washington, DC, can also be helpful.[14] For individuals contemplating working for charitable organizations as volunteers, whether in direct service or as board directors or trustees, it is imperative that they find out about the extent of their liability for conduct on behalf of their nonprofits.

After years of legislative futility, and out of concern about the growing unwillingness of volunteers to offer services in light of legitimate fears about frivolous, arbitrary, capricious lawsuits, and the high cost of liability insurance coverage, Congress passed the Volunteer Protection Act in 1997. This law provides an immunity shield as long as the volunteer was acting within the scope of his or her responsibilities, if appropriate or required, the volunteer was properly licensed, certified, or authorized by the state for the activities or practices in question, the harm was not the result of willful or criminal misconduct or a conscious indifference to the rights or safety of the individual harmed by the volunteer, or the harm was not caused by the volunteer operating a motor vehicle, vessel, or other craft for which the state requires a license.

The Volunteer Protection Act protects the volunteer, but not the nonprofit organization; nor does it wholly preempt state law. Neither does the act relieve board directors of their obligations, duties, and responsibilities to the organization.

---

[13] Nonprofit Risk Management Center, 1001 Connecticut Avenue NW, Suite 900, Washington, DC 20036, 202/785-3891, fax: 202/833-5747, www.nonprofitrisk.org

[14] Council on Foundations, 1828 L. Street NW, Washington, DC 20036, 202/466-6512 fax: 202/785-3926. www.cof.org

Fiduciary and Other Duties of Directors

Directors are expected to carry out their duties and obligations to the organization in good faith, with the care a prudent person would apply in the same or similar circumstances and the director reasonably believes to be in the best interest of the nonprofit organization. Directors can, of course, rely on the opinions of experts and on reports and statements presented by CEO, officers, or agency committees, unless the individual directors have knowledge to the contrary. This reliance, however, does not relieve directors from three general duties:

- diligence in accomplishing the purposes for which the non-profit was incorporated
- avoiding harmful effects that result from their negligence, and
- prudence, good faith, and the avoidance of self serving or personally enriching conduct

Diligence

The board of directors has a legal responsibility to accomplish the purposes set forth in the organization's articles of incorporation. This kind of accountability is not strictly or tightly defined, but the board can be taken to court if it appears it has failed to accomplish the purposes of the nonprofit in substantial ways, or if it has pursued purposes other than those defined by the articles.

As social conditions change and social problems become redefined, nonprofits are asked to respond. Despite perceived needs, the availability of new funding opportunities, or compelling arguments for intervention, the organization should not respond in ways that are outside the parameters of the nonprofit's purpose as articulated in its articles of incorporation or bylaws.

Negligence Risks

The board of directors is responsible for conducting the organization's affairs in such a way as to avoid harm to those who come in contact with the agency. Avoiding harm means that the organization's physical plant and service programs must be reasonably safe.

In this era of quality assurance, not only must directors of nonprofit organizations attend to their organizations' purposes and policies, but they should insist upon careful monitoring and evaluation of all programs. Directors should also review agency policies and procedures with regard to those who provide direct services, whether they are employees or volunteers.

Some states may protect directors for simple negligence, but none allow statutory immunity for gross negligence. This is one arena in which insurance becomes a must, not only for the organization, but also for directors who may be sued by third parties. It is incumbent on directors to have all insurance policies reviewed to ensure that the extent and amount of coverage is adequate and that policies are up to date in light of current law.

Several forms of liability insurance are available to cover the directors of nonprofit organizations. Directors and officers insurance covers acts deemed to be unreasonable or imprudent. Acts of omission or commission deemed to constitute malpractice may be covered by errors and omissions insurance. Beyond insurance, directors may be indemnified against liability in the nonprofit's articles of incorporation, if allowed by state law. Such indemnification, however, is limited to the assets of the charitable organization, meaning that if the losses are greater than the assets, the individual director may still be held personally responsible.

Prudence and Good Faith

Prudence and avoidance of self-enriching conduct implicates concepts of loyalty, good faith, acting in the organization's best interest, and monitoring and avoiding conflicts of interest. Perhaps the clearest area of board responsibility is avoiding personally enriching conduct. This most directly involves compensation beyond reimbursement for expenses or small honoraria—items such as cash loans or gifts in property from the agency to the director. This standard is frequently applied to any business relationships between directors and the agency.

Conflicts of interest may not always lead to problems, but they can and should be watched carefully. Conflicts occur when a director is involved in a transaction from which he or she derives some personal benefit from what the organization may be doing. In such cases, the director must withdraw from participating in the deliberations or action on the matter. Less clear is the popular practice in which some organizations seek professional opinions, such as legal or fiscal advice, for example, from directors serving on the board. When the board needs such knowledge and skills, it should, as a general rule, seek them from outside the organization, whether such service be for hire or pro bono. This does not mean that lawyers or other professionals should not serve on boards. Rather, directors should be appointed in their capacities as citizens instead of as professionals. The dual role of being a director and a disinterested professional is potentially a great source of conflict and mischief.

On occasion, a person may serve on two or more boards simultaneously. Here, conflicts of interest become especially ticklish. If the charitable organizations are in competition for fundraising, programs, grants, or contracts, what the director knows from serving on one board cannot be shared, directly or indirectly, with the other. Serving on multiple boards can place one in a very compromising position, involving vague and uncertain lines between loyalty and disloyalty. Before agreeing to serve on more that one board, one should fully explore the potential conflicts.

The Standard of Care

Directors of nonprofit corporations in New York State are required by statute to discharge their duties in "good faith with the degree of diligence, care, and skill which ordinarily prudent men would exercise under similar circumstances in a like position" [Consolidated Laws 1990]. This is similar to statutory language in other states. The standards of diligence and good faith require considerable interaction between the CEO staff and the board so that directors are up to date on purposes, intents, and implications of actions on which they are required to vote. Whatever the knowledge, involvement, or concern of a particular director, that director is legally responsible for the actions of the board unless he or she has statutory immunity. Diligence and good faith require an informed and involved board of directors. Fulfillment of this standard not only requires consistent attendance at board meetings, but also that directors insist on being fully informed on all matters within the parameters of the board's authority. Directors cannot just sit comfortably as figureheads or rubber stamps for CEO decisions. Directors are required to act with the same degree of prudence and judgment in advancing the financial and other business affairs of the organization as they would reasonably do in handling their own personal affairs. There is an objective standard of reasonableness here, so negligence in handling one's personal business affairs does not excuse negligence in handling the organization's business dealings.

Other Legal Responsibilities

Many other points are relevant to the legal responsibilities of volunteers, but these are best left to a nonprofit corporation attorney. The purpose here is to alert volunteers to some of the issues they may need to consider. Every board should consult a corporate counsel as soon as possible regarding its liabilities and whether current policies and practices conform to state law. Below are checklists for making choices and minimizing risks that apply to both directors and volunteers serving nonprofit, charitable organizations.

For Directors

Ask for a copy of and carefully read your organization's bylaws. Be clear about the organization's mission. These documents are not the most exciting reading you will encounter, but you should be clear about the purpose and organizational structure of the nonprofit, and the responsibility you undertake in becoming a director. If you do not understand some matters, ask for clarification.

Do not accept a position on the board if you do not take the responsibility seriously. Serving on a board is not a trophy or luxury appointment. It means hard work and dedicated commitment.

Be sure of your motivations for serving on a board. If your primary motivation is to promote your own entrepreneurial and professional advancement, you probably should not accept a board position.

Ask for clarification regarding your liability as a board director. The Volunteer Protection Act focuses primarily on direct service volunteers and does not wholly abrogate state law. Ask for a written legal opinion on state law. Make sure any liability that inheres to board directors is adequately covered by insurance.

Attend all meetings if possible. When you cannot attend a meeting, make sure you know what is on the agenda and provide feedback in absentia. The same caution applies to any committees on which you sit. As a general rule, you cannot vote by proxy unless permitted by state law.

Insist that all minutes, reports, or other documents on the agenda are received well in advance of meetings. Nonprofits, like other organizations, have a habit of producing last-minute reports for action by governing boards. Do not accept the "press of time" argument for tardy reports.

Do not go into a board meeting unprepared. Formulate concerns and questions in advance. Make sure that policy decisions are made on the basis of adequate information and are within the guidelines of the articles of incorporation and state and federal regulations, if any.

Always pay close attention to budgetary matters, and be reasonably certain that financial reports contain adequate information. Without access to the budget, a board director can be largely left in the dark about agency priorities, specific program allocations, and money trails. As with many organizations, allocations to cover administrative costs may outweigh moneys directed at service obligations.

Ask to see the agency's conflict-of-interest statement. Many agencies will not have one, but this is a special area of concern for board directors. They all have lives outside the boardroom, and they must be clear as to when to withdraw from particular decisions on grounds of conflict of interest.

Do not be overwhelmed by expertise nor fear that asking questions will expose your own ignorance. Be an active participant. CEO officers of nonprofits, like those of for-profit organizations, may prefer to have their way and hope to encounter a rubber stamp board. Do not rely totally on an expectation that organizational CEOs will always do the right thing.

When Hiring Volunteers

Obtain a careful personal history of each volunteer, including letters of recommendation. In some service programs, especially those dealing with children, a check of any criminal history may be advisable, if not mandated by state law. Checking a person's criminal history can, admittedly, be an expensive inquiry. In an ideal world, this expense should be provided by external sources, such as state government, but the lack of such support is no excuse for not protecting recipients of service.

Volunteers should receive a thorough orientation to the organization, including statements of mission, ethics, rules of conduct, agency policy and procedures, potential liability, and the limits of the organization's insurance coverage. Volunteers should receive a short course on safety issues, not only for themselves, but for those they serve as well. The agency should have an established inservice training program for all volunteers. The agency should take every reasonable means to integrate volunteers into the agency's organizational life. The organization should have written policies and procedures related to volunteers, including termination of service. The agency should supervise volunteers with the same care and concern as with paid employees.

The agency should establish a code of conduct for both volunteers and paid employees, including written policies that prohibit sexual harassment and other forms of discrimination. Volunteers, like employees, should receive annual evaluations, and the agency should establish annual performance awards.

Insurance is a must. Even where laws grant immunity to volunteers, the organization may be found liable. In addition, insurance is necessary to cover those acts of volunteers that fall outside federal or state immunity policy.

Know Your Legal Responsibilities

Knowledge of the legal responsibilities and commitments is one of the director's primary obligations, not only to him or herself, but also to the organization. Just wanting to "do good" is no longer sufficient, if it ever was. Indeed, these matters should be explored before one assumes a directorship or otherwise volunteers for a charitable organization. Similarly, the nonprofit organization itself has some responsibilities that involve the careful orientation and preparation of directors and other volunteers, risk management policies and procedures, and sufficient insurance to protect volunteers against personal loss.

Serving on a Nonprofit Board: Legal and Ethical Duties in an Age of Accountability

Lloyd Hitoshi Mayer
Associate Professor of Law
The Law School, University of Notre Dame

Introduction

This outline summarizes the legal and ethical duties of nonprofit directors and officers in light of the increasing public scrutiny of directors in both the for-profit and nonprofit sectors. Much of this material may be familiar to you if you have served on a nonprofit's board, but there have also been several recent developments that affect these duties. These developments include the Sarbanes-Oxley Act, the growing access to information through the Internet, and the increased scrutiny of nonprofit activities in the wake of 9/11.

The first part of this outline reviews the general duties of nonprofit directors under state law, the implications for those duties of the Sarbanes-Oxley Act, other federal government actions affecting nonprofit governance, and ethical considerations that extend beyond fulfilling legal duties. The second part of this outline briefly reviews the effect that the Internet has on the availability of information about nonprofits. While not strictly a legal issue, in many ways the increased access to information about nonprofits creates the greatest possible exposure to nonprofit directors by potentially identifying them with any controversial activities or misdeeds by the nonprofit or its officers and employees.

The third part reviews restrictions and prohibited activities for nonprofits, primarily under federal tax law, with a focus on those activities that either directly involve directors or may result in liability for directors. The third part also includes information about the increased focus on the international and domestic activities of nonprofits in the wake of 9/11. The fourth and final part of this outline briefly reviews various other legal issues for nonprofits that do not directly implicate directors but can have negative ramifications for a nonprofit and therefore its board if the nonprofit fails to address them adequately, including commonly overlooked legal issues.

Because each of the topics covered by this outline could easily be reviewed in greater depth, throughout the outline are references to additional resources that are accessible through the Internet. As indicated by these references, which are far from comprehensive, additional information is available from a variety of sources. These sources include both government agencies, such as the IRS (www.irs.gov/nonprofits/index.html) and state attorneys' general offices (for links to these and other relevant state government offices, see http://www.irs.gov/charities/article/0,,id=129028,00.html), and private organizations, such as the ASAE & The Center for Association Leadership (www.asaecenter.org), BoardSource (www.boardsource.org), the Council on Foundations (www.cof.org), Independent Sector (www.independentsector.org), the National Council of Nonprofit Associations (www.ncna.org), and state and local associations of nonprofit organizations. There are also often industry specific organizations with helpful resources for both their members and the public, such as the American Hospital Association (www.aha.org/aha/about), the Association of Governing Boards of Universities and Colleges (www.agb.org), the Evangelical Council for Financial Accountability (www.ecfa.org), and the National Human Services Assembly (www.nassembly.org). Finally, information on state law requirements is also available from the National Association of State Charity Officials (www.nasconet.org).

Duties of Directors

General Fiduciary Duties

The general duties of nonprofit directors under state law have not changed substantially in recent years, although the attention paid by the media and state attorneys general to such duties has significantly increased. (Note that while members of nonprofit governing boards are usually referred to as "directors," they may also be referred to as "trustees." All of the statements in this outline relating to "directors" apply equally to nonprofit board members who are referred to as "trustees.") Those duties are duties of care, loyalty, and obedience. These duties also generally apply to nonprofit officers.

Duty of Care

In general, state laws require directors to act in good faith and to use the degree of diligence, care, and skill which prudent people would use in similar positions and under similar circumstances. This duty requires directors to act responsibly in their roles as directors, which includes: attending and participating in board and committee meetings; reviewing materials provided to them about the nonprofit; overseeing the nonprofit's finances, including requiring and reviewing regular financial reports; and selecting and supervising the CEO and other key officers and employees.

Duty of Loyalty

In general, state laws require directors to be loyal to the nonprofit they serve. This duty requires directors to put the interests of the nonprofit above any personal interests they may, and includes: disclosing to the rest of the board any conflicts of interest they may have with the nonprofit; not participating in discussions or votes on transactions that may benefit the director or persons closely associated with the director; and not steering opportunities away from the nonprofit for the director's own benefit.

To ensure fulfillment of this duty, nonprofits should have a written conflict of interest policy that is distributed to all directors, officers, and employees. The IRS provides a sample conflict of interest policy as Appendix A to the instructions for the tax exemption application form (IRS Form 1023), available at www.irs.gov/instructions/i1023/ar03.html. The Council of Foundation has also published Conflict of Interest: IRS Sample Policy Annotated for Grantmakers to help grant making foundations develop conflict of interest policies, available at www.cof.org/files/Documents/Building%20Strong%20Ethical%20Foundations/Conflicts_of_Interest_IRS_Sample_Policy.pdf.

Duty of Obedience

Directors are prohibited from directing their organization to engage in ultra vires acts — acts that the organization is prohibited from performing by the applicable law or by its governing documents, such as its certificate of incorporation and bylaws.

Additional information about these three duties is often available from state attorneys general. For example, the New York Attorney General's office publishes Right from the Start: Responsibilities of Directors and Officers of Not-for-Profit Corporations, which provides an overview of the duties that directors of nonprofits are generally required to fulfill (available at www.oag.state.ny.us/charities/not_for_profit_booklet.pdf) The Minnesota Attorney General's office provides similar information at www.ag.state.mn.us/charities/FiduciaryDuties.asp. For general information on nonprofit governance, see the websites of the organizations listed in the introduction and the nonprofit governance books published by the American Bar Association, available at www.abanet.org/abastore/index.cfm search for "nonprofit governance". The Panel on the Nonprofit Sector also recently proposed draft principles for governance and related issues, available at www.nonprofitpanel.org/Report/principles/index.html. There is also growing trend to have different individuals serve as board chair and CEO, to help insure adequate board oversight of the CEO.

Finally, note that both federal tax law and some states differentiate between charitable nonprofits (commonly referred to as "charities" and sometimes as "public benefit" organizations) and non-charitable nonprofits (sometimes referred to as "mutual benefit" organizations). The latter type of nonprofits includes certain advocacy groups, such as the Sierra Club and the National Rifle Association, as well as labor unions and trade associations.

Implications of the Sarbanes-Oxley Act

The federal Sarbanes-Oxley Act generally only applies to publicly traded companies and so not to nonprofits. The only two exceptions are criminal penalties for:

(1) corruptly altering, destroying, mutilating, or concealing any document with the intent to impair the object's integrity or availability for use in an official proceeding or otherwise corruptly obstructing, influencing or impeding any official proceeding and

(2) Retaliating against a whistleblower for providing truthful information to a law enforcement officer about a possible federal crime.

While directors and officers should be aware of these legal rules, most are unlikely to face situations where they would apply.

Nonprofit boards should, however, consider the adoption of a formal whistleblower policy, particular in light of the second application of Sarbanes-Oxley to nonprofits listed above.

Various state legislatures have, however, considered bills that would apply some of Sarbanes-Oxley's other provisions to nonprofits, and in 2004 California adopted a law based in part on Sarbanes-Oxley. This new law requires certain governance procedures, including the creation of audit committee for nonprofits over a certain size and review of by the board or a board authorized committee of the compensation paid to certain CEOs. Most importantly, this new law generally applies to both nonprofits organized under California law and to nonprofits that operate in California, even if they are incorporated or otherwise organized under the laws of another state. The California Attorney General's summary of this new law can be found at http://ag.ca.gov/nonprofits/publications/nonprofit_integrity_act_nov04.pdf.

Congress and the IRS are also looking at a range of nonprofit governance and related issues based in part on Sarbanes-Oxley. In August 2006, Congress tightened a number of the rules relating to nonprofits, including requiring even small nonprofits (annual gross receipts of $25,000 or less) that are not required to file an IRS annual return to provide the IRS with an annual notice of their continued existence beginning in 2008. More information about this notice can be found at www.irs.gov/nonprofits/article/0,,id=169250,00.html. Congress has also changed the rules relating to various types of charitable contributions, including requiring additional documentation for charitable contributions that the donor wishes to deduct regardless of the size of the contribution. A brief description of these new rules is provided below. Summaries of the new laws affecting nonprofits that were contained in the Pension Protection Act of 2006 (Pub. L. No. 109-280) are also available at www.independentsector.org/programs/gr/nonprofitreform.html and at www.irs.gov/newsroom/article/0,,id=164997,00.html.

For a more detailed discussion of the ramifications of Sarbanes-Oxley for nonprofits, see The Sarbanes-Oxley Act and Implications for Nonprofit Organizations, available at www.boardsource.org/clientfiles/Sarbanes-Oxley.pdf.

Recent Federal Government "Suggestions" Regarding Governance

While regulation of nonprofit governance is generally a state law matter, overseen by the various state attorneys general, the federal government has in recent years issued voluntary recommendations for governance practices and, on the annual information return filed by most nonprofits with the IRS (Form 990), required increased reporting of such practices. One of the most prominent examples of these recommendations is a Treasury Department issued Guidelines on Charitable Best Practices, available at www.ustreas.gov/offices/enforcement/key-issues/protecting/nonprofits-intro.shtml. The other prominent example is a Governance and Related Topics- 501(c) (3) Organizations document issued by the IRS and available at www.irs.gov/pub/irs-tege/good_governance_practices.pdf. Listed "good governance practices" include:

- Adopting a mission statement, code of ethics, conflict of interest policy, whistleblower policy, document retention policy, investment policy, and fundraising procedures;
- Ensuring directors, officers and employees comply with their duties of care and loyalty to the organization and, if compensated, are paid no more than reasonable compensation;
- Providing full and accurate information to the public about the nonprofit's activities and finances; and
- When the size of a nonprofit's revenues or assets are substantial, hiring an independent auditor to conduct an annual financial audit

While conforming with either the Treasury Department Guidelines or the IRS document is purely voluntary, a number of funders, watchdog organizations, and government agencies are looking at the rules in these documents to determine whether they should be mandatory for some or all nonprofits.

Finally, on the annual information return that most nonprofits (churches being the big exception) are required to file with the IRS, the IRS now asks detailed questions about payments to insiders, including directors and those related to them, and about whether the organization has various governance policies in places. For more details, see the redesigned IRS Form 990, available at http://www.irs.gov/charities/article/0,,id=181091,00.html, especially Part IV (questions 25-28), Parts VI and VII, and Schedules J and L. The draft instructions for the redesigned form, which organizations must file for fiscal years beginning on January 1, 2008 or later, are also available at the same IRS website. The IRS asks similar questions as part of the tax exemption application process for charitable nonprofits; see Part V or IRS Form 1023, available on the IRS website.

Going Beyond the Law: Developing a Code of Ethics

Most nonprofits seek to hold themselves to a higher standard than simply mere compliance with the law. For example, many non-profits develop a code of ethics or a set of ethical principles to guide their activities in a manner that both promotes and is consistent with the ideals of the nonprofit. Because such a code or set of principles can have fundamental effect on how a nonprofit operates, it is often developed or, at a minimum, approved by the nonprofit's board.

While each nonprofit will have unique considerations that shape its ethics, a good starting place for developing a code of ethics or set of ethical principles is a collection of materials gathered by Independent Sector, including a Compendium of Standards, Codes, and Principles of Nonprofits and Philanthropic Organizations. It is available at www.independentsector.org/issues/accountability/standards2.html.Independent Sector also makes available its own Statement of Values and Code of Ethics as a sample at http://www.independentsector.org/PDFs/code_ethics.pdf.

Nonprofits should not rely, however, solely on policies and proce-dures to ensure good governance in both the legal and ethical sense. Compliance with the spirit as well as the letter of legal and ethical rules is required, and the character of a nonprofit's directors and CEOs is the greatest guarantee of proper behavior. For an insightful consideration of this point, see "What Makes Great Boards Great," written by Yale Professor Jeffrey A. Sonnenfeld and published in the Harvard Business Review. While written with a focus on for-profit companies, it also applies to nonprofits. It is available at www.ceolead-ership.org/sonnenfeld/articles/hbr_whatmakesgreatboards.pdf.

Living in the Information Age

The vast majority of nonprofits and their directors and officers seek in good faith to comply with their legal and ethical duties and so avoid any significant violations of the above legal standards. But increasing access to information about nonprofits can expose non-profits and their directors to allegations of both legal and ethical violations, as well as other criticisms, simply because incorrect or distorted information about a nonprofit is posted on the Internet. While nonprofits only have a limited ability to prevent others from posting inaccurate information, there is much that a nonprofit can do to ensure that accurate and positive information is made readily available.

Information the Nonprofit Releases

If you serve on the board of a nonprofit, have you looked at its website recently? Most nonprofits maintain websites, but many do not have procedures in place to ensure only appropriate information is placed on their website. For example, when the nonprofit posts materials such as newsletters, brochures, and fundraising requests on its website, often no one is reviewing such materials with an eye to the fact that not only supporters of the nonprofit but also its critics and the media will have access to them. If copy-righted material or personal information such as testimonials is posted, appropriate permissions may not have been obtained. If information relating to pending legislation or upcoming elections is posted, it may not be consistent with the restrictions on such information (see below).

Nonprofits are also required to provide the public with copies of their IRS Application for Recognition of Exemption (Form 1023 or, for non-charitable nonprofits such as certain advocacy groups and unions, Form 1024) and their IRS annual information returns (Form 990, 990-EZ or 990-PF) on request. All information on the returns must be disclosed, including the compensation paid to of-ficers, directors, and key employees. The only exception is the names and addresses of donors, which nonprofits other than pri-vate foundations may (and should) redact. In a recent change, nonprofits are also required to provide copies of the unrelated business income tax (UBIT) return (Form 990-T) upon request, if they file such a return (many nonprofits do not). The IRS has issued interim guidance regarding this new requirement, available at www.irs.gov.charities/charitable/article/0,,id=182722,00.html.

The Compliance Guide for 501(c)(3) Public Charities (IRS Publication 4221-PC), available at www.irs.gov/pub/irs-pdf/p4221pc.pdf, provides general information on recordkeeping, filing requirements and disclosure obligations for charitable nonprofits, other than private foundations, for which similar information is provided in the Compliance Guide for 501©(3) Private Foundations (IRS Publication 4221-PF), available at http://www.irs.gov/pub/irs-pdf/p4221pf.pdf. IRS Announcement 99-62, available at www.irs.gov/pub/irs-drop/a-99-62.pdf, also summarizes the disclosure requirements. There have been two significant changes in the disclosure requirements since this announcement: the requirements also now apply to private foundations; and they now extend to Form 990-T.

Information the Government Releases

Even if a member of the public does not ask a nonprofit directly for a copy of its IRS filings, those filings may still be available. The IRS provides copies of exemption applications and annual information returns on request, and has provided copies of all recent annual information returns for tax-exempt nonprofits, including both charities and other types of nonprofits such as advocacy groups, unions, and trade association, to Philanthropy Research Inc., which has posted the returns on its web site, www.guidestar.org. Nonprofits therefore need to treat these forms as public relations documents and not just tax forms.

Filings made with state agencies are also generally matters of public record, and some states have begun posting such filings on the Internet. Many states do not have procedures in place to redact the names and addresses for donors from such filings, so if a nonprofit other than a private foundation provides a state agency with a copy of its IRS annual information return, it should first redact the names and addresses of its donors. Philanthropic Research, Inc., is also working with state nonprofit officials to create a national database of information charitable and possibly other types of nonprofits file with state governments.

Little Brother Is Watching

Watchdog organizations are proliferating, taking advantage of this ready access to information to evaluate and rate nonprofits based on a range of sometimes inconsistent criteria. These groups have focused primarily on charitable nonprofits and include: the American Institute of Philanthropy, which publishes its ratings of over 500 national charities in its Nonprofit Rating Guide & Watchdog Report (available by mail for $3.00) and also lists the top-rated charities at www.nonprofitwatch.org; the BBB (Better Business Bureau) Wise Giving Alliance, which makes reports available at www.give.org on hundreds of charities that solicit nationally or have national or international programs; Charity Navigator, which rates more than 5,000 charities at www.charitynavigator.org/; and Ministry Watch, which rates over 400 large Christian churches and ministries at www.ministrywatch.org. The National Council of Nonprofit Associations and the National Human Services Assembly have co-published an overview of these organizations, Rating the Raters, available at www.nassembly.org/nassembly/documents/RatingtheRaters_004.pdf.

Some organizations have also begun introducing voluntary certification processes for nonprofits that choose to participate. These include a Standards for Excellence Seal program created by the Maryland Association of Nonprofits (www.marylandnonprofits.org/html/standards/index.asp), which has attracted so much interest that the program is now being replicated in several other states, and a National Nonprofit Seal program created by the BBB Wise Giving Alliance (www.giveorg/seal/index.asp).

Other Legal Restrictions and Prohibited Activities

Nonprofits face additional legal restrictions and prohibitions relating to certain types of activities. Such restrictions and prohibitions apply specifically to: transactions with directors, officers,

243

and other insiders; transactions with other parties generally; international activities; fundraising; investing; lobbying; and election-related activities. Most of these restrictions and prohibitions only apply to charitable nonprofits, as they arise from the fact that such nonprofits are tax-exempt under section 501(c)(3) of the Internal Revenue Code, although state laws may also impose their own restrictions and prohibitions.

Intermediate Sanctions on Transactions with "Insiders"
Background

Prior to 1996, the only penalty the federal government could impose when a nonprofit paid excessive compensation or gave a "sweetheart" deal to an insider was to revoke the tax-exempt status of the organization. In 1996, Congress enacted the intermediate sanctions rules, which gave the IRS the power to penalize the insider who benefited from such a transaction and, in some case, those who approved the transaction. The rules are codified at section 4958 of the Internal Revenue Code and the underlying regulations. They apply to insiders of both charitable nonprofits (tax-exempt under section 501(c) (4) of the Internal Revenue Code) and social welfare organizations (nonprofits that are tax-exempt under section 501© (3) of the Internal Revenue Code).

The IRS also announced on August 10, 2004 that it had launched a special audit program to contact almost 2,000 charities regarding their compensation practices. To the degree that the IRS uncovers excessive compensation payments to CEOs as part of these audits, such payments could be subject to intermediate sanctions. The IRS issued a report on a result of those audits in March of this year, available at www.irs.gov/pub/irs-tege/exec._comp._final.pdf. The report did not find many instances of clearly excessive compensation—only 25 organizations total so far, although about 80 examinations remain open. The IRS did find, however, widespread incorrect reporting of compensation and a significant number of loans to directors, officers, and other insiders either at better than commercial terms or that were not repaid according to their stated terms.

244

The Rules in a Nutshell

Disqualified Persons

Intermediate sanctions only apply to transactions with insiders known as "disqualified persons." A disqualified person is someone who, at any time during the five years prior to the transaction in question, was in a position to exercise substantial influence over the affairs of the nonprofit. Disqualified persons include the voting members of a nonprofit's board and the nonprofit's president, chief CEO officer, chief operating officer, treasurer and chief financial officer, as well as family members of these individuals. Disqualified persons also include any entity, such as a corporation, in which one or more disqualified persons and/or their family members own in the aggregate more than a 35% interest.

Excess Benefit Transactions

Intermediate sanctions also only apply to "excess benefit transactions." An excess benefit transactions is broadly defined as any transaction in which an economic benefit is provided by a nonprofit directly or indirectly to or for the use of any disqualified person if the value of the economic benefit provided by the nonprofit exceeds the value of the consideration (including the performance of services) it receives from the disqualified person in return. The IRS has interpreted this to mean that excess benefit transactions do not include payments made at fair market value in transactions resulting from arm's-length negotiations. Both compensation arrangements and business transactions with disqualified persons (such as sales of property or joint investments) can be considered excess benefit transactions.

Standard for Fair Market Value

The fair market value of property is the price at which the property would change hands between a willing buyer and a willing seller, neither being under any compulsion to buy, sell, or transfer the property and both having reasonable knowledge of the relevant facts. If a nonprofit pays a disqualified person no more than fair market value for property (or the right to use property), then the payment will not constitute an excess benefit transaction. A similar standard applies to payments for services.

Note that a nonprofit can compensate both its directors and its officers for their services as long as the amount of such compensation is reasonable in light of the services provided in return. However, the usual practice for nonprofits is not to compensate directors. California also has a special rule requiring that a majority of directors not receive compensation from the nonprofit for services other than as a director (e.g., for services as a consultant or employee). California Corporations Code § 5227.

Rebuttable Presumption of Fair Market Value

To aid organizations in making the fair market value determination, Congress directed the IRS to create a process under which a nonprofit could create a "rebuttable presumption" that the amount paid is in fact fair market value. Under the IRS process, an organization can invoke the presumption of reasonableness if the arrangement is approved in advance by an authorized disinterested body (for example, the board or a board-appointed committee if any members with an interest in the proposed transaction recues themselves from the discussion and vote on the transaction) that relied on appropriate comparability data and documented the basis for its determination adequately and contemporaneously.

Automatic Excess Benefit Transactions

There is one major trap for the unwary under intermediate sanctions. If a nonprofit provides an economic benefit to a disqualified person that would constitute reasonable compensation but the nonprofit and the recipient fail to contemporaneously document that benefit as compensation, that benefit will automatically be treated as an excess benefit transaction. For example, if a nonprofit pays each director a $1,000 a year for "expenses" but fails to require any documentation of those expenses, the $1,000 payment will be an automatic excess benefit transaction unless the nonprofit or the director contemporaneously document that the payment is compensation. Such documentation includes the nonprofit filing a federal information return (e.g., an IRS Form W-2 or IRS Form 1099) reporting the payment as compensation or reporting the payment as compensation on the nonprofit's annual return (e.g., IRS Form 990), or the recipient reporting the payment as compensation on her personal income tax return (e.g., IRS Form 1040).

Penalties on Disqualified Persons

Disqualified persons who participate in an excess benefit transaction are subject to a tax of 25% of the excess benefit and are required to repay the excess benefit to the nonprofit with interest. If the disqualified person refuses to repay the excess benefit within a certain period of time, he or she will be subject to a tax of 200% of the excess benefit.

Penalties on Those Who Approve Excess Benefit Transactions

Any director, officer or individual acting with similar authority who participated in or approved a transaction and knew or reasonably should have known that it was an excess benefit transaction is subject to a tax equal to 10% of the excess benefit (capped at $10,000 per single transaction), but only if that participation was willful and not due to reasonable cause. Reasonable cause might be reliance on a knowledgeable professional who actually gave incorrect advice. More specifically, this tax does not apply if the appropriate body followed the rebuttable presumption of reasonableness procedures with respect to the transaction or if the director or officer relied upon a reasoned

247

written opinion of an appropriate professional with respect to elements of the transaction within that professional's expertise.

Additional Materials

More detailed information about the intermediate sanctions rules is available at www.irs.gov/charities/charitable/article/0,,id=123298,00.html and at www.independentsector.org/programs/gr/intermediate-sanctions.htm.

Private Inurnment and Private Benefit Rules for Transactions with "Insiders" and Other Parties
Background

For charitable nonprofits that are exempt from federal income tax under section 501(c)(3) of the Internal Revenue Code, there is also a bar on the nonprofit using their income or assets for the benefit of private parties. The private inurnment rule, like intermediate sanctions, regulates transactions between a charitable nonprofit and its officers, directors and other "insiders." This rule also applies to social welfare organizations that are tax-exempt under section 501(c) (4) of the Internal Revenue Code. The private benefit rule, which applies to charitable nonprofits, regulates all other transactions.

Both of these rules establish a substantive standard for policing transactions between a covered nonprofit and other parties: the nonprofit may not transfer goods or services to other parties for less than fair market value and may not obtain goods or services from other parties for more than fair market value. Covered nonprofits are therefore permitted under these rules to pay compensation for services if such compensation is reasonable, and to enter into sale and lease transactions, whether with insiders or with other private parties, if such transactions are at fair market value. Covered nonprofits are also permitted to make grants and provide other financial assistance if doing so furthers their nonprofit purposes.

Violation of either of these rules can result in the revocation of a covered nonprofit's tax-exempt status, regardless of whether intermediate sanctions would also apply. Unlike intermediate sanctions, however, neither rule imposes a penalty on either the other participants or the approving directors or officers.

Private Inurnment

Under the private inurnment rule, which applies to both charitable nonprofits and social welfare organizations, the first dollar of value inappropriately transferred from a covered nonprofit to an insider is theoretically grounds for revocation of the nonprofit's exempt status. As a practical matter, the IRS has generally dealt with inurnment problems through agreements under which the nonprofits involved have retained their tax-exempt status but agreed to pay a financial penalty and/or to institute prophylactic measures to prevent future problems. The existence of the intermediate sanctions rules now also gives the IRS a strong tool for forcing insiders to pay back any excess benefit they received.

Private Benefit

For transactions with non-insiders, the IRS' position is that the private benefit rule compels revocation of exempt status only if the private benefit is more than incidental in relation to the public benefit arising from the transaction in question. To be incidental, a private benefit must be both qualitatively and quantitatively incidental.

Qualitatively incidental means that the private benefit is a "necessary concomitant" of an activity that benefits the public—in other words, the benefit to the public cannot be achieved without benefiting certain private individuals. For example, cleaning up a public park benefits the public but also necessarily and unavoidably benefits the private parties who own property near the park.

Quantitatively incidental means the private benefit is insubstantial when compared to overall public benefit conferred by the transaction in question. For example, any benefit to property owners near the now clean park would generally be insubstantial compared to the overall benefit to the public.

Increased Scrutiny of International Activities

Direct Effects on Nonprofits Engaging in International Activities

One major concern in the post-9/11 world is the flow of money to terrorists and organizations that support them. Treasury Department officials have repeatedly stated that charities are the second largest source of such funds (the first being wealthy individuals). The IRS is currently exploring whether to impose additional record-keeping, administrative, and reporting requirements on charities and possibly other types of nonprofits that engage in international activities. For more details about the current federal tax rules for such activities, see IRS Announcement 2003-29, available at www. irs.gov/pub/irs-drop/a-03-29.pdf.

Regardless of whether the IRS chooses to impose any new requirements, nonprofits need to be aware that there are a number of federal laws prohibiting financial support to identified terrorist organizations, individual terrorists, and other international criminals. For more information on these prohibitions, see the Handbook on Counter-Terrorism Measures: What U.S. Nonprofits and Grant makers Need to Know, published by the Council on Foundations, the Day, Berry & Howard Foundation, Independent Sector, and InterAction, and available at www.independentsector.org/media/counterterrorismpr.html.

Indirect Effects on All Nonprofits

In response to requests from Arab American and American Muslim organizations, the Treasury Department issued voluntary guidelines on charitable best practices with minimal input from the nonprofit community. These guidelines purport to apply to all charitable nonprofits, not only those involved in international activities. In response to comments from a variety of nonprofits, the Treasury Department recently modified those guidelines. The current version of the guidelines is available at www.ustreas.gov/press/releases/hp122.htm. As mentioned above, while these guidelines are completely voluntary a number of funders, watchdog organizations, and government agencies, are looking at them to determine whether some or all of them should be mandatory.

The Combined Federal Campaign (CFC), operating by the U.S. Office of Personnel Management (OPM), also recently attempted to require participating nonprofits to verify that they do not employ individuals or make grants to individuals with terrorist links by requiring that the nonprofits check all of these individuals against various lists of alleged terrorists and other criminals. After a number of participants in the campaign, led by the ACLU, filed suit asserting that this requirement placed improper burdens on participating nonprofits, the OPM modified its rules. The current rules on this issue are available at http://a257.g.akamaitech.net/7/257/2422/01jan20051800/edocket.access.gpo.gov/2005/pdf/05-22186.pdf. General information about the CFC is available at www.opm.gov/cfc.

Other Restrictions and Prohibited Activities
Increased Restrictions on Donors

Congress and the IRS have expressed growing concern that many donors are claiming inflated charitable contribution deductions. To counter this perceived abuse, Congress enacted a series of new restrictions on that deduction in 2006. These restrictions may have a significant effect on fundraising for those nonprofits that qualify as charities—that is, as tax-exempt under Internal Revenue Code section 501(c)(3) and so eligible to receive deductible contributions. These restrictions include:

- Contributions of clothing and household items may only be deducted if in good used condition or better, and a deduction of more than $500 for any single item must be supported by a qualified appraisal. This restriction is effective for donations made after August 17, 2006.
- Contributions of money must be documented by a bank or credit card record or a receipt from the charity showing the charity's name and the date and amount of the contribution; cash contributions that are not substantiated with a receipt from the receiving charity are therefore no longer deduct-

ible. This restriction is effective for donations made in tax-able years beginning after August 17, 2006. For individuals, this generally means this restriction applies to donations made in 2007 and later years.

- Revised definitions of "qualified appraisal" and "qualified appraiser," which are relevant for certain high-dollar donations of property that require a qualified appraisal in order to be deductible.
- Limitations on the deductibility of certain historic conservation easements.
- Limitations on the deductibility of donated taxidermy property.
- Limitations on the deductibility of donated fractional interests in tangible personal property (aimed primarily at the practice of some art museums to accept donations of partial interests in artwork, allowing donors to continue to display the art in their personal residences).

These new rules are the latest in a recent series of congressional imposed restrictions on such contributions, including provisions limiting deductions for donations of vehicles and donations of intellectual property. An IRS summary of the rules governing charitable contributions that reflects these changes can be found at www.irs.gov/newsroom/article/0,,id=164997,00.html. The IRS has also issued two publications addressing restrictions on car and other vehicle donations that become effective in 2005 (IRS Publications 4302 and 4303, available at http://www.irs.gov/pub/irs-pdf/p4302.pdf and http://www.irs.gov/pub/irs-pdf/p4303.pdf).

To offset, in a minor way, these restrictions Congress also recently enacted or extended certain charitable contribution incentives. These include a temporary provision permitting individual retirement account (IRA) owners who are 70½ years old or older to "rollover" up to $100,000 of their IRA assets to a charity without any negative tax effects and temporary extensions of certain favorable deduction rules for donations of food, books, and certain conservation property. These changes are also described in the IRS summary noted above.

Congress and the IRS have also been concerned with the use of various intermediary vehicles by donors, including donor-advised funds and supporting organizations. Congress therefore also recently enacted a series of new rules for those organizations, limiting their ability to serve as vehicles for making donations. The details of these rules are beyond the scope of this outline; for an IRS summary of them, see www.irs.gov/charities/article/0,,id=161145,00. html. The Council on Foundations has also published a summary, available at www.cof.org/action/content.cfm?itemnumber=5275&n avItemNumber=5276.

Increased Restrictions on Investments

Congress and the IRS have also been concerned that nonprofits that are tax-exempt might be lured into investment schemes that are in fact tax shelters used by the other investors to improperly evade taxes. To counter this perceived trend, Congress has enacted an excise tax that penalizes tax-exempt nonprofits that knowingly participate in such schemes. While not relevant for most nonprofits, any nonprofit considering participating in a complicated investment vehicle would be well advised to become familiar with this new tax to ensure they do not inadvertently trigger it. For an IRS description of this new tax, see www.irs.gov/pub/irs-drop/n-07-18.pdf.

Congress also recently required nonprofits that are tax-exempt to report information about life-insurance contracts they acquire in a manner that also gives private investors an interest in those contracts. Again, this new requirement will not be relevant for most nonprofits, but for nonprofits for which this may be of interest the IRS has issued a notice requesting comments regarding how this requirement should be administered, www.irs.gov/pub/irs-drop/n-07-24.pdf.

Other Federal Tax Law Prohibitions

There are other federal tax law prohibitions on the activities of charitable nonprofits, including a limitation on the amount of permitted lobbying and an absolute ban on supporting or opposing candidates for elected office, both provided by section 501(c)(3) of the Internal Revenue Code. While the primary ramification of violating either the lobbying limitation or the political activity ban is the possible revocation of the charity's tax-exempt status, a possible secondary ramification is personal financial liability for directors and officers who approved the prohibited activities. For excessive lobbying, under section 4912 of the Internal Revenue Code the IRS may impose a penalty of 5% of the amount spent on such excessive lobbying on a director who approved the expenditure, if, and only if, the director knew the expenditure was prohibited. For political activity, under section 4955 of the Internal Revenue Code the IRS may impose a penalty of 2½% (increased to 50 percent if the director refuses to agree to correct the violation) of the amount spent on such political activity on a director who approved the expenditure, again, if, and only if, the director knew the expenditure was prohibited. For political activity, the penalty is capped at $5,000 per expenditure ($10,000 if the director refuses to agree to correct the violation).

Additional information about these limitations is available from the IRS at www.irs.gov/charities/charitable/article/0,,id=120703,00.html and from the National Council of Nonprofit Associations, at www.ncna.org/index.cfm? fuseaction=Page.ViewPage&PageID=689. In 2004, the IRS created a special audit program to investigate reports and complaints of apparent violations of the political activity prohibition by charities relating to the 2004 elections. The IRS continued the program for the 2006 election and is continuing it for the 2008 election.

State Law Prohibitions

State laws may prohibit certain otherwise permitted transactions. For example, many states prohibit nonprofits from making loans to directors or officers even if the loans require reasonable interest payments by the borrower. Violation of this prohibition may lead to the approving directors being personally liable for the loan in the event that the borrower fails to repay it. See, e.g., California Corporations Code § 5237(a) (3).

Other Legal Requirements

Nonprofits are subject to a variety of other legal requirements. This section summarizes the most common such requirements relating to required filings, required disclosures, fundraising, commonly overlooked legal issues, and other common legal issues, although it necessarily is not exhaustive.

Required Filings
Federal

Application for Recognition of Exemption

Charitable nonprofits are generally required to file an Application for Recognition of Exemption (IRS Form 1023) to have their exemption from federal income tax recognized by the IRS. Only a few categories of organizations are exempt from this requirement, principally churches and some (but not all) church-related entities. The application may be filed anytime within 27 months of an organization's creation, but since an IRS letter granting the application is often a pre-requisite for various other filings, it is generally advisable to file the application as soon as possible. Other types of nonprofits are also effectively required to apply for tax exemption (by filing IRS Form 1024) because the IRS will refuse to accept an annual information return from such entities if there is no record that they are in fact tax-exempt.

Annual Returns

Nonprofits are generally required to file an annual information return (IRS Form 990 or 990-EZ, Form 990-PF for private foundations). Some nonprofits are exempt from this requirement, principally churches, some church-related entities, and nonprofits (but not private foundations) with annual gross receipts of no more than $25,000. Nonprofits that are exempt because they have annual gross receipts of $25,000 or less will, however, have to file an annual notice with the IRS starting in 2008. As mentioned above, more information about this notice requirement can be found at www.irs.gov/charities/article/0,,id=169250,00.html. Nonprofits that have more than a minimal amount of unrelated business taxable income (UBTI) are also required to file an annual tax return reporting that income (IRS Form 990-T). For more information about UBTI, see the instructions to Form 990-T available on the IRS website.

Materials

The Compliance Guide for 501© (3) Public Charities (IRS Publication 4221-PC), available at http://www.irs.gov/pub/irs-pdf/p4221pc.pdf, provide information on recordkeeping, filing requirements and disclosure obligations for charities other than private foundations. The Compliance Guide for 501© (3) Private Foundations (IRS Publication 4221-PF), available at http://www.irs.gov/pub.irs-pdf.p4221pf.pdf, provides similar information for private foundations.

State

Certificates of Authority

If a nonprofit has a significant presence in a state other than its state of incorporation, states generally require that the nonprofit apply for a Certificate of Authority.

Applications for Exemption

Similarly, most states require that nonprofits with a significant presence within their borders file an application for exemption. A favorable IRS ruling letter is often a pre-requisite for such an application. Some states do not require such filings.

Annual Returns

Most states that require an application for exemption also require nonprofits to file annual returns. The annual return requirement may range from simply providing a copy of the IRS annual information return to completing a separate state annual return form.

Fundraising Registration and Reporting

Most states require charities and often other nonprofits that ask state residents for donations to register and file regular reports. See Section IV.C.2 below for more information about this requirement.

Local

Nonprofits are often subject to various local filing requirements, including applying for licenses for various activities, obtaining certificates of occupancy for buildings, and similar items.

Required Disclosure

Federal Filings

Nonprofits are required to provide copies of their Application for Recognition of Exemption (IRS Form 1023 or 1024) and their annual information returns (IRS Form 990, 990-EZ or 990-PF) on request. The IRS also provides copies of these documents on request, and has provided copies of all recent annual information returns for charitable nonprofits and some social welfare organizations to Philanthropy Research Inc., which has posted the returns on its web site, www.guidestar.org. All information on the returns must be disclosed, including the amount of compensation paid to officers, directors, and key employees. The only exception is the names and addresses of donors, which nonprofits (other than private foundations) may (and should) redact.

The Compliance Guide for 501(c)(3) Tax-Exempt Organizations (IRS Publication 4221), mentioned above and available at www.irs.gov/pub/irs-pdf/p4221.pdf, provides provide additional information about these requirements for charities, as does IRS Announcement

99-62, available at www.irs.gov/pub/irs-drop/a-99-62.pdf, which summarizes the disclosure requirements. There have been two significant changes in the disclosure requirements since this announcement: the requirements also now apply to private foundations; and they now extend to Form 990-T.

State Filings

Filings made with state agencies are generally matters of public record. Some states also have begun posting such filings on the Internet. Many states do not have procedures in place to redact the names and addresses for donors from such filings, so if a nonprofit other than a private foundation provides a state agency with a copy of its IRS annual information return, it should first redact the names and addresses of its donors.

Fundraising and Other Communications

Fundraising Standards

There are both legal and ethical considerations that apply to fundraising appeals. The specific legal rules vary depending on the method used to make the appeal (in person, by advertisement, by mail, by telephone, etc.), but generally require, at a minimum, truthfulness and identification of the requesting nonprofit. Suggested standards for fundraising appeals are listed in the Compendium of Standards, Codes, and Principles of Nonprofits and Philanthropic Organizations, available at www.independentsector.org/issues/accountability/standards2.html (see especially the standards provided in Section III.A.1 of this webpage).

Federal Laws

Besides the new restrictions on deductible charitable contributions summarized above, other requirements for such contributions to be deductible including providing donors with receipts for their contributions when legally required. See Nonprofit Contributions: Substantiation and Disclosure Requirements (IRS Publication 1771), available at www.irs.gov/pub.irs-pdf/p1771.pdf, for more information about these requirements.

The Federal Trade Commission ("FTC") and the Federal Communications Commission ("FCC") also oversee rules governing the use of email, faxes and telephone calls. These laws may apply to communications by nonprofits, particularly with respect to sender and subject identification requirements, opt-out opportunities, email and fax communications that are "commercial" in nature (for example, because they offer to sell goods or services), and telephone communications made by a for-profit telephone solicitor on behalf of a nonprofit.

- For general information regarding the FTC's rules for emails, see www.ftc.gov/spam. For articles discussing the application of these rules to nonprofits, see www.independentsector.org/programs/gr/spam.htm, www.guidestar.org/DisplayArticle.do?articleId=791, and www.afpnet.org/ka/ka-3.cfm?content_item_id=17967&folder_id=2465.
- For general information regarding the FCC's rules for faxes, see www.fcc.gov/cgb/consumerfacts/unwantedfaxes.html. For an article discussing the application of these rules to nonprofits, see www.independentsector.org/programs/gr/donotfax.html.
- For general information regarding the FCC's rules for telephone calls, see www.fcc.gov/cgb/consumerfacts/tcpa.html. For an article discussing the application of these rules to charities, see www.independentsector.org/programs/gr/donotcall.html.

State and Local Laws

Most (approximately 40) states require charities and often other nonprofits that solicit contributions from their residents to register with the state (usually the Attorney General's office) and file annual reports. Some states also require reviewed or audited financial statements to be filed by such nonprofits with gross receipts above certain thresholds. A few counties have similar requirements. Exceptions to these requirements vary from state to state, but churches, alumni associations, and organizations that only solicit contributions from their members are often excluded from these requirements.

Failure to make such filings can result in civil penalties and a bar on soliciting contributions in that state. Information about these filings can generally be found on the Attorney General's web site of each state (for links to state AG and other relevant state government offices, see www.irs.gov.charities/article/0,,id=129028,00.html). General information is also available through the National Association of State Charity Officials at www.nasconet.org.

Some states also have laws that are similar to the federal laws governing emails, faxes, and telephone calls, including do-not-call and do-not-fax lists, although nonprofits are often exempt. Some states also extend these laws to mail, although again nonprofits are often exempt. More information about such laws is usually available on the website of the Attorney General or the consumer protection office of each state.

Donor Restrictions

Both for ethical and donor relations reasons, nonprofits should comply with restrictions and conditions placed on contributions by donors. It is particularly important not to let general financial pressures lead you to "borrow" money from restricted contributions, as this is both unethical and unwise. Failure to comply with donor restrictions can result not only in a public relations disaster, but also in lawsuits by donors and investigations by Attorneys General.

Commonly Overlooked Legal Issues

The federal tax laws and state nonprofit rules outlined above, along with everyday legal issues such as employment laws and liability concerns, usually receive the greatest attention from nonprofit directors and officers. There are, however, several legal issues that are commonly overlooked but can be devastating to a nonprofit if not handled properly.

Intellectual Property

A nonprofit's most valuable asset is often its name, logo, and related items. Yet many nonprofits do not recognize this fact and so leave these items unprotected by, for example, not registering them as trademarks and not challenging others who inappropriately use these items. Another issue that commonly arises is how to structure agreements when a nonprofit is willing to allow the use of its name, logo, or other intellectual property, including in cause-related marketing efforts.

It is beyond the scope of this outline to explore this topic in any depth, but for general information about intellectual property, including copyrights, trademarks, and patents, see the United States Copyright Office website (www.copyright.gov) and the United States Patent and Trademark Office website (www.uspto.gov). General information is also available from the American Intellectual Property Law Association (www.aipla.org).

Proper Classification of Service Providers

Many nonprofits misclassify service providers as independent contractors when they should instead be classified as employees. Such misclassifications can be costly, as for employees a nonprofit is generally required to withhold income taxes and withhold and pay Social Security and Medicare taxes. If the IRS discovers such misclassification, a nonprofit can therefore be held liable for all the amounts it failed to properly withhold and pay to the federal government, which can quickly add up to many thousands or tens of thousands of dollars, plus interest and penalties. Perhaps even more importantly, if the nonprofit is unable to pay the amounts owed the IRS can require the individuals at the nonprofit who were responsible for withholding and paying the taxes to pay those amounts. The IRS provides detailed information about properly classifying service providers at www.irs.gov/businesses/small/article/0,,id=99921,00.html.

A related problem that nonprofits sometimes face is failing to pay over amounts withheld to the federal government when due (and to the applicable state government(s) if state income or other taxes are also withheld). When a nonprofit is running on a tight budget, it is often tempting to tap into the significant amount of such funds that have been set aside to be transferred to the government. Don't do this—it is stealing from the government. Not surprisingly, the government is not very forgiving of this behavior. And, as noted above, if the nonprofit is unable to pay the amounts owed, the IRS can require the individuals who were responsible for the funds to pay those amounts instead.

Estate and Trust Disputes

One other legal area that catches many nonprofits by surprise is when they become involved in a dispute regarding the disposition of assets in an estate or trust. Yet nonprofits, particularly charitable nonprofits, often are beneficiaries of such entities without their knowledge and so unexpectedly find themselves involved in disputes regarding the proper distribution of such assets. For general information about the law in this area, see the American College of Trust and Estate Counsel (ACTEC) website (www.actec.org). The website includes extensive information about these issues, including information specifically related to charities and charitable trusts under the public resources tab. A nonprofit can also use the site to search for an ACTEC Fellow in its geographic area. ACTEC Fellows are nominated by other Fellows in their geographic area and must be elected by the membership at large based on the nominee's professional reputation and ability in the fields of trusts and estates.

Other Legal Issues

It is important to remember that nonprofits are also generally subject to the same legal rules that apply to other types of organizations. These rules include contract law, employment law, and tort law.

Contract Law

Nonprofits routinely enter into contracts with employees, vendors, and other third parties. Given the variety of transactions contracts can cover and the fact that state law usually governs contracts, it is impossible to provide a comprehensive guide here. That said, the National Council on Nonprofit Associations provides general guidance for contracting on its website, available at www.ncna.org/ index.cfm?fuseaction=page.viewPage&PageID=554. Many other nonprofit associations, including the ASAE & The Center for Association Leadership (www.asaecenter.org), provide additional information to their members, often including sample contracts for common situations.

Employment Law and Tort Law

While some states offer special protection to some or all nonprofits and their volunteer directors and officers, in general nonprofits and their directors and officers are subject to the same duties as other organizations under employment law and tort law and so are exposed to liability under those laws to the same extent as other organizations and other organization leaders. With respect to employment laws, it is therefore generally advisable for nonprofits to develop employment policies that are distributed to employees both to ensure that standards for employees are clear and prevent illegal employment activities, such as sexual harassment and illegal discrimination. Similarly for any activities that create a potential risk to staff or others, policies should be in place to minimize such risk as appropriate in order to protect the nonprofit from liability under tort law.

It is also generally advisable for nonprofits to have appropriate insurance to protect against liability for claims of violations of employment law or tort law and to pay for legal expenses incurred to defend against such claims. For most nonprofits this means at a minimum having both general liability insurance to protect the organization as a whole and directors and officers ("D&O") insurance to protect the nonprofit's directors and officers. The latter is particularly important when directors could be viewed by any allegedly injured party as potential "deep pockets."

For more information regarding risk management by nonprofits, see the Nonprofit Risk Management Center's website (www. nonprofitrisk.org). Another good source of such information is the nonprofit's insurance company and other insurance companies. For example, the Church Mutual Insurance Company offers an array of free safety resources to the public, available at www.churchmutual. com/index.php/choice/risk/page/intro/id/21. While aimed primarily at churches, these resources address many topics of interest to nonprofits generally, including facility safety, preventing child sexual abuse, youth safety generally, and so on.

Appendix 1.2

The Carver Model: Some Consideration

The book, *Nonprofit Boards: What to Do and How to Do It*, clearly presents itself as a practical tool to help nonprofit boards perform well. It is all about best practices. Such best practices include virtually every aspect of board functioning: agenda setting, time management, leadership selection, recruitment, decision making, and performance evaluation to name just a few. In recommending a best practice for many of these board roles and responsibilities, the authors did call upon various theories that support the recommendations. For example, theories of group process shed incredible light on when and why to hold a board retreat.

Thus, it is important for those involved in nonprofit, board governance to be familiar with the most prolific writer on the subject, namely, John Carver. His writings date back several decades in the 20th century. As such, the Carver Model of Board Governance has the type of name recognition in its field that other firsts enjoy in very different fields. For example, Xerox's early dominance in the field of photocopying led to its very name becoming a verb.

To Xerox means to photocopy. Kleenex is another example. It so pioneered and dominated the supply of paper tissues that all such tissues became known as Kleenex.

Thus it is important to understand the Carver Policy Governance Model in nonprofit organizations. This appendix will be an attempt to summarize it. Serious students of board governance should read John Carver's original texts, many of which are listed in the bibliography at the end of this book.

Carver sees the fundamental purpose for the existence of any board is to be accountable that its organization works. In other words, all authority within an organization resides in the board until or unless it is given away or delegated.

The theoretic Carver Model is not to design a best practice model structure or organizational behavior, but to keep the focus on authority and accountability. Carver seeks to develop "internally consistent principles, externally applicable and logical."

Carver finds it amazing that theorists have developed a whole variety of managerial theories in a continual effort to improve effectiveness of managers. In contrast, boards continue to act without such theoretical catalysts. In attempting to fill the void, Carver argues that his theoretical model must be taken as a whole and not selectively applied. He strongly advocates that his model will ensure an effective and measurable outcome that avoids the two extremes of rubber-stamping on the one hand and micro-managing on the other.

From Carver's perspective, the focus of the nonprofit board should be to meet the expectations of the owners, not the customers. In a for-profit corporation, the owners are easily identified. They are the investors. In nonprofits, the owners are less easily identified. They are part of society itself who cares about a particular value or need. The board acts on their behalf in identifying who the clients or customers are.

This brief statement itself begins the critique of many common practices wherein the staff recruit and recommend board members. The board should constantly reconnect with the "owners" to find new directors.

The second principle of the theory involves systematic delegation. Thus to be effective in mission attainment, the board must hire the right manager and articulate very clear expectations for this manager.

Carver sees the hiring of the Chief Executive Officer as the board's single most important role. For Carver, the board has one employee. He notes how common it is for this role to be reversed as when some charismatic individual forms a nonprofit organization and recruits the board. In such cases, the CEO usually exercises authority over the board itself.

In Carver's model, it is critically important to have measurable outcomes that are expected and to serve as the benchmarks for the performance evaluation of the executive.

This is the critical variable to the Carver Model. These outcomes that are expected are the "ends" for which the organization exists. Ends involve what results, for which recipients, and at what value? Thus, "ends" never describe an organization's programs or processes. These constitute the "means." Perhaps an example will make the point. If an organization exists to reduce illiteracy, the ends are about how much was illiteracy reduced. The ends are not about a new reading program.

Ends decisions involve board activity; means decisions involve management activity. The role of the board is to define the ends. These are all about the organization's mission. The role of staff is to produce the ends.

In light of this distinction between ends and means or between the unique roles of the board and management, one can understand that the Carver Model does not value such committees of the board as personnel or program committees. By definition, these involve the oversight of processes, which are the functions of management and staff.

The board is to keep its focus on the ends—why does this organization exist? The board meeting is where these ends are decided upon in a group setting facilitated by the chair. The chair should not have excessive individual authority. He or she should be the servant leader. As such, even the evaluation of the CEO should not be delegated to the chair. The board is responsible for the ends, i.e., the organization's effect. Thus, the board itself should evaluate whether the *ends* were as expected. In doing so, the board evaluates the CEO's performance. Simply stated, the products tell the story of what the nonprofit board is all about.

This is a capsule version of the theory. Boards that choose to embrace this theory would be well advised to consult with organizations already implementing the Carver Policy Governance Model. Because of its unequivocal call for a governance board to focus entirely on mission and ends, there will be a myriad of practical issues to decide. These include such basics as the size and composition of the board, the agenda, and structure of actual board meetings, clear expectations on all information to be shared at meetings, etc. The theory is relatively easy to comprehend. Delegating to management virtually all oversight of programs, budget, and staffing demands more, not less, defined expectations and very specific patterns of accountability.

Appendix 1.3

Mergers and Acquisitions[15]

Nonprofit Mergers: Considerations for Boards

In 2004, 12 Chief Executive Officers of large, nonprofit social service organizations gathered in Chicago for a strategic planning consultation. All represented nonprofit, member organizations of the Milwaukee-based National Association, The Alliance for Children and Families. Typically at the beginning of such sessions, the facilitator or chair asks participants to introduce themselves and respond to some open-ended questions. In this case the chair asked each CEO to mention the most difficult situation that he or she ever faced as a manager. Three responded that guiding their organizations through successful mergers far exceeded any other challenge that they had experienced.

This informal discussion actually highlighted not only the frequency of the phenomenon of nonprofit mergers, but also the challenge they impose. The results of a recent study, conducted by researchers at Stanford University, supports well the candid remarks of these Alliance CEOs concerning the difficulties involved in nonprofit mergers.

---

[15] See also John A. Yankey, Barbara Wester and David Campbell, (1998): Managing Mergers and Consolidations

The anecdotal observations and the researched findings align well. The Stanford Project on the Evolution of Nonprofits (SPEN) interviewed the leaders of 200 randomly selected nonprofit organizations in the San Francisco metropolitan area about mergers and other management practices. Of the 200 organizations involved, 17 had gone through a merger. Of these, 10 had gone through more than one such merger which raises the number of mergers in the sample to over 10% of nonprofits. Obviously this represents a significant trend in the nonprofit environment. As such, all nonprofit boards should consider the implications and forces driving the trend.

What are these forces?

Usually one of three forces, or some combination of the three, pressures an organization to merge with another nonprofit whose mission and program aligns well with it. The three include funder pressures, the explosive increase in the number of nonprofits and search for ways to maximize the cost effectiveness of administration.

The pressure from funders is most common. Funders—whether private philanthropies such as the United Way or a community foundation or a public sector vendor—assess that they can put more money into programs if they reduce duplication of administrative services and infrastructure costs through encouraging the merger of the providers involved. Some funders will even give a one-time incentive grant to cover the costs involved in a merger.

The second catalyst for more nonprofit mergers arises from the sheer increase in the number of nonprofit organizations in the United States. In his book, *The State of Nonprofit America*, Lester Salamon notes that 1.2 million formally constituted nonprofit organizations existed in the United States in 1997. This represents a 115% increase or 23,000 new nonprofits per year since 1977. With such growth, there will be an inevitable pressure for consolidation and merger within the sector. In addition to the numbers involved, many of these newer nonprofits provide a very narrow range of specialized services. This reality also increases the pressure for consolidation into larger organization with a wider range of services.

The third and perhaps most compelling pressure for nonprofits to merge comes from the organization's own leadership whether at the board or executive level. At some point good leaders in an overly competitive environment will consider the value of a merger with another nonprofit organization that offers similar services to clients who live in the same or nearby communities. Since most funding for services tend to be restricted to specific programs, a merger does offer the possibility of administering more programs at less cost and with greater depth.

This pressure for merger exhibits a rationale that is similar to the first identified source of pressure mentioned earlier, namely, the pressure which funders bring to bear to encourage or force a merger between nonprofit organizations. Nonetheless, the chance for a successful merger is qualitatively better if the process results from the vision of the organizations themselves, rather than from coercion from a funding source.

The success of a merger between two nonprofit organizations depends less on the logic of the fit and more on the process used to assess the feasibility of the merger and to guide the plan of implementation.

The authors of this book have drawn upon the results of the Stanford Study (SPEN), anecdotal feedback from colleagues in the nonprofit sector, and from their own experience in leading or advising nonprofit organizations to offer a checklist for nonprofit boards to use in assessing the merits of a merger.

The checklist of best practices for a successful nonprofit merger:
1.) The mission of each organization must align with that of the other.

The mission of any nonprofit organization involves its ultimate identity. Programs come and go as needs change and funding patterns shift. In contrast, the stated mission of the organization changes little. It is the stabilizing reality for the organization's continuing value to the community. The success of any merger will presume that the mission of each partner organization will actually be preserved or strengthened by their union.

Prior to an actual merger, both boards should be involved in drafting a new mission statement from the congruence of the two current mission statements.

This then can become the prism through which the value of all programs come to be measured to decide which will continue and which will not continue.

2.) The culture of each organization must align with that of the other.

One of the most difficult and demanding tasks of the due diligence process needed in a merger of nonprofit organizations involves the assessment of how well the organizations fit culturally. If the organizations offer similar services to different ethnic groups, they will usually realize the culture diversity of these client groups that must be considered for board composition and functioning as well as for staffing issues. However, cultural diversity includes much more that just issues of religion, race, or gender. It involves work expectations and the division of labor. If a nonprofit, service provider has a culture in which all staff are considered generalists, it will not fit well with a highly professionalized mental health provider that hires staff within very specialized areas of competence.

3.) A successful merger needs a realistic timeline for the due diligence and planning processes.

For large, complex organizations, the planning process for a successful merger may easily demand a two- or three-year timeline.

There is no greater obstacle to the successful merger of two nonprofits than rushing the process. In addition to promises of future cost savings and program efficiencies, mergers also involve the potential for conflicts and for feelings of loss. The process needs to confront knotty problems like differences in salary scales, in pension and other benefits, in expectations of what positions will be eliminated post-merger, etc. The rule is: resolve such conflicts before the actual merger.

4.) The vision which guides the mergers due diligence process will focus on the long term value of the new organization that results from the merger, not the merger, itself.

It is the big picture of a successful outcome that must drive the planning process. As one researcher in the Stanford Study (SPEN) opined, the two organizations must focus on the marriage, not just the wedding ceremony.

This is not just a cute metaphor. It cleverly invites those in the planning process for a merger to keep their focus where it should be.

5.) The financial analysis of the projected costs and savings that will result from the merger should be exhaustive in extent and detail.

Financial analysis constitutes one of the most obvious, and yet, most complicated activities in the due diligence process. The projected cost savings, economies of scale, and efficiencies that lead organizations to consider the merits of merging can seduce those involved to overlook hidden expenses of the merger process. Such expenses include the reassignment of key managers and staff from their normal income-generating work to do the activities demanded by the merger process. This analysis must also include firm projections of expected income post-merger. Many managers that have been through mergers report that often the funders do not fund the new entity at the levels projected during the planning process. This maybe especially true when the funder acted as the original force that drove the merger.

This leads to the next essential element in effecting a successful merger.

6.) All current funders must be considered key stakeholders and be supportive of the enterprise.

A successful merger will depend on the maintenance or expansion of funding, not a contraction of financial resources imposed by a non-supportive funding source. There is anecdotal evidence that some funders which so agree with the ultimate value of the merger to the local community will actually underwrite many of the real costs involved in the merger planning process to maximize the full benefit of the merger. It should be added that all donors to the merging organizations should be considered key stakeholders to the success of this efforts.

7.) Serious attention should be invested in the eventual brand of the organization that results from the merger.

Attention to the brand means more than just choosing a new name. Focusing on how to brand the newly formed organization gives an opportunity for how the total service package will now be developed for the good of clients and the good of the community. The brand then must be marketed to internal and external audiences. This process should be designed so that there is little risk that the new brand will merely become the merger itself.

8.) Choosing the executive leader for the new organization will be critical to the success of the entire enterprise.

This priority should not be a surprise. The most important decision made by virtually all nonprofit boards involves the selection of the best possible candidate for the role of Chief Executive Officer. In a merger, the board should not be intimidated to assign the new role to one of the current executives due to years of service, loyalty, or some other such measure. The success of the entire initiative may depend on leadership strengths and skills that were not necessarily needed in the pre-merged organizations. The selection of this leader must be based on managerial and program competencies, as well as on the political skills that will be essential to success.

9.) The board for the new organization should have some representation from each of the boards of the founding organizations, but should have a majority of newly recruited directors to guide the implementation.

As noted earlier in this Appendix, mergers involve loss for many of the stakeholders involved. This includes the board members who indeed constitute one of the categories of stakeholders most prone to

274

feelings of loss. Consider that they are losing the identity and, possibly, even the name of an organization in which they invested time, talent, and treasure. At one level every such director can acknowledge the logic of a merger while still wishing that it was not necessary. Some directors can work through this normal reality. Those that do it well should obviously be the ones selected to serve on the newly formed board. However, if a majority of the new board did not serve the pre-merger organizations, that group will more objectively make the decisions that will assure the success of the merger.

Appendix 1.4

The Governance Principles

Nonprofit Self Governance

A Draft Version of 29 Principles Suggested by the Independent Sector's Expert Panel

March, 2007[16]

A. PRINCIPLES FOR FACILITATING LEGAL COMPLIANCE

1. A charitable organization should be knowledgeable about and must comply with all applicable laws and regulations and international conventions.

2. A charitable organization must have a governing body that is responsible for reviewing and approving the organization's mission and strategic directions, annual budget and key financial transactions, compensation practices and policies, and fiscal and governance policies of the organization.

---

[16] http://www.independentsector.org/panel/main.htm

3. A charitable organization must adopt and implement policies and procedures to ensure that all conflicts of interest, or the appearance thereof, within the organization and the board are avoided or appropriately managed through disclosure, recusal, or other means.

4. A charitable organization must establish and implement policies and procedures that enable individuals to come forward with credible information on illegal practices or violations of organizational policies. This "whistleblower" policy must specify that the organization will not retaliate against individuals who make such reports.

5. A charitable organization must establish and implement policies and procedures to protect and preserve the organization's important documents and business records.

6. A charitable organization must make information about its operations, including its board members, finances, programs and activities, and methods used to evaluate the outcomes of work, widely available to the public.

B. PRINCIPLES FOR EFFECTIVE GOVERNANCE

7. The board of a charitable organization must meet regularly enough to conduct its business and fulfill its duties. The board should hold at least three meetings per year.

8. The board of a charitable organization should establish and review periodically its size and structure to ensure effective governance and to meet the organization's goals and objectives. The board should have a minimum of five members.

9. The board of a charitable organization should include members with the diverse skills, background, expertise, and experience necessary to advance the organization's ability to fulfill its mission. The board should include or have access to some individuals with financial literacy.

10. A substantial majority of the board of a public charity should be independent—that is, individuals (1) who are not compensated by the organization as an employee or independent contractor, (2) whose own compensation is not determined by individuals who are compensated by the organization; (3) who do no receive, directly or indirectly, material financial benefits from the organization except as a member of the charitable class served by the organization; and (4) who are not related to (as a spouse, sibling, parent or child) or do not reside with any individual described above.

11. The board must hire, supervise, and evaluate the performance of the chief executive officer of the organization, as well as approve annually and in advance the compensation of the chief executive officer unless there is a multi-year contract in force or there is no change in the compensation except from an inflation or cost-of-living adjustment.

12. The board of a charitable organization that has paid staff should ensure that the positions of chief executive officer, board chair, and treasurer are held by separate individuals.

13. The board should establish an effective, systematic process for educating and communicating with board members to ensure that the board carries out its oversight functions and that individual members are aware of their legal and ethical responsibilities.

14. Board members should evaluate their own performance as a group and as individuals no less frequently than every three years. The board should establish clear policies and procedures on the length of terms and on the removal of board members.

15. The board must review organizational and governing instruments no less frequently than every three years.

16. The board should establish or review goals for implementing the organization's mission on an annual basis and evaluate

programs, goals, and activities to be sure they are consistent with the mission no less frequently than every three years.

17. Board members are generally expected to serve without compensation, other than reimbursement for expenses incurred to fulfill their board duties. Charitable organizations that provide compensation to board members must make available to anyone, upon request, relevant information that will assist in evaluations of the reasonableness of such compensation.

C. PRINCIPLES FOR STRONG FINANCIAL OVERSIGHT

18. The board of a charitable organization must institute policies and procedures to ensure that the organization and, if applicable, its subsidiaries, manages and invests its funds responsibly and prudently. The full board must review and approve the organization's annual budget and should monitor actual performance against the budget.

19. A charitable organization must keep complete and accurate financial records and should have a qualified, independent financial expert audit or review them annually in a manner appropriate to the organization's size and scale of operations.

20. A charitable organization must not provide loans (or the equivalent) to directors or trustees.

21. A charitable organization must spend a reasonable percentage of its annual budget on programs in pursuance of its mission. An organization must also provide sufficient resources for effective administration of the organization, and, if the organization solicits contributions, for appropriate fundraising activities.

22. A charitable organization must establish and implement policies that provide clear guidance on its rules for paying or reimbursing expenses incurred when conducting business or traveling on behalf of the organization, including the types of expenses that can be paid for or reimbursed and the documentation required.

D. PRINCIPLES FOR RESPONSIBLE FUNDRAISING PRACTICES

23. Solicitation materials and other communications with donors and the public must clearly identify the organization and be accurate and truthful.

24. Contributions must be used for the purposes described in the relevant solicitation materials, in the way specifically requested by the donor, or in a manner that reflects the donor's intent.

25. Charitable organizations must provide donors with appropriate acknowledgements.

26. Charitable organizations should implement clear policies, based on the organization's exempt purpose, to determine whether accepting a gift is in the best interests of the organization.

27. A charitable organization should provide appropriate training and supervision of the people soliciting funds on its behalf to ensure that they understand their responsibilities and applicable federal, state and local laws, and that they do not employ techniques that are coercive, intimidating, or intended to harass potential donors.

28. Organizations should not compensate internal or external fundraisers based on a commission or a percentage of the amount raised.

29. A charitable organization must respect the privacy of individual donors and must not sell or otherwise make available the names and contact information of its donors without prior permission, except where disclosure is required by law.

The staff proposed two additional principles – one on adopting a code of ethics and another on establishing and following appropriate risk management practices.

Appendix 2

Tools for Analysis and Use

The thought provoking material in Appendix 1 surely gives non-profit/human service managers and directors food for thought, but perhaps food for worry as well. "How," a director might ask, "can our board address these issues?" Appendix 2 provides some tools to respond to this question.

First, programs need to be constantly analyzed in a strategic way, and the MacMillan Matrix is an excellent tool for this purpose. It provides a so-called "keep/kill" grid that allows boards to strategically consider the value of each program in a competitive analysis framework. Two approaches to using the Matrix are provided here.

Secondly, a Strategic Planning Questionnaire is presented to assist boards in thinking through the mission and purpose in connection with their products, as we suggested in the Overview.

Thirdly, we have included an excellent and simplified set of rules for Parliamentary Procedure, compiled by the League of Women Voters. For those boards that wish to use a set of meeting rules, this is the very best we have come across.

Lastly, we have included a set of web resources—selected to be sure—prepared by Catherine Christ Lucas, MSW, of the Willard Library in Battle Creek, Michigan.

Appendix 2.1

MacMillan Matrix[17]

Nonprofit staff are often uncomfortable discussing "competitiveness" or "resource allocation"—not because we don't understand these ideas, but because we like concentrating on the people we help through our work. Recent environmental changes—shifts in funding priorities, increased home computer usage, and a proliferation of community technology programs (CTC)—require us, however, to use these concepts to ensure that we are truly meeting the needs of the people we want to help.

The MacMillan Matrix can help your CTC discover the program areas that are most needed in your community and that you are in the best position to provide. The Matrix is based on the following assumptions:

- Nonprofits should avoid duplicating services. This will ensure that limited resources are used well and quality of service is maximized.
- Nonprofits should focus on a limited number of high-quality services, rather than providing many mediocre services.
- Nonprofits should collaborate so that a continuum of service can be provided with each partner focusing on specific pieces.

The MacMillan Matrix will help you assess current and prospective programs according to four criteria—fit with your organization's mission, attractiveness to funders and participants, whether the service is provided elsewhere, and organizational capacity. Below is an adapted MacMillan Matrix for CTCs.

---

[17] http://www.ctcnet.org/what/action/?page_id=39

282

MacMillan Matrix for CTCs	Program is Very Attractive to Funders and/or Community Participants		Program is Not Attractive to Funders and/or Community Participants	
	Several Orgs. Offer Similar	Few/No Orgs. Offer	Several Orgs. Offer Similar	Few/No Orgs.

		Programs	Similar Programs	Programs	Offer Similar Programs
G O O D	**High Org. Capacity and Credibility**	Keep and Complete	Keep and Grow	Keep and Collaborate	Keep and Subsidize
F I T	**Weak Org. Capacity and Credibility**	Give Away to Other Orgs.	Grow Your Capacity or Give Away	Give Away to Other Orgs.	Collaborate or Stop
	POOR FIT	**Give Away**		**Give Away**	

Each current and prospective program should be put into the appropriate square. Those program ideas that fall into top row (good fit and high capacity) should be kept. The programs in the top right-most cell are those programs that your CTC is well-suited to provide and that are most needed, but are difficult to fund. These are the programs that you should consider subsidizing with general operating funds. Those program ideas in the bottom two rows should usually not be undertaken.

Resources:
- Alliance for Nonprofit Management MacMillan Matrix FAQ
- MacMillan Matrix 15-page How-To Guide and Worksheet (free from the Forbes Group, but requires filling out a form)

Question[18]
How can we do a competitive analysis?

Answer

Nonprofits have not traditionally been thought of as organizations that need to be competitively oriented. Unlike for-profit businesses, which compete for customers and whose very survival depends on providing services or products to satisfied, paying "clients," many nonprofit organizations operate in a non-market, or grants, economy—one in which services may not be commercially viable. In other words, the marketplace may not supply sufficient resources to support an adequate, ongoing provider base. Moreover, the customer (client) does not decide which provider gets adequate, ongoing funding. (In fact, many nonprofits are considered "sole-source," the only place to get the service, so there is not necessarily any choice in which provider receives funding even if the client does have some say). Consequently, nonprofit organizations have not necessarily had an incentive to question the status quo, to assess whether client needs were being met, or to examine the cost-effectiveness or quality of available services.

The competitive environment has changed, however: funders and clients, alike, are beginning to demand more accountability; sole-sourced nonprofits are finding that their very success is encouraging others to enter the field and compete for grants; and grant money and contributions are getting harder to come by, even as need and demand increase. This last trend—increasing demand for a smaller pool of resources—requires today's nonprofits to rethink how they do business, to compete where appropriate, to avoid duplicating existing comparable services, and to increase collaboration, when possible.

---

[18] http://www.allianceonline.org/FAQ/strategic_planning/how_can_we_do_competitive.faq

The MacMillan Matrix for Competitive Analysis of Programs

The MacMillan Matrix is an extraordinarily valuable tool that was specifically designed to help nonprofits assess their programs in that light. The matrix is based on the assumption that duplication of existing comparable services (unnecessary competition) among nonprofit organizations can fragment the limited resources available, leaving all providers too weak to increase the quality and cost-effectiveness of client services. The matrix also assumes that trying to be all things to all people can result in mediocre or low-quality service; instead, nonprofits should focus on delivering higher-quality service in a more focused (and perhaps limited) way. The matrix therefore helps organizations think about some very pragmatic questions:

- Are we the best organization to provide this service?
- Is competition good for our clients?
- Are we spreading ourselves too thin, without the capacity to sustain ourselves?
- Should we work cooperatively with another organization to provide services?

Using the MacMillan Matrix is a fairly straightforward process of assessing each current (or prospective) program according to four criteria, described below.

1. Fit

Fit is the degree to which a program "belongs" or fits within an organization. Criteria for "good fit" include:

- congruence with the purpose and mission of the organization;
- ability to draw on existing skills in the organization; and
- ability to share resources and coordinate activities with programs.

2. Program Attractiveness

Program attractiveness is the degree to which a program is attractive to the organization from an economic perspective, as an investment of current and future resources (i.e., whether the program easily attracts resources). Any program that does not have high congruence with the organization's purpose should be classified as unattractive. No program should be classified as highly attractive unless it is ranked as attractive on a substantial majority of the criteria below:

- high appeal to groups capable of providing current and future support stable funding
- market demand from a large client base appeal to volunteers
- measurable, reportable program results
- focus on prevention, rather than cure
- able to discontinue with relative ease, if necessary (i.e., low exit barriers)
- low client resistance to program services
- intended to promote the self-sufficiency or self-rehabilitation of client base

3. Alternative Coverage

Alternative coverage is the extent to which similar services are provided. If there are no other large, or very few small, comparable programs being provided in the same region, the program is classified as "low coverage." Otherwise, the coverage is "high."

4. Competitive Position

Competitive position is the degree to which the organization has a stronger capability and potential to deliver the program than other agencies—a combination of the organization's effectiveness, quality, credibility, and market share or dominance. Probably no program can be classified as being in a strong competitive position unless it has some clear basis for declaring superiority over all competitors in that program category. Criteria for a strong competitive position include:

- good location and logistical delivery system;
- large reservoir of client, community, or support group loyalty;
- past success securing funding;
- superior track record (or image) of service delivery;

- large market share of the target clientele currently served;
- gaining momentum or growing in relation to competitors;
- better quality service and/or service delivery than competitors;
- ability to raise funds, particularly for this type of program;
- superior skill at advocacy;
- superiority of technical skills needed for the program;
- superior organizational skills;
- superior local contacts;
- ability to conduct needed research into the program and/or properly monitor program performance;
- superior ability to communicate to stakeholders; and
- most cost effective delivery of service.

After each program is assessed in relation to the above four criteria, each is placed in the MacMillan matrix, as follows. For example, a program that is a good fit is deemed attractive and strong competitively, but for which there is a high alternative coverage would be assigned to Cell No. 1, *Aggressive Competition*.

		High Program Attractiveness: "Easy" Program		Low Program Attractiveness: "Difficult" Program	
		Alternative Coverage *High*	Alternative Coverage *Low*	Alternative Coverage *High*	Alternative Coverage *Low*
G O O D	**Strong Competitive Position**	1. Aggressive Competition	2. Aggressive Growth	5. Build up the Best Competitor	6. "Soul of the Agency"
F I T	**Weak Competitive Position**	3. Aggressive Divestment	4. Build Strength or Get Out	7. Orderly Divestment	8. "Foreign Aid" or Joint Venture
P O O R F I T		9. Aggressive Divestment		10. Orderly Divestment	

Once all programs have been placed in the appropriate positions on the matrix, an organization can review its mix of programs, sometimes called a "program portfolio," and decide if any adjustments need to be made. Ideally, an organization would have only two types of programs. The first would be attractive programs (programs that attract resources easily), in areas that the organization performs well and can compete aggressively for a dominant position.

These attractive programs can be used to support the second program type: the unattractive program with low coverage. The unattractive program is considered unattractive by funders, with low alternative coverage, but makes a special, unique contribution and in which the organization is particularly well-qualified. These programs typically fall under Cell No. 6, the soul of the agency. These programs are known as the "soul of the agency" because the organization is committed to delivering the program even at the cost of subsidizing it from other programs. An organization cannot afford to fund unlimited "souls," and it might have to face some difficult decisions about how to develop a mix of programs that ensure organizational viability as well as high-quality service to clients.

For example, five years ago there was little funding for case management by AIDS Service Organizations. Unwilling to let clients fend for themselves in getting the help they needed, many organizations devoted staff time to this service. At the time this was a "soul of the agency" program. These days, this program is more attractive (i.e., fundable) though there is also growing alternative coverage. Therefore, organizations in a strong position to serve the clients well, with cultural competence and program expertise, should aggressively compete: those in a weak competitive position should get out of the business.

Articulating Previous Strategies

Most organizations operate within the guidelines of certain program and organizational strategies, although often these have neither been recognized or articulated as actual strategies. Once an organization is in the process of strategic planning, however, it is time to make explicit these unspoken strategies and incorporate them into this deliberate consideration of the organization's future directions. This should happen as part of the situation assessment: look for past patterns of operation or allocation of resources—these are your previous strategies; analyze whether those strategies were effective, and why; and consider whether or not they should be held as strategies for the future.

Identification of Critical Issues

Upon completion of the situation assessment, a planning committee should be in a position to identify all of the critical issues, or fundamental problems or choices, facing the organization, and then begin to address those issues and identify priorities. A first attempt will probably result in a very long list of "critical" issues. Some might indeed be critical, but require no action at present and should, therefore, be monitored; some will require immediate attention, and as such should be dealt with accordingly; and some will be of critical importance to the long-term viability and success of the organization. Those are the issues (usually no more than six to eight issues qualify) that become the framework for the decisions that must be made next: decisions regarding strategies, long-range goals and objectives, and financial requirements.

To arrive at this final list of true critical issues, the planning committee should brainstorm a list of issues that might qualify and then assess each issue by asking: Why is it an issue? What are the consequences of not responding to this issue in the near future ? Why does the issue need immediate attention? Why is it a critical issue? Again, the final list should include no more than six to eight items; beyond that, the organization is in danger of losing focus and sabotaging its own best intentions.

Finally, additional research may be needed, in order to gather specific information about new opportunities which can be pursued. This might include: description of new target markets and their needs; description of new products and/or services with descriptions of start-up costs, competitor analysis, long-term financial projections, and break-even analysis.

Appendix 2.2

Strategic Planning Process Guide Self-Assessment Questionnaire

Copyright© 1997-2001

This questionnaire is designed to help you critique your strategic planning and management process. It is structured to allow review of the process to determine which strategic planning steps the organization now performs well, not so well, or not at all. Even if your organization does no strategic planning at present, a review of this questionnaire should be instructive as the individual questions identify those considerations that are primary in designing and implementing an effective process.

For each question below, enter the appropriate number to indicate the degree of improvement your organization needs in order to function effectively in that planning step or area.

Institutionalizing the Planning Function	Improvement Needed		
	Little	Some	Much

1. Do top CEOs take formal responsibility for the organization's strategic business planning?

    1 2 3 4 5 6

2. Is strategic planning a top priority activity, performed on a regular basis, e.g., each year?

    1 2 3 4 5 6

3. Does the organization provide resources (managers' time, money, staff support, etc.) earmarked specifically for strategic planning?

    1 2 3 4 5 6

4. Does the organization follow a defined set of procedures in its strategic planning process?

    1 2 3 4 5 6

5. Do all managers whose work might be affected significantly by strategic planning participate in the planning process?

    1 2 3 4 5 6

Establishing the Strategic Foundation	Improvement Needed		
	Little	Some	Much

6. Does the organization have a written mission statement?

    1 2 3 4 5 6

7. Are all management and higher-level staff aware of the mission? Do they understand it?

    1 2 3 4 5 6

8. Does the organization have written longer-term (3-5 years) and short-term (1-year) goals?　　1　2　3　4　5　6

9. Do the goals list quantified, measurable targets (e.g., volume, market share, growth rate, profitability)?　　1　2　3　4　5　6

10. If appropriate, do the goals specify targets by location or geographic area?　　1　2　3　4　5　6

11. When appropriate, do the goals list quality, time frame, and cost targets? Are they observable or measurable?　　1　2　3　4　5　6

12. Do the goals appear realistic yet challenging, based upon experience and/or research?　　1　2　3　4　5　6

13. Does the organization systematically measure actual performance vs. goals?　　1　2　3　4　5　6

14. Do management and higher-level staff whose responsibilities are affected participate in setting goals?　　1　2　3　4　5　6

Conducting the Strategic Situational Diagnosis	Improvement Needed		
	Little	Some	Much

15. Does the organization periodically gather and analyze data about market and other external factors which affect the business?　　1　2　3　4　5　6

16. Does the external/market   1   2   3   4   5   6
analysis identify key threats to the
business? Key opportunities?

17. Does the analysis include detailed   1   2   3   4   5   6
analysis of market or other
geographic and/or demographic
and/or psychographic segments?

18. Are the business' performance   1   2   3   4   5   6
and operational characteristics
compared with those of competitors?

19. Are demographic, behavioral, and   1   2   3   4   5   6
other consumer trends analyzed?

20. Does the organization assess the   1   2   3   4   5   6
industry as a whole in terms of
new competitors and concepts,
new technologies, procurement
practices, price trends, labor
practices, etc.?

21. Does the organization assess   1   2   3   4   5   6
institutional factors such as cost
and availability of capital, government regulations, and the economy?

22. Does the organization have know-   1   2   3   4   5   6
ledge of and access to sources of
information about the industry,
markets, and other external factors?

23. Does the organization analyze its   1   2   3   4   5   6
own business objectively?

24. Does this internal analysis identify key strengths and weaknesses in the organization? 1 2 3 4 5 6

25. Does the analysis include profitability factor trends, e.g., after-tax earnings, return on assets, cash flow? 1 2 3 4 5 6

26. Does it include marketing/advertising? 1 2 3 4 5 6

27. Does it include pricing strategy and its effects on customer behavior? 1 2 3 4 5 6

28. Does it include quality of customer service and customer satisfaction/loyalty/defection data? 1 2 3 4 5 6

29. Does the organization assess its human resource development and management programs? 1 2 3 4 5 6

30. Does the organization's management information system provide relatively easy access to the internal data discussed above? 1 2 3 4 5 6

31. After completing its external and internal analyses, does the organization review the mission and goals in light of the apparent threats/opportunities and strengths/weaknesses? 1 2 3 4 5 6

32. Based upon such a review, does   1   2   3   4   5   6
the strategic diagnosis culminate
in identifying key strategic issues,
e.g., outlet expansion, profitability
improvement, positioning change?

Developing Strategic Plans	Improvement Needed		
	Little	**Some**	**Much**

33. Does the organization use the   1   2   3   4   5   6
strategic (situational) diagnosis to
formulate strategic plan options?

34. Does it consider business perfor-   1   2   3   4   5   6
mance options, e.g., cost reduction,
alternative suppliers, production
improvements, etc.?

35. Does it consider market penetration   1   2   3   4   5   6
options, e.g., pricing/ promotion,
market expansion, segmentation?

36. Does it consider organization and   1   2   3   4   5   6
management options, e.g., restruc-
turing, purchasing competitive
businesses?

37. Does the organization consider   1   2   3   4   5   6
product/service enhancement
options?

38. Is the planning process based on   1   2   3   4   5   6
criteria by which options can be
compared and selected?

39. Does the organization decide its   1   2   3   4   5   6
strategic plan(s) based on
feasibility and risk/return criteria?

Managing Strategic Plan Implementation	Improvement Needed		
	Little	Some	Much

40. Does the organization make   1   2   3   4   5   6
strategic decisions (implemen-
tation action plans) based upon
the strategic plan?

41. Does the organization clearly   1   2   3   4   5   6
assign lead responsibility for
action plan implementation to a
person or, alternately, to a team?

42. Are sufficient resources allocated   1   2   3   4   5   6
for implementation?

43. Does the organization set clearly   1   2   3   4   5   6
defined and measurable
performance standards for each
plan element?

44. Does the organization develop an   1   2   3   4   5   6
organized system for monitoring
how well those performance
standards were met?

45. Does the organization review   1   2   3   4   5   6
monitoring data regularly, and
revise strategic decisions as
appropriate?

46. Are individuals responsible for   1   2   3   4   5   6
     strategic planning and imple-
     mentation rewarded for successful
     performance?

Scoring Summary

To perform a summary analysis of the quality of your organization's performance in each of the broad areas of the strategic planning process, calculate the average score for each of the Self-Assessment Questionnaire categories in accordance with the following instructions.

Institutionalizing the Planning Function (items 1-5)   Score
Total of numbers for items 1-5 = _____ divided by 5 =

Establishing the Strategic Foundation (items 6-14)   Score
Total of numbers for items 6-14 = _____ divided by 9 =

Conducting the Strategic Situational Diagnosis (items 15- 32) Score
Total of numbers for items 15-32 = ___ divided by 18 =

Developing Strategic Plans (items 33-39)   Score
Total of numbers for items 33-39 = _____ divided by 7 =

Managing Strategic Plan Implementation (items 40-46)   Score
Total of numbers for items 40-46 = _____ divided by 7 =

Examine the scores for the major categories. Those with relatively high scores (4-6) indicate that the organization needs significant improvement in these categories. Within the high-scoring categories, note any specific items that rated "5" or "6" for special attention.

Matrix Management | Strategic Planning |
Cross-Functional Teams | Visit Our Library!
Training & Facilitation | Customer Service Training |
Management Consulting
Marketing Services | Who We Are | Contact Us | Home

Appendix 2.3

Selected Web Sources
by Catherine Christ Lucas, MSW

Organization: BoardSource
Information Type: FAQs and resources
URL: http://www.BoardSource.org

Organization: Alliance Online
URL: http://www.allianceonline.org/ARC/search?search=&type=Website+and%2For+Organization&category=Governance%2FBoard+Development&submit=Search

Organization: Board Café (Compass Point)
Information Type: E-newsletter with archives
URL: http://www.compasspoint.org/boardcafe/

Organization: BoardNetUSA (Volunteer Consulting Group)
Information Type: Board matching
URL: http://www.vcg.org/

Organization: Free Management Library (Carter McNamara)
Information Type: Exceptional, comprehensive site with content by noted authority, Carter McNamara. One of the last sites to continue to provide extensive free information. Includes a complete toolkit for boards.
URL: http://www.managementhelp.org/boards/boards.htm

Organization: Governance Matters
Information Type: Resources for Boards
URL: http://www.governancematters.org/index.cfm?organization_id=56&section_id=801&page_id=3271

Organization: Leadership Skills for Board Members
(Enterprise Foundation)
Information Type: Publication
URL: http://www.practitionerresources.org/cache/
documents/36790.pdf

Organization: Michigan Nonprofit Alliance
Information Type: Assessment Tool including Board principles
URL: http://www.mnaonline.org/pdf/principles.pdf

Organization: Midwest Center for Nonprofit Leadership
URL: http://bsbpa.umkc.edu/mwcnl/board%20resources/
intro.htm

Organization: Minnesota Council of Nonprofits
URL: http://www.mncn.org/info_govern.htm

Organization: Nonprofit Boards and Governance
Review-Charity Channel
Information Type: FAQs and resources
URL: http://two.charitychannel.com/enewsletters/nbgr/

Organization: Nonprofit Center at Seattle University
Information Type: downloadable outlines and materials for
board training sessions online
URL: http://www.seattleu.edu/artsci/npl/modules.asp

Organization: Nonprofit Good Practice
Information Type: FAQs and resources
URL: http://www.npgoodpractice.org/Topics/Governance/
BoardManagement/BoardDevelopment/Default.aspx

Organization: Policy Governance (John Carver)
Information Type: Overview of the Carver Model
URL: http://policygovernance.com/

Appendix 2.4

Simplified Rules for Parliamentary Procedure

Based on: Robert's Rules of Order Newly Revised
League of Women Voters®

The application of parliamentary law is the best method yet devised to enable assemblies of any size, with due regard for every member's opinion, to arrive at the general will on a maximum number of questions of varying complexity in a minimum time and under all kinds of internal climate ranging from total harmony to hardened or impassioned division of opinion.

From the Introduction to
Robert's Rules of Order
Newly Revised. *

*Robert's Rules of Order Newly Revised, Tenth Edition, the most commonly used parliamentary manual, is published by Perseus Books Group and can be obtained through most bookstores.

Organizations

An organization and the way it functions are governed by its charter (if it is incorporated), its bylaws, and parliamentary rules or rules of order. Nothing in the bylaws may conflict with the corporate charter; the bylaws, in turn supersede the rules of order. Bylaws are considered so important that special requirements are set for changing them. These usually include advance notice and a larger-than majority vote for the adoption of amendments.

Most organizations use as their parliamentary authority a published manual, such as *Robert's Rules of Order Newly Revised*, which they may modify to meet their particular need by adopting special rules of order.

Governing an organization

In any organization, final authority rests with the members assembled in regular or annual meetings or conventions, though they may not, of course, take any action that conflicts with the charter or bylaws.

The business of most organizations is managed by a board of directors that is responsible to the membership and acts under its general instructions and guidance. The officers and members of the board are usually elected at an annual meeting, although the board is sometimes empowered to choose some of its own members. Other members may serve *ex officio* usually because of another position they hold. *Ex officio* members have all privileges, including the right to vote and make motions.

Work is often carried on by committees that are either provided for in the bylaws (standing committees) or appointed for a special purpose (ad hoc committees, task forces). Their powers are limited to those specifically given them by the bylaws or by direction of the board or the members. Usually they report to the board or to the membership meeting and may not be authorized to act on their own in the name of the organization.

Officers

The president:

❐ Supervises the conduct of the organization's business and activities.

❐ Serves, *ex officio*, on all but the nominating committee.

❐ Presides at meetings.

The vice-president:

❐ Acts in place of the president when necessary and presides at meetings when the president temporarily vacates the chair. In the absence of the president, the vice-president should not change rules, cannot fill vacancies required to be filled by the president and does not serve as an ex officio member of committees.

❐ Upon the death or retirement of the president, assumes all the duties and privileges of the president, unless the bylaws provide another method of filling the vacancy, in organizations with more than one vice-president, these duties and responsibilities are assumed by the first vice-president.

The secretary:

❐ Is the recording officer.

❐ Handles correspondence.

❐ Issues notices of meetings.

❐ Informs those elected or appointed to office or committees.

❐ Receives and files committee reports.

❐ Keeps the minutes of meetings. At each meeting, the secretary should have the minute book, a copy of the bylaws, a book on parliamentary procedure and a list of the unfinished business from the previous meeting.

Minutes should reflect what was *done* not what was *said*, at a meeting. The common tendency is to report too much detail. Minutes should contain:

• The date, place, time and type of meeting (regular, special).

• The names of the presiding officer, the secretary and, in boards and committees, the names of those present.

• Action taken on the minutes of the previous meeting and corrections, if any.

• Exact wording of each motion, the name of the maker and the disposition.

• The name and topic of guest speakers (their speeches need not be summarized).

• Time of adjournment.

The Treasurer

Receives funds.

❐ Deposits them in financial institutions approved by the board.

❐ Pays bills for expenses that have been authorized. If any appreciable sums of money are involved, the treasurer should be bonded to protect the organization from loss. It is customary for the treasurer to report to the board at each of its meetings and to make a full financial report to the annual meeting or convention. (In larger organizations, this report should be reviewed by an independent auditor. If the auditor's report's available at the time of the annual meeting or convention, it should be presented immediately after the treasurer's report. Adoption of the auditor's report, on motion, signifies acceptance of the treasurer's report.)

Meetings

At all meetings (referred to in Robert's Rules as "assemblies"), it is up to the presiding officer to use the rules of parliamentary procedure appropriately so that good order and reasonable decorum are maintained and the business of the meeting goes forward. At times, the technical rules of parliamentary procedure may be relaxed, as long as the meeting accomplishes its purpose and the rights of absentees and minorities are protected. Conventions and large meetings are conducted more formally than the meetings of small board and committees.

The role of the presiding officer

The presiding officer (chair) should:

❐ Be ready to call the meeting to order at the time set.

❐ Follow the agenda and clarify what is hap¬pening and what is being voted on at all times.

❐ Deal firmly with whispering, commotion and frivolous or delaying debate and motions.

❐ See that debate is confined to the merits of the question and that personal comments are avoided. No one should speak more than twice on a subject, and no one should speak a second time until all who wish to speak have had a chance to do so.

❏ Talk no more than necessary. Except in small boards and committees, the presiding officer should not enter the debate without giving up the chair to a substitute until the motion under debate has been voted on.

❏ Remain calm and deal fairly with all sides regardless of personal opinion. To preserve this impartiality, the presiding officer abstains from voting except by ballot or to cast the deciding vote on an issue.

Order of business

A minimum number of voting members (quorum), as prescribed in the bylaws, must be present before business can be legally transacted. The presiding officer should determine that there is a quorum before beginning the meeting. Every organization is free to decide the order in which its business will be conducted, but most agendas follow a standard pattern:

1. Call to order.
2. Secretaries Report: Minutes are read by the secretary and corrections requested. The presiding officer says: If there are no corrections, the minutes stand approved as read.
3. Treasurer's Report is given and questions called for: The Treasurer s Report will be filed.
4. Reports of officers, the board and standing committees. Recommendations in reports should be dealt with as motions at this point.
5. Reports of special committees.
6. Unfinished business. Items left over from the previous meeting and business postponed to this meeting are brought up in turn by the presiding officer.
7. New business: Is there any new business?
8. Program. The program chairperson is called upon to introduce speakers, film or other presentation.
9. Announcements.

10. Adjournment: Is there any further business? (Pause) The meeting is adjourned.

Motions

Business is conducted by acting on motions. A subject is introduced by a main motion. Once this has been seconded and stated by the presiding officer, nothing else should be taken up until it is disposed of Long and involved motions should be submitted in writing. Once a motion has been stated, the mover may not withdraw it without the consent of the meeting. Most motions must be seconded.

While a main motion is being considered, other parliamentary motions, which affect either the main motion or the general conduct of the meeting, may be made. The ones most frequently used are described in general below, but it should be noted that there are exceptions and modifications that cannot be included in this brief text.

1. Amend. Debatable; majority vote

Used when the intention is to change, add or omit words in the main motion.

Amend the amendment: Used to change, add or omit words in the first amendment. This motion cannot itself be amended.

Method: The first vote is on the amendment to the amendment. The second vote is on the first amendment either as changed or as originally proposed, depending on the first vote. The third vote is on the main motion either as introduced or as amended.

2. Refer. Debatable; majority vote

If a motion becomes too complicated through amendments or if more information is needed, a motion may be made to refer it to a committee for study or redrafting. This committee reports back or acts as instructed.

3. Postpone. Debatable; majority vote

Consideration of a motion can be delayed until a more suitable time, until other decisions have been made or until more information is available by a motion to postpone to a stated future time.

4. The previous question. Not debatable; two-thirds vote

I move the previous question. This motion is used to end debate that has become lengthy or repetitious. When it is seconded, the presiding officer immediately puts the question on closing debate. If this receives a two-thirds vote, the pending motion is voted on at once without further discussion.

5. Lay on the table. Not debatable; majority vote

I move that we table this motion. In order when something more urgent needs consideration. This postpones consideration in such a way that the motion can be taken up again in the near future if a majority decides to "take it from the table."

6. Reconsider. Usually debatable; majority vote

A vote may be reconsidered through this motion, which must be made on the same day or the day following the vote by someone who voted on the prevailing side. A motion can be reconsidered only once. The first vote is on whether the motion should be reconsidered. If this passes, the second vote is on the motion itself

7. Point of order and appeal.

A member who feels the rules are not being fol¬lowed may call attention to the breach by rising and saying: Point of order. The chair says: State your point of order Upon hearing it, the chair may say: Your point is well taken, or Your point is not well taken.

One dissatisfied with the ruling may appeal to the meeting for a final decision: Shall the decision of the chair be sustained? This appeal is debatable, and the presiding officer may enter the debate without giving up the chair. A majority of no votes is necessary to reverse the ruling; majority sustains it.

8. Questions and inquiries.

Whenever necessary, advice may be asked as to correct procedures (parliamentary inquiry), facts may be requested (point of information), or a change may be sought for comfort or conve¬nience (question of privilege). The presiding of¬ficer responds to the question, or refers it to the proper person.

9. Adjourn. Usually not debatable; majority vote

If the time set for adjournment has arrived or there is no further business, the presiding officer declares the meeting adjourned without waiting for a formal motion. A member may move to adjourn at any time except when a speaker has the floor or a vote is in process. If the motion carries, the meeting is immediately adjourned.

Voting

The vote needed to pass a motion or elect an official is based on the votes actually cast, unless the bylaws or rules provide otherwise. Thus, a majority is more than half of those voting; abstentions and blank ballots are disregarded.

❐ By using general consent, a formal vote can be avoided on routine matters where there is no opposition. The president officer says: If there is no objection (Pause)... and declares the decision made.

❐ A voice vote (aye and no) is common practice but should not be used where more than a majority is needed.

❐ A show of hands is a good alternative in small groups.

❐ If unsure of the result, the presiding officer should order a rising vote or an actual count. If this is not done, a member can insist upon a rising vote by calling out "division"; a count can be forced only by a motion made, seconded and approved by a majority vote.

❐ A motion for a ballot (secret written vote) can be made if the bylaws do not already require one. This motion is not debatable and requires a majority vote.

Nominations and elections

Normally, a nominating process is used for elections, although any eligible member may be elected whether nominated or not. Most organizations use a nominating committee to prepare a slate of nominees for the offices to be filled. Service on a nominating committee does not prevent a member from becoming a nominee.

After presentation of the nominating committee's report to the assembly, the presiding officer calls for nominations from the floor. Many organizations require that the consent of the nominee be obtained in advance to avoid a futile election. Seconds are not necessary for either committee nominations or nominations from the floor.

When all nominations appear to have been made, the presiding officer declares that nominations are closed—or a motion to this effect may be made. It is not debatable and requires a two-thirds vote. A motion to reopen nominations requires a majority vote.

The method of voting usually is fixed in the bylaws. A ballot is the normal procedure if there is more than one nominee for an office. If there are several nominees and the bylaws do not provide for election by a plurality vote (that is, the largest number, but not necessarily more than half the votes cast), several ballots or votes may be needed before one candidate achieves a majority.

Where election is by ballot, the presiding officer appoints tellers (or an election committee) to collect and count the votes. The tellers' report, giving the number of votes cast for each nominee, is read aloud and handed to the presiding officer. The presiding officer rereads the report and declares the election of each official separately. Tellers' complete report is recorded in minutes.

A postscript to the presiding officer:

The rules of parliamentary procedure are meant to help, not hinder. Applied with common sense, they should not frustrate the meeting or entangle it in red tape. Retain control at all times, give clear explanations, and keep things as simple as possible. Good advice from the chair as to the wording of motions and the best way to proceed will avoid needless complications. When in doubt, your rule should be: Respect the wishes of the majority, protect the minority and do what seems fair and equitable.

Order from: League of Women Voters of the United States. Pub #138; 888-287-7424; pubsales@lwv.org; fax: 202-429-4343. Revised and reprinted 2006

Bibliography & References

Alexander, J.A., & Weiner, B.J. (1998). The adoption of corporate governance model by nonprofit organizations. Nonprofit Management & Leadership, 8, 223-42.

Austin, D.M., & Woolever, C. (1992). Voluntary association boards: A reflection of director and community characteristics? Nonprofit and Voluntary Sector Quarterly, 21, 181-193.

Axelrod, N.R. (1994). Board leadership and board development. In R.D. Herman (Ed.). The Jossey-Bass handbook of nonprofit leadership and management (pp. 119-136). San Francisco: Jossey-Bass.

Bell, P.D. (1993). Fulfilling the public trust: Ten ways to help nonprofit boards maintain accountability. Washington, DC: National Center for Nonprofit Boards.

Bradshaw, P.; Murray, V.; & Wolpin, J. (1992). Do nonprofit boards make a difference? An exploration of the relationships among board structure, process, and effectiveness. Nonprofit and Voluntary Sector Quarterly, 21, 227-248.

Bradshaw, P.; Murray, V.; & Wolpin, J. (1996). Women on boards of nonprofits: What difference do they make? Nonprofit Management & Leadership, 6, 241-254.

Bramson, R.J. (1981). Coping with difficult people. New York: Ballentine Books.

Carver, J. and Carver, M.M. (2006a) Boards that Make a Difference. San Francisco: Jossey Bass

Carver, J. and Carver, M.M. (2006b) Reinventing Your Board. San Francisco: Jossey-Bass

Carver, J. (2006c). Boards that make a difference. San Francisco: Jossey-Bass.

Carver, J. (1996a). Chairperson's role as servant leader to the board. San Francisco: Jossey-Bass.

Carver, J. (1996b). Planning better board meetings. San Francisco: Jossey-Bass.

Carver, J. (1996c). Strategies for board leadership. San Francisco: Jossey-Bass.

Carver, J. & Carver, M.M. (1996d). Basic principles of policy governance. San Francisco: Jossey-Bass.

Carver, J., & Carver M.M. (1996e). Your roles and responsibilities as a board director. San Francisco: Jossey-Bass.

Carver, J., & Carver, M.M. (1997). Reinventing your board: A step-by-step guide to implementing policy governance. San Francisco: Jossey-Bass.

Casey, R.W. (1998). Best practices for nonprofit boards: Managing finances and investments. Homewood, IL: Irwin Professional Publishers.

Child Welfare League of America (1996). CWLA board self-assessment checklist. Washington, DC: CWLA Press.

Child Welfare League of America (1996). CWLA standards of excellence for the management and governance of child welfare organizations. Washington, DC: CWLA Press.

Cleese, J. (1988, May 16). No more mistakes and you're through. Forbes, 141, 126, 128.

Clifton, R. I. & Dahms, A A M (1980). Grassroots administration: A handbook for staff and directors of small community-based social service agencies. Prospect Heights, IL: Wavelin Press.

Code of Alabama (1993). Vol 5, Art 6-5-336. Charlottesville, VA: Michie Co.

Cohen, M.; March, J.G.; & Olsen, J. (1972, March). A garbage can model of organizational choice. Administrative Science Quarterly, 17, 1-25.

Colorado Revised Statutes. (1996). 1996 Cumulative Supplement, Title 13, Vol. 6A, Sec. 13-21-115.7(b)(2)(3). Denver: Bradford Publishing Co.

Conrad, W.R., Jr., & Glen, W.E. (1983). The effective voluntary board of directors. Athens, OH: Swallow Press.

Consolidated Laws of New York Statutes (1997). Book 37, Art. 7, Sec. 717. St. Paul, MN: West Group.

Delaware Code Annotated (1996). Vol.4, Tit. 8, Sec. 102(d)(7). (1996 Supplement). Charlottesville, VA: Michie Co.

Drucker, P.F., & Rossum, C. (1993). How to assess your nonprofit organization with Peter Drucker's five most important questions: User guide for boards, staff, volunteers, and facilitators. San Francisco: Jossey-Bass.

Duca, D.J. (1986). Nonprofit boards. Phoenix: Oryx Press.

Duca, D.J. (1996). Nonprofit boards: Roles, responsibilities and performance. New York: John Wiley & Sons.

Eadie, D., & Daily L. (1994). Boards that work: A practical guide to building effective association boards. San Francisco: Jossey-Bass.

Emenhiser, D.L.; King, D.W.; Joffe, S.A.; & Penkert, K.S. (1998). Networks, mergers, & partnerships in a managed care environment. Washington, DC: CWLA Press.

Flamholtz, E.G. (1986). How to make a transition from entrepreneurship to a professionally managed firm. San Francisco: Jossey-Bass.

Greenleaf, R. (1973). Trustees as servants. Peterborough, NH: Windy Row Press.

Hardy, J.M. (1990). Developing dynamic boards: A proactive approach to building nonprofit boards of directors. Erwin, TN: Essex Press.

Harper, E. & Dunhom, A. (1959). Community Organization in Action. New York: Association Press

Hart, P. (1990). Groupthink in government. Bristol, PA: Taylor & Francis.

Harvey, J.B. (1974, Summer). The Abilene paradox. Organizational Dynamics 63-80.

Herman, R.D. (1988). Nonprofit board of directors: Analyses and applications. New Brunswick, NJ: Transaction Publishers.

Herman, R.D. Renz, D.O.; & Heimovics, R.D. (1997). Board practices and board effectiveness in local nonprofit organizations. Nonprofit Management & Leadership, 7, 373-385.

Herman, R.D. & Van Til, J. (1989). Nonprofit boards and directors: Analysis and applications. Washington, DC: National Center for Nonprofit Boards.

Hirk, C. (1960). The Effective Board. New York. Association Press.

Houle, C.O. (1989). Governing boards: Their nature and nurture. San Francisco: Jossey-Bass.

Ingram, R.T. (1989). Ten basic responsibilities of nonprofit boards. Washington, DC: National Center for Nonprofit Boards.

Janis, I. (1972). Victims of groupthink. Boston: Houghton Mifflin.

Janis, I. (1983). Groupthink: Psychological studies of policy decisions and fiascos. Boston: Houghton Mifflin.

Janis, I., & Mann, L. (1997). Decision making: A psychological analysis of conflict, choice, and commitment. New York: The Free Press.

Kaner, S.; Lind, L.; Toldi, C.; Fisk, S.; & Berger, D. (1996). Facilitator's guide to participatory decision-making. Branford, CT: New Society Press.

King, C. (1938). Social Agency Boards and How to Make Them Effective. New York: Harper & Brothers.

Koontz, Harold (1967). The Board of Directors and Effective Management. New York. McGraw Hill.

Kornhauser, W. (1959) The Politics of Mass Society. Glencoe, IL: The Free Press.

Kluger, M.P., & Baker, W.A. (1994). Innovative leadership in the nonprofit organization: Strategies for change. Washington, DC: CWLA Press.

Kluger, M.P.; Baker, W.A.; & Garval, H.S. (1998). Strategic business planning: Securing a future for the nonprofit organization. Washington, DC: CWLA Press.

League of Women Voters. (1979). Simplified parliamentary procedure. (Pamphlet). Washington, DC: Author.

Leifer, J.C., & Glomb. M.B. (1997). Legal obligations of nonprofit boards: A guidebook for board directors. Washington, DC: National Center for Nonprofit Boards.

Levy, L. (1981, January/February). Reforming board reform. Harvard Business Review, 59, 166-172.

Long, Fern (1967). All About Meetings. Dobbs Ferry, New York: Oceona Publications.

Margolis, R.J. (1989, September). In America's small town hospitals.... Smithsonian, 20, 52-67.

Mintzberg, H. (1994). The rise and fall of strategic planning. New York: Free Press.

Moynihan, D.P. (1969). Maximum feasible misunderstanding. New York: Free Press.

Mueller, R.K. (1981) The Incomplete Board. Lexington, MA: Lexington Books.

Murray, D. (1998). Nonprofit budgeting step by step: A practical workbook for managers and boards. San Francisco: Jossey-Bass.

Myers, R.J.; Ufford, P.; and McGill, M. (1988). On-site analysis: A practical approach to organizational change. Etobicoke, ON: On Site Consultant Associates.

Naisbitt, J., & Aburdene, P. (1985). Reinventing the corporation. New York: Warner.

National Information Bureau (1979). The volunteer board director in philanthropy. New York: Author.

Nonprofit Risk Management Center (1993, 1995). State liability laws for charitable organizations and volunteers (2nd edition with 1995 modifications). Washington, DC: Author.

Nelson, Bob (1994). 1001 Ways to Reward Your Employees. New York. Workman Press

Parkinson, C.N. (1957). Parkinson's law. New York: Houghton Mifflin.

Perkins, K.B., & Poole, D.G. (1996). Oligarchy and adaptation to mass society in an all-volunteer organization: Implications for understanding leadership, participation, and change. Nonprofit and Voluntary Sector Quarterly, 25, 73-88.

Pious, S. (1993). The psychology of judgment and decision making. Philadelphia: Temple University Press.

Portnoy, R.A. (1986). Leadership: What every leader should know about people. Englewood Cliffs, NJ: Prentice-Hall.

Rittel, Horst and Melvin Weber (1973). "Dilemmas in a General Theory of Planning" Policy Sciences (July), 4 (2) : 155-169

Schmid, H.; Dodd, P.; & Tropman, J.E. (1987). Board decision making in human service organizations. Human Systems Management, 7, 155-161.

Schwarz, R.M. (1994). The skilled facilitator: Practical wisdom for developing effective groups. San Francisco: Jossey-Bass.

Sims, R. (1992). Linking groupthink to unethical behavior in organizations. Journal of Business Ethics, 11, 651-652.

Sorenson, Roy (1950). The Art of Board Membership. New York: Association Press.

Stebbins, R.A. (1996). Volunteering: A serious leisure perspective. Nonprofit and Voluntary Sector Quarterly, 25, 211-224.

Stein, T.J. (1998). Child welfare and the law (Rev. ed.). Washington, DC: CWLA Press.

Strauss, B. and F.(1951). New Ways to Better Meetings. New York: The Viking Press.

Stoesz, E., & Raber, C. (1997). Doing good better! How to be an effective board director of a nonprofit organization. Intercourse, PA: Good Books.

Tichy, H., & Devanna, M.A. (1990). The transformational leader. New York: John Wiley & Sons.

Tjosvold, D. (1986). Working together to get things done. Lexington, MA: Lexington Books.

Tropman, J.E. (1984). Policy management in the human services. New York: Columbia University Press.

Tropman, J.E. (1995). The role of the board in the planning process. In J.E. Tropman, J. Erlich, & J. Rothman (Eds.), Tactics and techniques of community practice (3rd ed.) (pp. 157 - 171). Itasca, IL: F.E. Peacock.

Tropman, J.E. (1996a). Effective meetings: improving group decision making. Thousand Oaks, CA: Sage Publications.

Tropman, J.E. (1996b). Making meetings work: Achieving high quality group decisions. Thousand Oaks, CA: Sage Publications.

Tropman, J.E. (1998). Managing ideas in the creating organization. Westport, CT: Quorum Books.

Tropman, J. and Johnson, H.R. and Tropman, E.J. (1979) The Essentials of Committee Management. Chicago: Nelson-Hall.

Tropman, J.E.; Johnson, H.R.; & Tropman, E.J. (1992), (1979) Committee management in the human services (2nd ed.). Chicago: Nelson-Hall.

Tropman, J.E., & Morningstar, G. (1989). Entrepreneurial systems for the 1990s. Westport, CT: Quorum Books.

Tropman, J.E., & Tropman, E.J. (1995). Index of dissimilarity and the professional unit method of analysis. In J.E. Tropman, J. Erlich, & J. Rothman (Eds.), Tactics and techniques of community intervention (3rd ed.) (pp. 467-470). Itasca, IL: F.E. Peacock.

Tropman, John (2001) The Compensation Solution. San Francisco. Jossey Bass

Tropman, J. E.and L.Shaefer. (2004) Flameout at the Top: - CEO Calamity in the Nonprofit Sector") Administration in Social Work28¾ (2004).

Tropman, J.E. (2002)"Managerialism in Social Work" Hong Kong Journal of Social Work , 36, 1 & 2, Summer & Winter.

Tropman J. E, H. Shaefer, L. Zhu,(2004 "The Crow and the Cheese: From Derailment to Calamity in the CEO Suite" Proceedings of the International Applied Business Research Conference San Juan, Puerto Rico, March, 2004. The Ciber Institute. http://www.wapress.com/

Tropman, J. "Organizational Theory" in *The Comprehensive Handbook of Social Work and Social Welfare* , edited by Dr. Karen M. Sowers (University of Tennessee) and Dr. Catherine N. Dulmus (SUNY- Buffalo) forthcoming, 2008 Public Law 105-19, Volunteer Protection Act of 1997. (1997, June 18). 105th Cong., 1st sess.

Vaill, P. (1982, Autumn). The purposing of high performing systems. Organizational Dynamics.

Waldo, C.N. (1985). Boards of directors: Their changing role, structure, and information needs. Westport, CT: Quorum Books.

Widmer, C. (1993). Role conflict, role ambiguity, and role overload on boards of directors of nonprofit human service organizations. Nonprofit and Voluntary Sector Quarterly, 22, 339-356.

Wood, M. (Ed.). (1995). Nonprofit boards and leadership: Cases on governance, change, and board-staff dynamics. San Francisco: Jossey-Bass.

Yankey, J.; A.B. Wester and D. Campbell (1998). "Managing Mergers and Consolidations" in R. Edwards and J. Yankey, Eds., Skills for Effective Management of Nonprofit Organizations. Washington, D.C.: NASW Press.

Zander, A. (1982). Making groups effective. San Francisco: Jossey-Bass.

Zander, A. (1993). Making boards effective. San Francisco: Jossey-Bass.

Zelman, W. (1977). Liability for social agency boards. *Social Work*, 22, 270-274.

Internet Resources

Council on Foundations: www.cof.org
National Center for Nonprofit Boards: www.ncnb.org
Nonprofit Risk Management Center: www.nonprofitrisk.org

About the Authors

JOHN E. TROPMAN is a professor of human services management and organizational behavior at the University of Michigan, Ann Arbor. He coordinates the MSW-MBA program at the School of Social Work and School of Business and serves as faculty associate for the university's program in American Culture. In addition, he teaches in the CEO Education Programs at both the Michigan Business School and Carnegie Mellon University, Pittsburgh, Pennsylvania. He is a lecturer and author and consults with government, nonprofit, and commercial organizations. He received his bachelor's degree in sociology from Oberlin College, Oberlin, Ohio; his master's in social work from the University of Chicago; and his doctorate in social work and sociology from the University of Michigan.

THOMAS J. HARVEY began his professional social work career with Catholic Charities in his hometown of Pittsburgh, Pennsylvania, and went on to become the CEO of Catholic Charities USA, in Washington, DC. When he completed that assignment, he became Senior Vice President for Member Services at the Alliance for Children and Families in Milwaukee, Wisconsin. During these years of executive leadership, Harvey also served on some of the nation's best known nonprofit boards, Independent Sector, National Human Services Assembly, National Committee of Responsive Philanthropy, and Catholic Health East. He is currently Director of the Master of Nonprofit Administration Program, Mendoza College of Business, University of Notre Dame.